IN
NIXON'S
WEB

IN NIXON'S WEB

A YEAR IN THE CROSSHAIRS OF WATERGATE

L. PATRICK GRAY III

with Ed Gray

TIMES BOOKS

HENRY HOLT AND COMPANY   NEW YORK

Times Books
Henry Holt and Company, LLC
Publishers since 1866
175 Fifth Avenue
New York, New York 10010
www.henryholt.com

Henry Holt® is a registered trademark of Henry Holt and Company, LLC.

Copyright © 2008 by LPGIII Pages LLC
All rights reserved.
Distributed in Canada by H. B. Fenn and Company Ltd.

Library of Congress Cataloging-in-Publication Data

Gray, Louis Patrick, 1916–2005
In Nixon's web : a year in the crosshairs of Watergate / L. Patrick Gray III with Ed Gray. — 1st ed.
   p. cm.
Includes index.
"Times Books."
ISBN-13: 978-0-8050-8256-2
ISBN-10: 0-8050-8256-5
   1. Gray, Louis Patrick, 1916–2005.   2. Watergate Affair, 1972–1974—Personal narratives.
3. United States. Federal Bureau of Investigation—Officials and employees—Biography.
4. Government executives—United States—Biography.   5. Police—United States—Biography.
6. United States—Politics and government—1969–1974.   7. United States—Politics and
government—1974–1977.   I. Gray, Ed.   II. Title.
   E860.G73 2008
   353.5092—dc22
   [B]   2007037518

Henry Holt books are available for special promotions and premiums.
For details contact: Director, Special Markets.

First Edition 2008
Designed by Meryl Sussman Levavi
Printed in the United States of America
   1   3   5   7   9   10   8   6   4   2

For Bea

Contents

Cast of Characters

NOTE: Names in italics denote those individuals who were convicted of a crime, pled guilty, pled nolo contendere, or were named as an unindicted co-conspirator, according to the following key:

*	Convicted of a Watergate-related crime
**	Pled guilty to a Watergate-related crime
***	Pled guilty to a non-Watergate misdemeanor
****	Convicted of a Watergate-related crime, later overturned
*****	Convicted of a non-Watergate crime; pardoned by Ronald Reagan
******	Convicted of a non-Watergate crime
*******	Pled nolo contendere to a non-Watergate crime
********	Unindicted co-conspirator; pardoned by Gerald Ford

White House

RICHARD M. NIXON, president of the United States********
SPIRO T. AGNEW, vice president of the United States*******
H. R. "BOB" HALDEMAN, chief of staff*
JOHN EHRLICHMAN, assistant to the president for domestic affairs*
JOHN W. DEAN, counsel to the president**
CHARLES W. COLSON, special counsel to the president**
RON ZIEGLER, press secretary

CLARK MACGREGOR, congressional liaison; later chairman of the Committee to Re-Elect the President

DWIGHT CHAPIN, deputy assistant to the president; appointments secretary*

FRED FIELDING, associate counsel to the president

HENRY KISSINGER, assistant to the president for national security affairs

DAVID YOUNG, administrative assistant to Kissinger; cofounder of White House Special Investigations Unit (the "Plumbers")

DICK MOORE, special counsel to the president

Committee to Re-Elect the President (CREEP)

JOHN MITCHELL, chairman; former attorney general*

MAURICE STANS, finance chairman; former secretary of commerce**

JEB STUART MAGRUDER, deputy director; former Haldeman aide**

HERBERT KALMBACH, associate chairman; Nixon's personal attorney**

ROBERT MARDIAN, deputy director; former assistant attorney general****

FRED LaRUE, campaign aide; former consultant to White House**

DONALD SEGRETTI, campaign aide**

HUGH SLOAN JR., treasurer

KENNETH DAHLBERG, campaign contributor

MANUEL OGARRIO, Mexican attorney with clients in Texas branch of CREEP

Watergate burglars and accomplices

JAMES W. McCORD, chief of security, CREEP*

BERNARD BARKER, Watergate burglar*

G. GORDON LIDDY, general counsel, CREEP*

E. HOWARD HUNT, White House consultant*

Department of Justice

RICHARD KLEINDIENST, attorney general (acting attorney general until June 1972)***

RALPH ERICKSON, assistant attorney general, Office of Legal Counsel; later deputy attorney general

HENRY PETERSEN, assistant attorney general, Criminal Division

DONALD SANTARELLI, administrator, Law Enforcement Assistance Administration; former associate deputy attorney general

Prosecutors

EARL SILBERT, assistant U.S. attorney; later U.S. attorney

SEYMOUR GLANZER, assistant U.S. attorney

DONALD CAMPBELL, assistant U.S. attorney

JAY HOROWITZ, assistant special prosecutor

FRANK MARTIN, assistant special prosecutor

PHILIP HEYMANN, associate special prosecutor

Federal Bureau of Investigation, pre-1972

J. EDGAR HOOVER, director; died May 2, 1972

CLYDE TOLSON, associate director; retired May 3, 1972

CARTHA "DEKE" DELOACH, assistant to the director; retired 1970

WILLIAM C. SULLIVAN, assistant to the director after DeLoach; retired 1971

JOHN MOHR, assistant to the director after Sullivan; retired June 1972

HELEN GANDY, executive assistant to Hoover; retired May 1972

Federal Bureau of Investigation, 1972–73

L. PATRICK GRAY III, acting director

W. MARK FELT, acting associate director*****

ED MILLER, assistant director, Domestic Intelligence Division*****

DWIGHT DALBEY, assistant director, Office of Legal Counsel

TOM BISHOP, assistant director, Crime Records Division; retired 1973

CHARLIE BATES, assistant director, General Investigative Division; voluntarily transferred to San Francisco field office as special agent in charge

BOB GEBHARDT, assistant director, General Investigative Division after Bates

DICK BAKER, assistant director, Office of Planning and Evaluation

WESLEY GRAPP, special agent in charge (SAC), Los Angeles; demoted

BOB KUNKEL, SAC, Washington field office; transferred to St. Louis

JACK McDERMOTT, SAC, Washington field office after Kunkel

JOSEPH TRIMBACH, SAC, Minneapolis field office

ANGELO LANO, Watergate case agent, Washington field office

CHARLES BOLZ, special agent, General Investigative Division; voluntarily resigned

TOM SMITH, section chief, Domestic Intelligence Division

DONALD GUTHRIE, special agent, Birmingham field office

DAVE KINLEY, executive assistant to Gray

MACK ARMSTRONG, special assistant to Gray

BARBARA HERWIG, special assistant to Gray

CHUCK LICHENSTEIN, special assistant to Gray

MARGE NEENAN, personal secretary to Gray

TOM MOTEN, special agent; driver for Gray; former driver for Hoover

Central Intelligence Agency

RICHARD HELMS, director of central intelligence***

VERNON "DICK" WALTERS, deputy director

United States Congress

JAMES EASTLAND, senator (D-Mississippi), chairman of Senate Judiciary Committee

SAM ERVIN, senator (D-North Carolina), chairman of Senate Select Committee on Presidential Campaign Activities ("Ervin Committee")

HOWARD BAKER, senator (R-Tennessee), ranking minority member of Ervin Committee

ROBERT BYRD, senator (D-West Virginia), member of Senate Judiciary Committee; later elected Senate majority leader

EDWARD KENNEDY, senator (D-Massachusetts), member of Senate Judiciary Committee

PHILIP HART, senator (D-Michigan), member of Senate Judiciary Committee

ROMAN HRUSKA, senator (R-Nebraska), member of Senate Judiciary Committee

LOWELL WEICKER, senator (R-Connecticut), member of Ervin Committee

EDWARD GURNEY, senator (R-Florida), member of Ervin Committee

LUCIEN NEDZI, congressman (D-Michigan), chairman of House Select Committee on Intelligence

SAM DASH, chief counsel, Ervin Committee

FRED THOMPSON, minority counsel, Ervin Committee

Journalists

JACK ANDERSON, syndicated columnist

CARL BERNSTEIN, *Washington Post*

JOHN CREWDSON, *New York Times*

ROBERT NOVAK, syndicated columnist

JEREMIAH O'LEARY, *Washington Star*

SANDY SMITH, *Time* magazine

SANDY UNGAR, *Washington Post*

BOB WOODWARD, *Washington Post*

Gray's Attorneys

STEPHEN SACHS

ALAN BARON

Foreword

ON MAY 1, 1972, L. PATRICK GRAY III WAS AT THE PINNACLE OF a classic American success story. From his well-appointed offices as the deputy attorney general of the United States, Pat Gray could look back at age fifty-five with justifiable pride at what he had accomplished in the service of his country and as a beneficiary of the opportunities and freedoms he had fought for his entire adult life. It had been an improbable climb, but it was about to end.

The eldest son of a Texas railroad worker who had lost his job in the Depression, Gray worked three jobs while bootstrapping himself through high school, graduating at sixteen after skipping two grades. He enrolled at Rice University, where the tuition was free for a student good enough to be admitted, played football in the Houston Parks League to bring in a few more dollars for his family, and kept trying for four years to get what he wanted most: an appointment to the United States Naval Academy. That appointment came in 1936, his senior year at Rice, and he dropped out immediately to accept it. Unable to afford bus or train fare to Annapolis, Gray hired on as an apprentice seaman on a tramp steamer out of Galveston where he taught calculus to the ship's master, a naturalized Bulgarian named Frank Solis, in return for basic lessons in navigation. The steamer got him to Philadelphia and he hitchhiked to the Academy, where he walked onto the football field and became a starting quarterback, played varsity lacrosse, and boxed as a light heavyweight. His class of 1940, graduating just in time for World War II, would suffer more wartime losses than any other class in Academy history. Pat Gray made five submarine war patrols in the Pacific; at the start of his sixth, he suffered a ruptured appendix in mid-ocean and couldn't get it removed until he reached the Galápagos Islands seventeen days later. It should have killed him, but it didn't.

Soon he would make the two most important decisions of his life. In 1945, on his way back from the war in the Pacific, he paid a visit to Beatrice Kirk DeGarmo, the young widow of his classmate Ed DeGarmo, a highly decorated naval aviator who had been shot down over Okinawa just weeks before the war ended. A year later Pat and Bea were married and he adopted her two sons. They would have two more. Also in 1946, he was selected as one of eighteen out of 625 applicants to be sent by the navy to law school at George Washington University. He graduated Juris Doctor with honors, Order of the Coif, and a member of the Law Review.

While he was studying in Washington, he met a freshman congressman named Richard Nixon.

By 1960 he was a navy captain at the front of a fast field of soon-to-be admirals. Having chosen to stay with submarines as a line officer rather than switching to the Judge Advocate General corps, Gray commanded three submarine war patrols in the Korean conflict and had been given his four captain's stripes two years before the regulations allowed him to be paid for them. Promoted to high-level staff duty at the Pentagon, he was congressional liaison officer for the secretary of defense, the chairman of the Joint Chiefs of Staff, and the chief of naval operations, the famed Arleigh Burke, for whom the navy's top-of-the-line Burke-class guided missile destroyers would later be named. When Gray told the two four-stars that he wanted to retire and go to work as a military adviser for Nixon, who was then vice president under Dwight Eisenhower, both strenuously tried to talk him out of the decision. "If you stay," said Burke, "you'll have my job some day."

Pat Gray left anyway, betting that Nixon would defeat John F.

Kennedy in that year's presidential election and that he might then be able to rise even higher on the civilian side than he might have in the navy. Nixon lost, of course, but Gray had a hole card: a standing offer from a Connecticut law firm. He accepted, but when Nixon ran again in 1968, Gray stayed in Connecticut. His interest was in government service, not partisan politics. When Nixon won, Gray applied for a job. Bob Finch, the newly appointed secretary of health, education and welfare, hired Gray as his executive assistant. Gray moved to Washington for a year, but the financial demands of four college tuitions forced him back to the law firm in January 1970.

In December 1970, he was drawn back into the Nixon administration, this time as assistant attorney general in charge of the Civil Division of the Department of Justice. When John Mitchell resigned as attorney general in order to run Nixon's 1972 reelection campaign, Deputy Attorney General Richard Kleindienst was elevated to attorney general and Pat Gray was elevated to the number-two slot at the Justice Department. And it was there, as deputy attorney general–designate of the United States, his nomination already reported unanimously out of the Senate Judiciary Committee and awaiting a certain full-Senate confirmation vote, that Pat Gray found himself on May 2, 1972, the day that J. Edgar Hoover died. The next day, Nixon and Kleindienst appointed Gray to be acting director of the Federal Bureau of Investigation, a job he would hold for just 361 days before he was forced to resign.

Watergate was his undoing. Though he had not been part of any of the conspiracies, it would take him the next eight years to prove it. Five federal grand juries, four committees of Congress, dozens of magazine articles, hundreds of newspaper accounts. The cover of *Time* magazine. The dust jacket of *All the President's Men*. All of them lumping him in with the actual criminals, all of them assuming his guilt. None offering any proof.

In June 2005, the accusations came flooding back to the front pages when Mark Felt, the former acting associate director of the FBI, identified himself as "Deep Throat" and his defenders claimed that he had had no choice but to leak information to the *Washington Post* because his boss was L. Patrick Gray, one of the conspirators. After Pat Gray heard Ben Bradlee, Carl Bernstein, and Terry Lenzner trot out their old falsehoods on national television talk shows, he called me from Florida. He was incensed. "Ed," he said, "I think we need to get back in the book business."

"Pop," I answered, "I was hoping you'd say that."

Two days later my brother Alan and I met in Connecticut to retrieve his papers, enough to fill a midsized panel truck. Among them, intermingled with the memos, phone logs, personal notes, and formal documents—a treasure trove in themselves—were all of his personal narratives of the events that had swirled around him like a storm for those terrible eight years following Watergate. He had written the narratives primarily for his lawyers, Stephen Sachs and Alan Baron. Like all good advocates, the first thing each of them had said to him was, "Tell me what happened."

He did. Several hundred pages of first-person accounts, handwritten, then typed by his secretaries and delivered to the two lawyers who would become his lifelong friends. No one else has ever seen them. They formed the basis for his sworn testimony before the television cameras of the Ervin Committee and behind the closed doors of the Watergate grand juries, but the narratives themselves were never shown. They named names, offered opinions, and made conjectures. They were too personal and far too dangerous for a courtroom.

Thirty-five years have passed since the events he wrote about. "Watergate Affair, 1972–" is now a stand-alone category in the Library of Congress catalog system. John Ehrlichman's icy suggestion to let Pat Gray "twist slowly, slowly in the wind" has been enshrined in *Bartlett's Familiar Quotations*. Most of the major figures, like my father, have now died and the others won't be far behind, each leaving behind a different version of the story. They can't all be true.

This one is. It has already been verified by all those doubting prosecutors and investigators who sought to incriminate him but ended up exonerating him when they reluctantly concluded that everything he told them was the truth.

This is my father's book, told in his own words. To those who knew him, it may seem at times that he is speaking out loud, so familiar will be his voice. Others, meeting Pat Gray here for the first time, may be taken aback by the undiluted—some would even say naive—patriotism and respect for authority in that voice, especially coming from such a highly placed government official. But patriotism and respect for authority weren't just at the core of the self-made man who succeeded J. Edgar Hoover, they were the very attributes that got him there.

My father came to the end of his life with no illusions about his place in American culture. He had read history all his life and knew how often the biased newspaper stories of the day became primary sources for historians. But he also knew that those histories are subject to change. All it takes is the truth.

ED GRAY
Lyme, New Hampshire
September 2007

IN
NIXON'S
WEB

Prologue

April 26, 1973   *White House Telephone, 5:56–6:17 p.m.*

PRESIDENT NIXON: All right. On the Gray thing, it seems to me that Gray, that you should have your meeting with Gray immediately, the three of you. Don't have him make a statement, however, until—I don't know if he should even make one tonight. You know what I mean.

ASSISTANT ATTORNEY GENERAL HENRY PETERSEN: Yes.

PRESIDENT NIXON: I'm not sure I would react that soon. I don't know, but at least that was Dick's feeling, that maybe we shouldn't act tonight. But under the circumstances with the destruction of the documents story, even though it was done with no venal intent, this is stupidity of an unbelievable degree.

PETERSEN: I agree.

PRESIDENT NIXON: And he'll have to resign. And who would be the best—who is the second man over there?

PETERSEN: Mark Felt's the second man at the Bureau. Let me say one thing, Mr. President. You know, I don't give a damn whether I get that job or not.

PRESIDENT NIXON: I understand.

PETERSEN: You know, I think, next to the presidency of the United States, it may be the toughest job in America. . . . I don't want to see anybody from the inside take that job. . . .

> PRESIDENT NIXON: It's got to be cleaned out. But my point is, my
> point is, this is not the time, this is not the time. I'm not ready
> to name Gray's successor. I'm still searching, you know.
> PETERSEN: I agree . . .

As I left my office on the evening of April 26, 1973, and walked down to the parking garage with my driver, Special Agent Tom Moten, neither of us spoke as we went down the steps. Tom held the silence as he pulled the Mercury out toward the officer on duty at the gate.

At the gate the guard had none of his usual pleasantries, but instead hurriedly told me that Assistant Attorney General Henry Petersen had called and left word that it was urgent that I contact him.

Getting out of the car, I thanked the guard and stepped into his shack to call Henry.

"Pat," he said, "I just got a call from Dick Kleindienst. The president just called him and said that the story of your burning the Hunt files is going to be all over the news tomorrow and he wants to get the story himself first. Dick is coming back into the office from Burning Tree and wants to meet with the two of us at seven."

Word of Senator Lowell Weicker's selected leaks was out.

"Fine, Henry," I replied. "I'll go up to my office first, and I'll meet you in the AG's office at seven."

I hadn't expected this activity until the next day, when I knew that the news stories would appear, but I was just as prepared to deal with it tonight as I would be the next day. Perhaps even more so.

Shortly before seven I walked over to the attorney general's office. The main double doors were locked, so I went around through the circular alcove and foyer to his conference room, intending to use the key I had for that door. These doors, however, were open, so I walked through the conference room to the secretaries' offices and picked up a telephone to call Henry and tell him I was there.

Just at that moment I heard footsteps and I turned to see Dick Kleindienst striding into his office. I called Henry and told him that both the attorney general and I were in the office and that I would place a leather thong on the double doors so that he could come in that way. Henry said he would be right up.

Then I walked into the attorney general's office. Without preamble, Dick went right to the heart of the matter.

"Pat, I've been talking to the president about your burning of the Hunt files. The news inquiries are coming in thick and fast and the president wants a recommendation right now."

Before I could respond, Henry Petersen came into the room, and Dick repeated what he had just told me. Henry didn't say anything, just nodded his head, and took a seat in one of the chairs in front of the attorney general's desk. Dick sat in his chair behind the desk and waved toward the remaining chair in front of me. It was clearly my turn to speak.

"The news stories are coming from Lowell Weicker," I told them. Both of their faces went blank.

"I've already told Lowell the truth about the files," I went on. "And this afternoon at about 2:30 the senator came over to my office to tell me that he had relayed the entire story to four of his handpicked journalist friends. He said I may hate him for leaking this story but that he did it in my own best interests."

Kleindienst was visibly shaken. "I think we'd better go into my smaller office and have a drink," he said.

So the three of us went into the attorney general's small private office where Dick and I took seats while Henry went to the cabinet and fixed drinks. I declined.

I explained to them what I knew about the two files, which had come from the safe of E. Howard Hunt, one of the Watergate conspirators. Though I hadn't studied them in detail, it had been clear to me that they were copies of some sort of top-secret State Department cables, as well as some flimsy copies of muckraking correspondence about Senator Ted Kennedy's car accident at Chappaquiddick in 1969. I told them both, again, that when White House counsel John Dean had given me the files in the presence of John Ehrlichman, the assistant to the president for domestic affairs, both men had assured me the files were in no way connected with Watergate and that they had national security overtones. When I asked Ehrlichman and Dean if these files should be placed in the FBI files Dean responded, "These should never see the light of day." I took their statements at face value, so that when I actually went to burn the files I casually flipped through them and noted for myself that these indeed were not related in any way to our investigation of the break-in.

All of this I had carefully laid out for Senator Weicker, and at this point, sitting in the attorney general's office with these two grim-faced men, I still fully expected that the news stories the next morning would be factual.

Dick Kleindienst apparently knew better. Or perhaps he knew something else.

"Pat," he said, "I don't see how you can remain acting director of the FBI."

"I don't agree, Dick," I replied. "It will be perfectly clear that these files had nothing to do with Watergate. And certainly the people in the FBI know that I haven't in any way tried to stifle the investigation."

"That may be true," Dick stated. "But the timing of this just couldn't be worse. I think that the president will want you to step down."

Henry was nervously pacing back and forth in the small office while Dick and I remained in our chairs. The three of us discussed the pros and cons of the newspaper stories that would appear the next day, and then Dick abruptly got up.

"I'm going to telephone the president," he said, and he left the room.

April 26, 1973   *White House Telephone, 7:44–8:02 p.m.*

ATTORNEY GENERAL RICHARD KLEINDIENST: Henry and I are down here at my office with Pat Gray. . . . Let me give you his version of it before we discuss the ramifications of it and I describe his attitude. Several days after the apprehension of the Watergate burglars, he was asked to come over and met in John Ehrlichman's office with him, and there was Dean. Part of the conversation was with John Dean, Ehrlichman saying nothing. John Dean says, "Pat, here are some highly sensitive and very secret files that were in the possession of Howard Hunt that had nothing to do with the Watergate case. They are of a very, very secret, sensitive nature." He did not describe their contents. "They should not be put in the FBI files and they should never see the light of day. Here, you take them." That's the substance of it. Pat took the documents from John Dean. Then he stayed there with John Ehrlichman. Ehrlichman said nothing about the documents, and they were talking about the apprehension and concern that you had about leaks from the FBI. Pat then left that office, went home, had a few trips to make, left them at home. When he came back on a Sunday night—I think this occurred on a Thursday or a Friday. When he came back on a Sunday night, he then took the documents down to his office without looking at them, tore them into bits, put them in his burn basket, and they were destroyed. That's Pat's story. . . .

PRESIDENT NIXON: He will not say that he was ordered to destroy them?

KLEINDIENST: No. Pressed upon cross-examination as a result of what Dean said, he said that, "I had to gather from Dean as being, you know, a representative of the President of the United States, that I had to just infer from his remarks that, since they were never to see the light of day, they were of such a highly sensitive nature, and could not be put in the FBI files," he just concluded himself he ought to destroy them. Now, that's quite a bit different, you know, than getting a specific direction,

PRESIDENT NIXON: Yes.

KLEINDIENST: I think if you know Pat as I do, you press him to the wall and Pat would say that the only fair inference that I could gain from my conversation with John Dean with Ehrlichman present was that they had to be destroyed. He would not say—

PRESIDENT NIXON: It was Dean that told him this?

KLEINDIENST: Yes, yes. But he would not say that he was specifically ordered to destroy them. . . . So now we are talking in this vein: Pat, if you testify before a grand jury, we all have to assume that that's going to go out and hit the streets. . . . So suppose that this very statement that you gave us, that you made public tomorrow. You just got the press in and said, this is what happened. What would that do with respect to your ability to look after, manage, the Federal Bureau of Investigation? He said it would be a disaster. So I said, "Pat, that's where we are logically. If it should come out—and indeed it is because of all the leaks that we have—isn't that where we are?" He feels that for him to resign is an admission of guilt of some kind.

PRESIDENT NIXON: Right.

KLEINDIENST: And I said, "Pat, as far as I can see you haven't done anything criminally wrong. But in light of all the facts and circumstances of the Watergate case—"

PRESIDENT NIXON: His ability to conduct the office.

KLEINDIENST: "It creates just an impossible situation for you to manage that Bureau." And that is where we wound up before I called you, because I told him—

PRESIDENT NIXON: Right, I understand, I understand.

KLEINDIENST:—that I wanted to—he's in the other room with Henry—to report to you what he said and the context of it. Pat Gray, as you know, is a soldier and he's going to do any goddamn thing [you ask of him].

PRESIDENT NIXON: I know, I know.

KLEINDIENST: Henry and I . . . feel and we're trying to get across to Pat without just denuding him is he's got to resign. How do you want us to proceed tonight?

PRESIDENT NIXON: But how would we do it? He should say nothing tonight.

KLEINDIENST: Oh, I'm not talking about tonight. I'm trying to make a decision tonight.

PRESIDENT NIXON: Yeah. . . .

Henry was still pacing the floor, back and forth behind the leather chair I was in. My mind was going over the conversation we just had with the attorney general. Henry's pacing stopped.

"Pat, I'm scared," he said.

"Of what?" I asked.

"Well, it appears to me that you and I are expendable and Haldeman and Ehrlichman are to be saved."

The import of what he said didn't hit me right away. I answered him casually. "Henry, I think you're stretching the importance of this thing."

"Pat," he said, "I'm not kidding. We're in deep trouble here."

I thought for a moment. There was one question I could ask that would put it in perspective.

"All right, Henry. All right. Then let me ask you point-blank: Do you think I ought to retain a lawyer?"

"Yes," he said, "I think you should."

Now I knew Henry was offering me serious advice indeed, and yet I was not alarmed. Not as much as I should have been. But in my own analysis of the situation, I just could not see how I could be viewed as being liable to the point of requiring an attorney.

I did know that men in the White House and in the Committee to Re-Elect the President had recently hired some of the best criminal lawyers in Washington, although many of them had not yet been indicted. I also knew, ever since John Ehrlichman's phone call to me on April 15, that John Dean had been talking to the federal prosecutors. And certainly I knew that destruction of evidence was obstruction of justice.

But I knew that I was not involved with the Watergate wrongdoings. I knew that there had been nothing illegal in my dealings with John Dean, that I had dealt with him only in his official capacity as counsel to the president of the United States. And I knew that the files I had destroyed were most definitely not Watergate evidence. Furthermore, the files had been destroyed on the direct orders of John Ehrlichman, who was certainly acting for the president.

I also knew Henry Petersen to be a thoroughly experienced federal prosecutor who was in charge of the government's investigation of Watergate. And now he was offering me serious advice as a friend. I had to listen.

"Okay, Henry," I said, "but I don't know any criminal lawyers here in Washington. Aren't all the good ones already taken up by all these other fellows? Who would you suggest?"

"Pat, the best man you could find anywhere, and the man I would get for myself, is my good friend Stephen H. Sachs, over in Baltimore. He was an assistant United States attorney for the District of Maryland and then United States attorney for the same district for four years. Steve is an experienced prosecutor and an extremely competent attorney. He hates corruption. He's also a warm and compassionate human being, and if you can convince him that you've done nothing wrong, then you'll have a strong and very loyal advocate in your corner."

"Thanks, Henry," I said. "I know I've done nothing wrong. But if you think that I should do it, then I'll call Steve Sachs."

"I think you should do it," he said.

At that point the attorney general came back into the small office.

"Well, Pat," he said, "the president wants you to stay on as acting director. But there must be no implication of a cover-up at the White House in regard to the burning of the files."

"Dick," I said, "I burned those files at the clear direction of Dean and Ehrlichman, and John Ehrlichman has known since April fifteenth that I carried out his orders. There's nothing to cover up."

By now it was nearly 8:30 and time to go home. The three of us closed the office and moved out into the hall. Henry Petersen was six or seven steps ahead in the broad Justice Department hallway and Dick Kleindienst and I were walking together.

"You know, Pat," he said suddenly, "there are some things we will all have to take to our graves."

We walked quietly a few more steps.

"Not I," I said to him. "Not I."

The next day, I resigned as acting director of the FBI. I had held the job for less than a year. What follows is the story of that year.

"I don't want to add to your troubles."

I was told five times that Hoover would be fired.
The last time, for sure, they told me was on October
5, 1971. Five of his six top people were in my office,
waiting for the call from the White House that they
finally got it done. We never got it.

—Robert Mardian, Assistant Attorney General
The Nixon Presidency: An Oral History of the Era, 2003

ON A MAY EVENING IN 1971, I WENT TO ATTORNEY GENERAL
John Mitchell's office at just about six to report to him on the status of
civil litigation arising out of the various anti–Vietnam War demonstrations that had been occurring with some frequency that spring in
the District of Columbia. Though I had been the assistant attorney
general in charge of the Civil Division for six months, I had never reported directly to Mitchell on any matter. My reports normally went
through the deputy attorney general, so I was surprised when I heard
that the attorney general wanted to see me in person.

I walked into Mitchell's office, stood in front of his desk, and gave
him a thumbnail sketch of the demonstration notices filed and objected

to by the government. Mitchell was seated behind his large desk, which was literally overflowing with papers of all sizes, stacked in neat piles and lined up in rows. He was puffing slowly on the pipe that always seemed to be in his hand or in his mouth.

As I talked to him, it seemed to me his mind was elsewhere and that receiving my report was merely a duty he had to perform. When I finished, the attorney general motioned to one of the red leather chairs to the right of his desk.

"Sit down, Pat," he said. "I want to talk to you about another matter."

I sat down.

"I don't want to add to your troubles right now," he said, "but how would you like to be considered for the position of the director of the Federal Bureau of Investigation?"

Clearly he expected an answer from me, but I was literally speechless. There was no time to put together a reasoned response. "General," I merely said, "I will serve in whatever capacity you or the president may desire." Though his question had hit me like a bolt of lightning, that would have been my response in any event.

Mitchell then said that he just wanted to learn whether or not I was interested, and told me quite clearly that no immediate changes were planned. He didn't tell me to treat our conversation as confidential and said that he would talk to me later in the event that it became necessary for the president to make a decision regarding J. Edgar Hoover.

I didn't know what to think of our conversation. Until then my only dealings with the FBI had been to defend it and Hoover against civil suits. Despite the fact that most of us in the Department of Justice were well aware of the mounting waves of criticism directed against Hoover, I hadn't heard anyone chatter even covertly about a move to bring about his departure.

Several presidents, it was rumored, had tried to do without Hoover's services. None had succeeded. John F. Kennedy was supposedly prepared to choose a new director on New Year's Day 1965, the day Hoover was to reach compulsory retirement age at seventy. But Lyndon Johnson, six months after Kennedy's assassination, signed an executive order exempting Hoover, telling him that the country could not afford to lose him. And on this evening, as I left Mitchell's office to return to my own, I was absolutely certain that President Nixon, close friend of J. Edgar Hoover since the celebrated Alger Hiss espionage investigations of the late 1940s, was not inclined to dismiss the legendary chief of the FBI.

In my office, I began to place papers in my briefcase to take home for my evening work. I was hurrying to meet my wife, Bea, who would be waiting for me in our car. Before I left, though, I asked Marjorie Neenan, my private secretary, to come into the office. "Marge," I said, "how would you like to go to the FBI?"

She was as astonished as I had been when I heard Mitchell's words to me, and she could only say, "Oh, Mr. Gray!"

Then I described my conversation with Mitchell and said to Marge that I really didn't believe this move would ever occur and that we could look forward to many more months in the Civil Division. I could tell she wasn't so sure. Marge and I had moved before.

Marjorie Neenan had been working at the Department of Health, Education and Welfare when the new Republican administration took over in 1969. In my first meeting with her, I asked her if she thought she could work with me, a Republican. She replied that she would give it a try and see how it turned out. I agreed that she might not like me, the secretary, or our other staff people in the front office and that we might not get along with her. It was on this basis that we started, and those who served in HEW came to know Marge as an invaluable member of a front-office team that turned in many an eighteen-hour day in support of HEW secretary Bob Finch as he sought to get a handle on the most monstrous bureaucracy ever invented by accident and the hand of man.

When I left HEW in January 1970 to return to my law firm in New London, Connecticut, Marge remained in the front office at HEW. At Bob Finch's request, she moved with him and his longtime personal secretary, Doris Jones, to the White House when Bob resigned as secretary and became counselor to the president.

When I returned to government in December 1970 as assistant attorney general in charge of the Civil Division, I telephoned Marge at the White House to ask if she would like to work with me again as my private secretary. I wasn't at all sure that she would want to leave the aura of the White House to join me at Justice, but I knew that I had to try. Her competency and ability to work with people had been demonstrated time and again, and I knew she would become a key member of my personal staff if I could convince her to leave. To my delight she told me that she had accompanied Bob Finch to the White House with the understanding that she would be free to leave in the event I ever returned to government and offered her a position. I made the offer and she accepted.

It was dusk when I left the Department of Justice, walking through the inner courtyard and out the 10th Street gate. I crossed the street to where Bea and my youngest son, Stephen, then eighteen, had been waiting patiently for me. After I got behind the wheel, I turned to Bea. "Honey," I said, "how would you like your husband to be the next director of the FBI?"

Bea just looked at me, as did Stephen from the backseat. Then Bea and I broke into laughter and agreed that the suggestion was ludicrous, impossible. We agreed not to let ourselves think about the unthinkable and I drove through downtown Washington to Trader Vic's for the dinner that the three of us had planned.

Not for one minute did we consider the possibility that the president and the attorney general might try to force Hoover's departure from his beloved FBI. Hoover was the FBI and the FBI was Hoover; this was the legend, the myth, and the fact that had existed for more than forty-seven years. As we talked on the drive home to our apartment after dinner, Bea and I agreed that Hoover would not leave the FBI alive.

Little did we know how right we were. The next day I went back to work as usual. A year later, almost to the day, J. Edgar Hoover died in his sleep.

two

"Everyone knows the director of the FBI."

"All the News That's Fit to Print"

The New York Times

LATE CITY EDITION
Weather: Showers likely today and tonight. Partly cloudy tomorrow. Temp. range: today 65–75; Tuesday 60–75. Full U.S. report on Page 94.

VOL. CXXI . No. 41,738   © 1972 The New York Times Company   NEW YORK, WEDNESDAY, MAY 3, 1972   15 CENTS

**Story of Joe Gallo's Murder:
5 in Colombo Gang Implicated**

*Informant, in Fear,
Goes to the F.B.I.*

By NICHOLAS GAGE

*Suspects Abandon
Hideout in Nyack*

J. Edgar Hoover

**J. Edgar Hoover, 77, Dies;
Will Lie in State in Capitol**

By FRED P. GRAHAM

WASHINGTON, May 2

**BASES NEAR HUE ATTACKED;
SOUTH VIETNAMESE TROOPS
FLEE QUANGTRI IN DISORDER**

*Retreat Leaves Small Unit
Of Marines Facing Enemy*

By SYDNEY H. SCHANBERG

NEW ASSAULT DUE

U.S. General Expects
Enemy Step-Up in
Next Few Days

By HENRY KAMM

Humphrey Indiana Victor; **24 POLICE INDICTED**

Pessimism in Saigon

Front page of the *New York Times,* May 3, 1972.

Viewed from the exterior, the Department of Justice resembles a huge stone fortress placed between Constitution and Pennsylvania Avenues and 9th and 10th Streets. The architectural style, like that of the other government buildings lined up in a row from the Federal Triangle to the White House, is heavy and foreboding, yet its overall impact on the viewer is a structure of beauty and majesty. Inside this six-story building, erected around a central courtyard, are high ceilings and long corridors running parallel to the avenues and streets that form its boundaries. Offices are located along the main corridors and the many little corridors that branch off from them, leading into a labyrinth known only to longtime occupants of the building.

Inside the building the decorative scheme of the principal offices is warm, inviting, and symbolic of prestige and power: rich wood paneling, ornate drapes, heavy carpeting, and elegant furniture like that found in the best private law offices. Leaving the area of the principal offices, the steel-rimmed doors and opaque or frosted glass entrances to all other offices nestle in a forest of painted concrete walls stretching the length of the high-ceilinged corridors. To walk these is a dreary experience. The corridors are poorly lighted, the paint anything but colorful, and certainly not calculated to raise the human spirit. As I moved through the department on Wednesday, May 3, 1972, I noted people talking in hushed tones and in small groups. The entire building seemed to exude grief and sorrow. Or maybe that was just my imagination.

Since the day I talked to him in his office, John Mitchell had resigned as attorney general in order to run President Nixon's 1972 reelection campaign. I was now the deputy attorney general–designate, awaiting what seemed to be certain full-Senate confirmation, and I knew that Acting Attorney General Richard Kleindienst, whom I was now replacing as deputy attorney general, was going up to the Capitol at noon that Wednesday with others high in the government to honor Hoover as his body arrived to lie in state.

The day before, Dick Kleindienst had called me into his office to tell me that Hoover had just been found dead at his home. While I was there Dick called John Mohr, now the number-two man in the FBI, to instruct him that Hoover's private office was to be sealed and his personal files safeguarded. Dick and I discussed the funeral arrangements for Hoover and he asked me to talk with John Mohr about them and keep him advised of the details.

It seemed to me that I had spent most of that Tuesday in and out of Dick's office, as did numerous other officials of the Department of Justice. At one gathering in Dick's office that day, the obvious question of a successor to Hoover was raised. John Mohr and Mark Felt, now the number-three man at the Bureau, were presented as being obvious and natural successors to Hoover. After all, John had spent the vast majority of his FBI career at Hoover's side and Felt had been chosen earlier by Hoover and Clyde Tolson to be Tolson's deputy. Tolson was, of course, Hoover's devoted friend and companion as well as his associate director. Tolson was now the ranking official of the FBI, but he was not well and it was readily apparent to all of us at this meeting that he did not have the physical stamina to follow in Hoover's footsteps.

The names of various leading law enforcement officials of the country were discussed and their careers considered. I believe it was Richard Moore who said, "Why not Pat Gray?" Dick Moore had been John Mitchell's special assistant, adviser, and counselor in the Justice Department and was now serving at the White House as a special assistant to the president.

"No way," I countered. "The president just nominated me to be deputy attorney general and it isn't going to happen." Dick Kleindienst said he needed me at his side in the department.

After more discussion regarding the capabilities of Mohr and Felt, this impromptu gathering broke up, and I left with the clear impression that Dick Kleindienst would select Mohr, Felt, or one of the other leading law enforcement officials to succeed Hoover.

On Wednesday morning, I met John Mohr for the first time. I had some difficulty locating his office because assistant attorneys general did not go wandering about the corridors of the FBI area, even though their offices were in the same building as ours. This was Hoover's preserve and visitors from the Justice Department were neither encouraged nor welcomed. In our meeting Mohr and I discussed Hoover's funeral arrangements. Though I was there in my capacity as the second ranking official of the Department of Justice, I had the distinct impression that Mohr was far too busy to engage in what he obviously considered to be idle chatter on the part of someone who did not belong there. He was courteous, but blunt, and quickly conveyed the message that department interference in the arrangements for Hoover's funeral would not be tolerated, that the funeral was an FBI matter to be conducted by the FBI. I told him that wasn't true, and our discussion became a bit heated.

"Mr. Gray," he said, "I am a hardheaded Dutchman and nobody pushes me around."

"Well, Mr. Mohr," I answered, "I am a hardheaded Irishman and nobody pushes me around, either. These are the wishes of the Department of Justice and either you carry them out or we will find someone else who will."

Tempers were understandably short. In the end, civility and calm prevailed and the funeral arrangements were made. Obviously, John was acting under great stress and deep sorrow, and after that meeting I thought it best to remove myself from any involvement with the funeral arrangements. I later reported this to Dick Kleindienst, and I believe that he and John Mohr had more than a few telephone conversations and meetings with regard to Hoover's funeral arrangements.

Shortly before noon that same Wednesday, Dick called me from his automobile on his way back from the Capitol and asked if I could be in his office at 2:15 to meet with him. It was a normal request and I believed that it would involve our continuing turnover of matters handled by the deputy attorney general, which had been going on for at least a month as I prepared to assume the duties of that office.

I was in Indianapolis on business for Pepsico, the company I'd joined after leaving the bureau almost two years earlier. At 9:30 that morning, the attorney general, Richard G. Kleindienst, called me in Indiana, after getting my number from our corporate headquarters in New York.

"Deke," he said, "the director died last night, apparently of a coronary. His body wasn't found until this morning . . . Nobody knows about this except Hoover's household staff, a few top FBI people, and me. Please don't say anything until we issue a press release at noon."

"Of course not," I said hoarsely.

"Deke, I'm going to recommend to President Nixon that you be appointed interim director . . . I know you don't want to return permanently, but please consider coming back as acting director. It's important that we have somebody of your experience and stature . . . In the meantime," Kleindienst said, "whom would you recommend to hold the organization together?"

"John Mohr," I said instantly. "You couldn't find a better man."

"A good choice," he said. "I'll get right on it. Could you call me back shortly after noon? By then the news will be public and I'll know a little more about the president's frame of mind."

At 12:15 I called the attorney general back. He was apologetic. He had discussed my possible assignment with President Nixon, who had another candidate in mind as acting director. Kleindienst, a good friend, promised to give me the details later.

—Cartha D. "Deke" DeLoach
*Hoover's FBI: The Inside Story by Hoover's
Trusted Lieutenant*, 1995

At 2:15 p.m. I walked into Dick's outer office and was waved into his private office by his secretary, Trixie Landsberger. I knocked and entered. Dick was standing in front of his desk facing me. Ralph Erickson, the assistant attorney general in charge of the Office of Legal Counsel, was sitting at the corner of Dick's desk with books and papers spread out before him.

Dick's first words were, "Pat, I am going to appoint you acting director of the FBI."

"You have to be joking," I said.

"He's not," said Ralph. "I'm looking at the enabling statutes right now."

I was again thunderstruck, dumbfounded, and speechless. Finally, I said that it just could not be. Again I pointed out that I was serving as assistant attorney general in charge of the Civil Division. I was the deputy attorney general–designate, and I just could not wear another hat and take on a third set of responsibilities. We talked with Ralph briefly about the applicable laws and the legality of the appointment, and then Dick said, "Pat, let's go. We're on our way to the White House to meet with the president."

Five minutes after I entered his office, Dick and I were in the private elevator going down to the first floor, then out the door into the attorney general's black Cadillac limousine and on our way to the White House. Neither of us said much on the way over, but Dick did indicate to me that the president wanted to talk to me before the appointment was announced.

While riding over to the White House, I assumed that mine was to be a temporary appointment while the president made a choice and sent the name of a nominee for the permanent position to the Senate. Dick and I didn't have time to discuss it, but I felt certain because I had already been nominated to fill the second ranking position in the department, the Senate Judiciary Committee had reported out my nomination with a favorable 13–0 vote, and I knew that Dick wanted me to serve as his deputy attorney general.

When we arrived at the White House, we were moved right through the checkpoint at the gate, left the car in the care of Dick's chauffeur, and entered the Executive Office Building. Dick and I arrived in the reception room of the president's hideaway office and waited just a few minutes before going in to meet him.

After greeting us, the president sat down in a stuffed chair at one end of a coffee table. I sat on a sofa to the president's left and along the lengthy side of the coffee table and Dick took a chair across from the president. John Ehrlichman, the president's chief domestic adviser, had

From left: John Ehrlichman, H. R. Haldeman, President Nixon, L. Patrick Gray III, Richard Kleindienst. May 3, 1972.

been with the president when we entered and H. R. "Bob" Haldeman, the president's chief of staff, came in a few minutes later. Both sat in chairs arrayed along the other side of the coffee table.

The president did most of the talking. He commented that I would probably rather be deputy attorney general but that he wanted me to serve as acting director of the FBI. I said that I would serve in whatever capacity the president wished. Nixon said that after my service as acting director was completed, there would be another position of equal rank in the Nixon administration for me. He was careful to point out that no commitment was being made to me, but that my name would be among those considered when a permanent director was named. That wouldn't happen until after Election Day in order to keep the nomination free from any partisan debate in an election year. The president also directed me to continue the policy of operating the FBI without regard to any political influence or political considerations. Nixon also stated that I would be expected to work closely with members of his staff and that John Ehrlichman was designated as the staff member with whom I should maintain contact and to whom I should report.

This was not surprising. In the Nixon administration, designated White House staffers spoke for and in behalf of the president. Not too many of us even questioned this method of management, believing it to be that which best suited the president whom we served. Moreover, we were also quite certain that Haldeman and Ehrlichman and the other high-level White House staff persons were indeed conveying the president's instructions when speaking in his behalf. That was the way this president worked. He gave the orders to designated staffers who were to transmit them and monitor their execution so that "people did not fall between the seats," to use the president's own expression.

After about fifteen minutes Nixon arose and said that Press Secretary Ron Ziegler was in the White House pressroom and was expecting me and Dick Kleindienst over there any minute so that Dick could announce my appointment.

As the two of us walked to the pressroom, I said to Dick that I was just not going to be able to answer any questions from the newsmen because my confirmation as deputy attorney general was still pending before the Senate. When we arrived, we met Ziegler and he agreed with our position. It was in fact a long-standing Washington custom in deference to the power and prestige of the Senate, and we simply followed it.

Actually, I don't believe that anyone on this afternoon of May 3, 1972, including the president, knew whether I was going to be confirmed as deputy attorney general, whether my nomination would be withdrawn and I would serve only as assistant attorney general in charge of the Civil Division, whether I would serve only as acting director of the FBI, or some combination of the three. A few months later Senator William Proxmire, enlisting the support of the General Accounting Office, which found my appointment and service beyond a thirty-day period to have been illegal, charged that I had been illegally appointed and that I should return to the government all of the salary paid to me. Happily, I didn't have to do that.

In front of the reporters, Ziegler introduced Dick, who announced that he was going to name me as acting director of the FBI. I then said that I was proud yet humbled to have been named, and I praised the legacy bequeathed to our country by J. Edgar Hoover and the dedicated men and women of the FBI. Questions were in the air as soon as I stopped talking and I turned them all aside by saying that my nomination as deputy attorney general was still pending before the Senate. Then Dick and I left the room.

As the chauffeur moved us with practiced ease through the Washington traffic, neither Dick nor I noticed our surroundings as we rode in silence—a silence that was broken suddenly by the sharp buzz of the telephone in the car. Dick grabbed the handset, answered, then pushed the phone to me: "It's Marnie. She wants to talk to you."

It was Dick's wife calling to say that she had just heard the news of my appointment and wanted to be the first to congratulate me. I thanked Marnie and asked her if she knew where Bea could be found, saying that I had tried her at home but there was no answer. She told me that Bea was in the beauty parlor and gave me the number.

I dialed and asked to speak to Mrs. Gray. The lady who answered asked if she could tell Mrs. Gray who was calling. "Yes," I said, "I am her husband."

"Oh, Mr. Gray, isn't the news wonderful?" she blurted through the phone's static. "Mrs. Gray already knows! We heard it on the radio!"

Eventually I talked to Bea. She was thrilled. J. Edgar Hoover had been one of her favorite people. Even though she had met him only twice, that distinguished gentleman of the old school had charmed and captivated her completely. Hoover could be charming, gracious, and the soul of gallantry on social occasions. I too stood in awe of him; indeed, I had been careful not to chat too much with him, lest I bore him with trivia. I always had the feeling that he looked upon assistant attorneys general as bothersome fellows in the Department of Justice who for some reason or another did not understand the role of the director and the FBI in the department.

As the limousine turned into the Department of Justice gate in the middle of the block between Pennsylvania and Constitution Avenues, I said, "Dick, I just don't know that I really want to take on this assignment if it means I'm not going to be able to serve with you as your deputy."

"Pat," he replied, "there is no more important position in our government than the director of the FBI. No one knows who the deputy attorney general of the United States is, but everyone knows the director of the FBI."

After that, he and I were silent again. We left the car and went separately to our offices.

My personal staff greeted me with warm smiles and hearty words of congratulation. Surely they hadn't expected this honor to come to me and to them any more than I had. Each of us had been heavily involved in the planning necessary to move up and assume the role and the responsibilities of the office of the deputy attorney general of the United States. Today's announcement had cranked a big turn into the planning. None of us knew exactly how many offices I would be occupying or which members of my personal staff would be with me and in what office. I left them in my outer office and went into my private office.

Closing the door, I walked to my desk chair, leaned against it, and looked up Constitution Avenue toward the Capitol. For the first time that day I had a few moments to think about the impact the death of Hoover would have upon the men and women of the FBI. Being an outsider, I was in no position to attempt such an evaluation other than in a most general way and from the vantage point of a fellow human being, not a fellow professional. I finally sat down in my desk chair, put my feet up, and began to think in depth about any action I should take before Hoover's funeral, which was scheduled for the following morning.

Hoover had led the FBI for almost forty-eight years. He had become an international figure of renown, and the FBI was an institution honored and respected at home and abroad. He had raised the special agents of the FBI to a professional stature not enjoyed by any other law enforcement officers, had achieved for them salary benefits that no other government law enforcement agency, state or federal, had obtained. True, he had disciplined his agents with biblical severity, but he had also defended his brood with the sharp, fighting talons of a mother eagle. I fully expected the men and women of the FBI to be sorrowed and saddened by their great loss.

I debated what to do. I felt a duty to go to the senior executives of the FBI, the men who had worked with Hoover over the years, to let them see me, and to let them hear me. At the same time, I didn't want to be insensitive to their grief, and I didn't want to burst upon them like some jack-in-the-box, an interloper bent on pushing Hoover into the pages of history and remolding the FBI in my own likeness.

The plain truth of the matter was that I just did not know enough about the customs and traditions of the FBI, its inner workings, or the background and character of its senior executives to reach a reasoned judgment. I had talked with Mark Felt, the deputy associate director, on the telephone on several occasions; I had been in John Mohr's office the day before discussing the funeral; and I had met with Assistant Director Dwight Dalbey on two occasions to discuss lawsuits against Hoover and the FBI, which were being defended by the Civil Division. This was the extent of my prior contact with the senior executives of the FBI.

Finally, I decided that my heart and my instincts must control. I telephoned Mark Felt and asked him if he believed the senior executives of the FBI would be offended if I asked them to meet with me on this very afternoon. I said to Mark that I didn't want to appear insensitive to their grief, but that I did believe I had a duty to go to them, to let them see me, and to let them hear me. Mark assured me that these men would not react unfavorably to such a meeting. The meeting was set for 4:30 that afternoon in Hoover's personal conference room located in his office suite.

Mark offered to escort me from my Civil Division office. I declined and told him that I would come up alone to meet with them. Then I called Dick Kleindienst to tell him what I proposed to do. Dick asked me if I wanted him to accompany me and I told him no. He asked if I minded telling him why.

"Dick," I said to him, "you are the admiral. I am one of your captains, and if I cannot do the job, you had better get yourself another captain. I am going up alone." He said he understood and asked that I tell him later about the meeting.

As I prepared to go from my office on the third floor to the FBI on the fifth, I was thinking that this short walk would be taking me back into the nonpartisan service of our country, a return to a band of brothers similar in many respects to the one I left behind on my retirement from the U.S. Navy twelve years before. Though I believed firmly in supporting a presidential decision, not undercutting it, civilian service in the Nixon administration involved partisan, political considerations that were not particularly palatable to me. But I also knew our very existence as a democracy depends upon a strong two-party system functioning well. The alternative is chaos or a totalitarian state. The American political scene is a partisan arena, and no amount of hand-wringing is going to change that.

As I walked nearly half a city block before crossing the invisible border into FBI territory, I wondered about the kind of reception I might receive from the assembled executives of the FBI and the words that I would say to them. I paused a moment before the opaque glass door framed in rich wood that read "Office of the Director, Federal Bureau of Investigation." To this day, I cannot recall the room number.

I opened the door and stepped for the first time into the director's reception room. It was filled with memorabilia of the FBI's battles with the criminal bands roving the land in Hoover's early days, but I didn't idle there to admire the scenery. Mark Felt met me, we shook hands, and he led me through a polished wooden door that opened into a long interior corridor. On the right side were what appeared to be private offices. On the left hung pictures, awards, mementos, and citations along with testimonial scrolls and honorary degrees. At the end of this corridor, which was about forty feet long, we came to another highly polished door. Before going through it, I glanced up to see a very large multicolored seal of the Department of Justice, nearly three feet in diameter.

Mark preceded me into the director's conference room. Though I didn't yet know the full extent of it, this had to be the center ring of the Hoover extravaganza, opulent and impressive by any standard. But I wasn't devoting too much attention to the physical surroundings. My eyes instead were drawn to the group of fifteen men who rose from the large conference table as I entered the room. I noted their chiseled faces, their impeccable dress, their clean, crisp appearance overall. These were the assistant directors of the Federal Bureau of Investigation, men molded by Hoover, advanced by Hoover, and occupying their present positions by his mandate.

After being introduced to each man and shaking his hand, I stood at the head of the table, asked them to take their seats, and said that I wanted to chat with them for just a few moments. Famous FBI names were borne by this group: Felt, Mohr, Rosen, Bates, Bishop, Callahan, Casper, Cleveland, Conrad, Dalbey, Miller, Ponder, Soyars, Waikart, and Walters. Whether they were all there on this momentous occasion, I do not know; I didn't count noses nor could I remember each name. I never asked if any one of them dictated a Bureau memorandum for the record of this first meeting with their new acting director.

As I stood before them, I very carefully and slowly looked each man in the face and held his eyes for just a few seconds. I saw in their faces a grief and a grimness, and I sensed that they were wondering who this usurper might be who dared to come among them. I explained that I didn't want to tread upon their sensibilities, nor did I wish to intrude upon their private mourning on this sad occasion. Duty had brought me to them and I touched upon their duty to the people of the United States to join with me in preserving and protecting Hoover's legacy and in building upon that legacy as we moved forward together to maintain the traditions of the FBI. I concluded by directing that Hoover's personal staff have all the time they required to remove his personal effects and memorabilia, and I told them that I was assuming command of the FBI from this moment on and that I would exercise that command from my Civil Division office until such time as the director's office was ready. I then left the conference room and walked back to the Civil Division.

> Gray is an excellent speaker and his remarks on this
> occasion attested to that fact. . . . As the group broke
> up there was considerable discussion and
> everything I heard was favorable to our new boss.
>
> —W. Mark Felt
> *The FBI Pyramid From the Inside*, 1979

Earlier in the afternoon I had telephoned Clyde Tolson, but was advised that he was too grief-stricken to talk to me. I knew that he was not well physically and hadn't been for some time but I wanted to tell him personally of my appointment. Shortly after my brief meeting with the senior executives, Mark Felt telephoned to say that Tolson's resignation had been delivered to the FBI and that he was sending it down to me. I received it shortly after 5:00 p.m. I sent a warm letter to Tolson accepting his resignation, and then I called Dick Kleindienst to let him know.

There was no hint in the letter or in Mark's telephone call that Tolson would oppose my appointment or lead any opposition to it. Later there were rumors and allegations and even news stories indicating that he was leading a well-structured campaign supported by the "Hoover old boys" to discredit me, but I didn't receive any solid information or evidence at any time during my year in the FBI that Clyde Tolson was engaged in this type of activity. As far as I know, he never did.

But it wouldn't take me long to learn that the Bureau was, by its very nature, a spawning ground for all kinds of gossip, rumors, stories, and choice tidbits of information that got freely passed along the FBI grapevine. I would come to see this as an insidious parasite gnawing away at our soft underbelly, but I was never able to stop it, control it, or reduce it to an acceptable level.

Unfortunately, I never did get the opportunity to meet with Clyde Tolson, and he refused again to talk with me when I extended an invitation to him to meet with the president of the United States along with Helen Gandy, who had been Hoover's personal secretary and executive assistant for more years than anyone was able to remember.

(Official records indicate she was Hoover's secretary since March 1931 and was appointed as his executive assistant in 1939.) Nixon wanted to thank both of them personally for their long and dedicated service to our country, but they both refused to meet with him. This shocked me because I had been trained to treat presidential invitations as command performances. An American does not refuse a presidential invitation unless physically unable to be present. When I asked, I was told that Tolson was not well enough to leave his home.

Shortly after I called Dick with Tolson's resignation, a call came from the White House: Bea and I were invited by the president to accompany him and Mrs. Nixon to and from Hoover's funeral on the following day. Naturally, I was thrilled and I knew that Bea would be, too. Obviously, as acting director of the FBI, I knew I would be attending Hoover's funeral with my wife, but I had made no special arrangements for myself and fully intended to be there with Dick, the other assistant attorneys general, and their wives in the spaces reserved for officials of the Department of Justice. I probably called Mark Felt myself or had Marge Neenan call his secretary to let him know that Bea and I would accompany President Nixon to the funeral.

I had before me an almost impossible task. I had to learn all there was to know about the FBI as fast as possible and without the benefit of a no-holds-barred briefing from the man whom I had been appointed to succeed. That night I went home with two full briefcases containing papers involving Civil Division work as well as excerpts from prior news articles and the *Congressional Record* concerning attacks made on the FBI and Hoover. I had asked my personal staff earlier in the day to begin pulling some of these together for me and had asked one of my three principal assistants, Barbara Herwig, to begin scouring the Justice Department library for books written about the FBI.

Bea and I later joked about these evenings and the ever-present briefcases laden with papers and books to read and letters and documents to sign, but on that first night neither of us realized that I was destined to spend three and four hours each evening for the next year of our lives with the contents of these briefcases. Many in the FBI would probably say that I was the cause of a sudden increase in the flow of paper to the acting director's office because of the innumerable questions I asked in those early days at the Bureau. And they would be right. Unless they were thrown away, there must be hundreds of notes from me in the FBI's files asking questions on all phases of operations, which were reported to me in the form of the standard Bureau memoranda.

I think it was Attorney General Ramsey Clark who said that one must know the right question to ask, or at least the right manner in which to ask it, if one expects to get a clear, full answer from the FBI. Hoover had trained his headquarters staff to be very careful in answering outside questions and to answer them in such a way as not to embarrass the Bureau. This same training had been passed along to the field offices, the fifty-nine regional FBI divisions to which most of the FBI's special agents are assigned and through which most of its work is accomplished. As the days passed into weeks and into months, I began to learn firsthand of the policy known as "Don't Embarrass the Bureau." I never did learn how to ask the right questions.

On this first evening, I handled the paperwork easily and then began to think of the vast scope of FBI operations and the principal problems I faced. First, I recognized that I was an outsider, not one of the Bureau's own. I was a political appointee serving in the Department of Justice and not a career law enforcement professional. In the eyes of Bureau officials, I was probably suspect. This was brought home to me, and hard, much later on when one of the top Bureau officials said to me, "Mr. Gray, we just don't believe you are for real." To this day I am not certain what message he meant to convey.

By nature I had no taste or desire for bureaucratic infighting and maneuvering for power as Hoover had done throughout his life. It may have been necessary for Hoover's personal survival, but not for that of his organization. The record of FBI accomplishments spoke for itself and was there for all the world to see. I believed that Hoover, supposedly the world's master in imaginative public relations, had not really come to grips with the need to work effectively and openly with the members of the press and the communications media of all forms.

Hoover's style, I knew, was not going to be mine. I had been trained from my earliest days as a naval officer to take care of my men. Discipline them, yes, when required, but fairly and commensurate with the offense committed. The style of my leadership would be a product of my own family upbringing and my understanding of leadership principles, which had worked well for me for so many years in the navy.

Although I knew that Hoover's style would not be mine, I believed strongly that this man had served our country and our presidents honorably and faithfully for all his life. I would not permit these differences to be raised to a level that would amount either to criticism of Hoover the man or to condemnation of his method of directing and regulating the operations of the FBI. Because of the repeated attacks made against him in the last years of his life, I vowed that these same critics would not use me to take one piece of flesh from Hoover and would not rip, tear, or bend the fabric that was the Federal Bureau of Investigation. I resolved that neither I nor the FBI would respond to our critics with venom and personal insults. Fact and reason would be our counterpunches.

three

"You've got to remember, they're all enemies."

THE FOLLOWING DAY, THURSDAY, MAY 4, 1972, WAS TO BE ANother eventful day in our lives. Bea met me at the Justice Department and we were driven in my official car to the diplomatic entrance of the White House. Limousines, headed by the president's own, were parked in a row along the wide circular driveway. Secret Service men and presidential aides were guiding invitees to the appropriate vehicle in the procession. Bob Haldeman was there, busy with his movie camera. Ron Ziegler was moving from car to car assisting members of the press. Steve Bull, who assisted Dwight Chapin, the president's appointments secretary, gathered Bea and me under his wing and said we were to ride in the limousine directly behind the president, who rode with his wife and with Mamie Eisenhower, the widow of the late president. We watched as President and Mrs. Nixon and Mrs. Eisenhower walked from the Oval Office to their limousine. Once they were settled comfortably the column of vehicles began to move.

Neither Bea nor I had ever traveled in a presidential motorcade. The police, mounted on motorcycles, carved a path through the always dense Washington traffic and we began to gather speed, and then more speed as we ate up the miles between the White House and the National Capital Presbyterian Church, located in northwest Washington on Nebraska Avenue in the midst of a beautiful residential area.

Later on I heard stories that the entire funeral had been stage-managed by the White House as a public relations sop to those who had believed so strongly in Hoover and all the fundamental American principles he espoused. The implication was that the Nixon administration was fed up with Hoover and would have greeted his demise with business as usual were it not for the vast constituency of Hoover and FBI who also happened to be a vital part of Nixon's constituency. The White House may have stage-managed Hoover's funeral, but if that was the case they weren't allocating the seats in the church.

Bob Mardian, a former assistant attorney general who had recently left the Justice Department to work for Nixon's reelection committee, had called me the day before the funeral to say that several former FBI "biggies," among them Cartha "Deke" DeLoach, a former associate director to Hoover, did not have reserved seats and would I intervene with John Mohr to obtain seats for them. I called John, and he assured me that these former FBI executives would be greeted properly and seated. Certainly there was liaison and coordination between the FBI, the Justice Department, and the White House, but I saw no evidence then or since that Hoover's funeral was anything other than what it was—a state funeral in honor of a great American.

As the presidential motorcade turned from Ward Circle to Nebraska Avenue, Bea and I saw the first of thousands of police officers lined along each side of the street. We tried to identify their home-city shoulder patches as we passed, but our limousine was moving too fast. One colorful, handsome uniform blended into another as we turned into the driveway of the church and stopped immediately behind the presidential limousine, where we were met by other White House aides who escorted us to the president's vehicle. Mrs. Eisenhower, Mrs. Nixon, and the president emerged. Nixon was immediately told by an aide that television cameras had been placed in the church and he reeled off their locations. It was plain that these electronic eyes were going to have a clear view of the presidential party in the front pew.

Neither Bea nor I knew where we were going to sit in the church. Before I could ask, we were whisked off by another presidential aide and were walking down the center aisle of a very crowded church. I could see at a glance that all pews were filled on both sides of the aisle. Then I knew that we must be on our way to the front pew. It was a long way, and as we walked I could see familiar faces from the Department of Justice and other departments of the government. Soon we were there. Bea entered the pew first and I followed her, moving over as far as we could.

Looking to my right I could see that the front pew on the other side of the aisle was occupied by Dick Kleindienst and the top executives of the FBI. In death, Hoover had united the FBI and the Department of Justice, as if all of the walls had come tumbling down. I knew this was not really the miracle of the moment, but the symbolism was there and must have been obvious to longtime observers of the FBI and the Department of Justice. Dick Kleindienst looked out of place in that pew with those men, whom I had met for the first time only the day before. I didn't know whether he had been invited to sit there or had chosen to. He, too, was an intruder, and had picked the worst time and place to do it, on the day the FBI was burying its chief.

My thoughts were interrupted by the entry of Mrs. Eisenhower, Mrs. Nixon, and the president. Dr. Edward Elson, Hoover's pastor and friend of many years, immediately began the hauntingly beautiful service. I was aware of the roving eye of the television camera and resented that it was there. The serenity and dignity of the church at a time like this should have been spared the presence of its hyperactive lens. It was not to be. The president delivered the eulogy, Dr. Elson the concluding prayers, and then we were on our way again, striding down the aisle in the wake of the president, Mrs. Nixon, and Mrs. Eisenhower, and followed by Vice President and Mrs. Agnew. In the sea of faces, I saw a few I recognized as we moved swiftly toward the waiting limousines. Again the motorcycle officers of the Metropolitan Police Department guided us swiftly through the lovely streets of northwest Washington, past Embassy Row, through Rock Creek Park, and then to the White House.

As we left the limousines, I asked Steve Bull if I might use his phone to call for my own car at the Department of Justice. Bea and I walked with him across the White House lawn to his office where he asked his secretary to call the department for my car. His office was located next to the Oval Office, and the door between the two was wide open. As Bea and I chatted with Steve we could see President Nixon through the open doors. The president motioned with his arm for us to come in. Bea and I looked at each other and then at Steve, who merely nodded his head. I took Bea by the arm and we walked in.

We were elated to find ourselves alone in the Oval Office with the president of the United States. I reintroduced Bea to the president. At any moment, I expected an aide to enter to break up what was so obviously a spur-of-the-moment act. The president had thrown a monkey wrench into his appointments, and I expected to see Bob Haldeman, Dwight Chapin, or Steve Bull come through the door to advise the president that he had more important commitments.

"Now, I think the thing is," Nixon said to me, getting quickly to the point, "are you going to be the nominee later? You can say you're one, and you know that the president is going to select the best man for the job and you just are not going to comment on it at this point. As you well know, that could well be what we want to do."

I tried to answer, but just then we did get interrupted. It was the White House photographer, who came in and starting taking pictures. Nixon continued as if he wasn't there: "You could say the president has a number under consideration and that you're one, and that you want to do whatever the president desires."

The photographer left after a few minutes and Nixon closed the door behind him.

The president seated Bea to his right at the desk and I moved around to sit in the chair to his left. After he sat down, I did, and then proceeded to tell him about my meeting with Mark Felt and the other senior men at the FBI. Nixon listened and nodded, then said, "Well, the housecleaning has got to come later because you don't want to mess with it. But it should not come now."

The conversation turned to Hoover's friendship with Nixon and how I should compare that relationship to my own.

Nixon with Bea and Pat Gray in the Oval Office. May 4, 1972.

"You could say—because they always like this—'Well, it's common knowledge that Director Hoover was a very close personal friend of the president and his family.' Which is true. My God, I've been in his house a dozen times. He's been, you know, to the White House and to great numbers of occasions I've put on through the years. Out of office I had seen him in California. And I'd say that: 'My relationship with the president is not like that.'"

It certainly wasn't. And then Nixon turned abruptly to the press itself.

"You've got to remember, they're all enemies," he said. "They're all enemies. One or two exceptions, but generally speaking, whenever they say they're enemies of the Bureau, they're enemies of law and order, they're enemies of the administration. They were enemies of Hoover's, blood enemies, and they know it. . . . Just consider them as the enemy, but don't let them know that you're considering them that way. Hoover was a master at it. He hated the press. Hated them, except for a few that he, you know, people like Dick Berlin and others that he got along with. But his favorite words: 'They're scum. Scum!' And, so you should do the same thing. Never, never figure that anyone's your friend. Just don't do it. That doesn't mean that you don't do things with them socially, but let them think that you're their friend, that you're being taken. But never, never, never do that. That's the best advice I can give. Some of our boys around here have to learn the hard way. They say, 'Oh, we can change them.' Hoover hated 'em, and yet he had very good press relations. Rather curiously, because they had enormous respect for the old man, and he was clever as the dickens. With his enemies he'd, you know . . . he would in private talk very boldly. Publicly, except for the last when he did fall off a bit and he lost his judgment, you know. . . . Hoover really never missed. But you do the same thing. Play it. Play it. You've got to be a conspirator, you've got to be totally ruthless, you've got to appear to be a nice guy, but underneath you've got to be steely tough. That, believe me, is the way to run that bureau."

Nixon then asked about Clyde Tolson's health, and I said that he'd resigned. The president suggested I call a meeting of all the special agents in charge, each of whom ran a field office, and if I did, he might "pop over." But that was just an interlude before he turned back to the press.

"Well," he said, "we all have to put on the veneer. Like the press. I can hardly stand 'em. They have no loyalty to the country. They're a bad, bad bunch."

I mentioned that Ron Ziegler had had an inquiry from Dan Rather of CBS about a speech I had made, but before I could relate my response, Nixon was off again:

"Rather's a son of a bitch. Don't ever see him. Don't ever, ever, ever see him. I can assure you, because he will cut you up. I would not say anything at all. Cut him off totally. Recognize that Hoover hated CBS with an utter passion, you hear? . . . Rather is a smart rat, but not as smart as someone who's more of a pundit. But he's clever. Have nothing to do with CBS, I can assure you. Nobody. Never do it. They are out to get the Bureau. . . . There's one thing for the memory of Edgar Hoover: Don't do anything for those sons of bitches at CBS. They hated him.

They maligned him. Another group: Time-Life. Never see anybody from Time-Life. Never. Never. Never. You may have it in your head to, but remember: they're really, really out to get us. Now, on this, *Newsweek* is worse, but Time-Life, I just . . . They have total, total hatred of the Bureau. The *New York Times*, never let 'em in the office. They must not be in that office. Have nothing to do with them."

After that outburst, Bea asked about an upcoming interview she had with Bonnie Angelo of *Time* magazine. Nixon relaxed. "She's all right," he said. "Bonnie Angelo's all right. When I said *Time*, I meant Sidey, Checker, people like that. Bonnie Angelo is a nice little girl. But it won't come out the way you expect because they vet it in New York."

Emboldened by Nixon's direct answers, Bea then asked another question. She had volunteered for one of Nixon's reelection committees and now she wanted to know if it was still proper for her to do that.

The president turned toward the window, looked out over the Ellipse, and said to Bea that this would be political work and that she should not do it. He went on to say that she should let the newspapers know that she asked this question and that she could quote the president directly on his response. I considered this strange at the time because I had always been trained that one never quoted the president directly, that conversations with the president were privileged. I wondered why Nixon was so insistent in giving Bea permission to tell the newspapers. Indeed, he was urging her to tell the newspapers.

After that, the visit was quickly over. It had lasted perhaps fifteen minutes. We left the Oval Office, still amazed that it had even occurred. As we drove to the Sans Souci for lunch, I found it hard to believe that my dogged determination to serve the nation and this president had brought me to this day. I had worked hard and long in the navy, in civilian life, and in the Nixon administration and I had achieved a measure of success. I was confident of my ability to tackle the tough assignments. I was content to serve and not to be served, and I had never asked this president, or anyone connected with his administration, for a specific assignment. After Nixon was elected in 1968 I asked only that I be permitted to serve, that I be considered for a position in the administration. Now I was the acting director of the Federal Bureau of Investigation.

While assistant attorney general and deputy attorney general–designate, I had lunched at Sans Souci from time to time. The food was five-star, Monsieur Paul DeLisle the perfect and charming host, and the waiters courteous, friendly, and eager to serve, but I had not yet taken Bea there. So that morning before going over to the White House I asked Marge to call Monsieur Paul and ask if he could possibly find two places for lunch for me and for my wife. It was the first and last time Bea was ever in Sans Souci. If any of the regulars wondered what the new FBI chief was doing there in the company of a beautiful woman, none were so coarse as to display their wonderment in any manner. They were to see more of me, but without a beautiful woman at my side. Hoover had his lunch every day in the dining room at the Mayflower Hotel, but when Gray went out for lunch he visited Sans Souci.

four

"So few moist eyes."

RUMORS FLOW FREELY IN WASHINGTON. THAT SPRING IT WAS whispered that the liberals on the Senate Judiciary Committee were determined to work over the Nixon administration just as soon as a permanent director of the FBI was nominated. News reports claimed that regardless of whom the president chose to succeed Hoover, liberal senators were determined to force the FBI to face the most thorough public investigation in its history. Their official target was said to be J. Edgar Hoover and his abuse of power; the objective, of course, was the continued embarrassment of the Nixon administration. It was business as usual in the company town whose only real industry is the government of the United States.

From my first day as Hoover's successor, I knew that the windows of the FBI had to be opened if for no other reason than to counter the hue and cry now being raised by its critics. I was all but certain that Congress would move at once to set in motion a full-scale investigation of the Bureau, so I resolved to be immediately accessible to the press and to Congress. Despite the rumors, Congress showed little interest. The press, however, was ready and moved in on me like locusts ravaging a field of corn.

"Nixon Names Gray Acting FBI Director in Effort to Avoid Senate

Confrontation" read the *Wall Street Journal*'s headline, typical of the early newspaper reaction.

The syndicated columnists Rowland Evans and Robert Novak, in a column headlined, "The FBI After Hoover," labeled me "competent and colorless" and declared that the FBI had been paralyzed by Hoover's tyranny. Agents in the field were said to be consumed with fear and afraid to send official reports of their problems back to Bureau headquarters in Washington. Evans and Novak concluded that this damaging paralysis inside the FBI accounted for there being "so few moist eyes in the Bureau's headquarters on Pennsylvania Avenue after the stunning news that Hoover was dead at age 77." These two "experts" on the FBI, and on nearly every other institution of government in Washington, also reported that many FBI officials agreed with the bitter words of an unnamed veteran FBI agent: "It was fitting that the director died in his sleep. That was the way the Bureau was run lately." This was harsh commentary by a pair of men who never carried the responsibility of making a decision beyond "Who do we attack today?"

The *Philadelphia Inquirer* was more accurate. "How do you replace an American institution in what could be the second most powerful job in the Nation?" asked reporter Davis Merritt. "Very cautiously, if you're L. Patrick Gray 3d." He was correct. I was proceeding very cautiously and I intended to continue in that manner until I began to feel that my personal staff and I knew the names, reputations, and capabilities of the high-level players at FBI headquarters. I believed these men to be professionals in the service of their country, and I was certain that they would recognize me as being the same. It was just a matter of time and getting to know each other.

Most of the reporters didn't know me at all. So they adopted the oldest tactic in Washington: they turned to their "sources."

The Washington staff of the Scripps-Howard newspapers, in a weekly analysis sent out over their wires just after my appointment, reached the conclusion that "President Nixon's swift move to install his man— L. Patrick Gray, III—as acting head of the FBI has set off a wave of bitterness and suspicion between senior FBI officials and The White House." This same analysis reported: "The FBI men wanted one of their own to be appointed interim director to succeed the late J. Edgar Hoover. They say Nixon went outside the ranks of the Bureau in an effort to grab control of the traditionally non partisan, apolitical investigative agency."

This analysis, and a column in the *Washington Daily News* of May 6, 1972, touched on what appeared to be a very sensitive nerve as far as certain members of the press were concerned: the files of the FBI. The Scripps-Howard staffers put it this way:

> The Administration was clearly concerned about the storied files Hoover's agents allegedly collected on the private lives of many prominent people, in and out of government.
>
> On Tuesday afternoon, only a few hours after Hoover's death was announced, Gray, the man whom Nixon the next day would pick as acting head of the FBI, called top Hoover aide John P. Mohr and demanded that he turn over all files in Hoover's office "which pertain to the activities of congressmen, Justice Department officials and other important public officials."
>
> Mohr told Gray he didn't know what Gray was talking about. "I don't know of any such files," said Mohr.
>
> Gray angrily hung up and within 30 minutes called back to say that under orders of Acting Atty. Gen. Richard G. Kleindienst, Hoover's office was to be sealed and the keys to all doors and filing cabinets immediately brought to Kleindienst's office. This was done.

The confidential sources relied on by the Scripps-Howard staffers and the *Washington Daily News*, whoever they were, certainly did not have any facts to pass along to their journalistic friends. John Mohr knew that his orders to seal Hoover's office had come directly to him from Dick Kleindienst well before I had been named acting director, which he attested to in a personal memo to me after the story appeared.

> I have no idea who is responsible for the column, and as you well know, the facts are not correct. . . . The first knowledge that I received of Mr. Hoover's death was when I received a telephone call from Miss Gandy asking me to come to her office immediately, which I did. She told me she had received a telephone call from Mr. Tolson to the effect that Mr. Hoover was dead and Mr. Tolson asked if I would take charge of the funeral arrangements for Mr. Hoover and if I would be kind enough to notify the Acting Attorney General. I told her that I would. I promptly notified Mr. Kleindienst as you are well aware, and to put it mildly, he was in a state of shock. He said he would immediately have to notify the White House.
>
> Subsequently in talking to Miss Gandy, she told me that Mr. Tolson had instructed that any official files in Mr. Hoover's office were to be delivered to Mr. Felt, and to my knowledge all official files in Mr. Hoover's office have been delivered to Mr. Felt. I understand from my conversation with Miss Gandy that the only thing she destroyed was the personal correspondence of Mr. Hoover, and to my knowledge there are no other files in existence anywhere relating to the work of the Bureau.

I sent the original of his memorandum back to him with these words in my own hand: "You are a diamond in the rough and a proud member of the FBI whom we cannot afford to lose. I expect you to continue to turn in, and deliver, an outstanding performance for our citizens and the FBI."

But John Mohr was finished with the FBI. He would submit his retirement request on June 15.

Long before this incident, I had resolved not to tangle with the Washington press corps regarding the contents of a story. Despite their protests to the contrary, my early experience in Washington led me easily to the conclusion that the press is always right and the facts are what they say they are. I did not even consider showing John Mohr's memorandum to Scripps-Howard or the *Washington Daily News*. Though both had written highly inaccurate stories that now repose uncorrected in their archives I knew that there was little or nothing I could do about it without becoming a leaker myself. That I would not do.

What I would do was talk to reporters on the record. Less than a week after I took office, even before I moved to the FBI spaces, I started giving one-on-one interviews. Among the first was to Robert Smith, a young reporter for the *New York Times*. His article ran on May 12 and its lead sentence encapsulated almost perfectly what I had set about doing at the FBI:

> L. Patrick Gray 3d, acting director of the Federal Bureau of Investigation, disclosed today a series of steps that may radically change both the appearance and substance of an agency held rigidly to a single pattern by J. Edgar Hoover for nearly 50 years.

Bob would leave the newspaper later that fall to go to law school. By that time we had become quite friendly and he and I had lunch together at Sans Souci just before he left.

On May 10, I gave a long interview to Sandy Ungar of the *Washington Post* in which I told him I was about to announce my decision to allow women to apply to become special agents of the FBI. I also told him that I had ordered the Bureau to look into how we could increase the number of black, Spanish-speaking, and American Indian special agents. "I want to convince these people that the Federal Bureau of Investigation belongs to all the people of the United States," I told him, and he quoted me directly in his May 12 front-page article. I had just discovered that the FBI had only 120 black and native

Spanish-speaking agents out of 8,600, less than 1.5 percent. That had to change.

Any reporter who wanted an interview was granted one, time permitting. I played no favorites, selected no individuals to promote my message. I granted in-office and telephone interviews, ate lunch with individual reporters, invited others to my home in Connecticut to meet and write about me and my family, let them accompany me as I worked out in the FBI gym. I talked with them on the street, at press conferences, and whenever I visited a field office away from Washington. My assistants spoke to them in my absence and provided background material as needed. I gave permission to senior FBI executives to talk to the press as well. My logs and calendars record more than 1,000 press availabilities, both scheduled and spur-of-the-moment.

Though I was always successful in getting press coverage when I wanted it, the results were rarely what I expected. As time passed, it seemed that every time I made a policy change, instead of getting accurately reported the decision would be criticized, usually based on distorted "facts" from some unnamed source. Attempts at correction would be futile. By the time of my Senate confirmation hearings the following February, I would stop giving interviews altogether.

five

"You heard it.
I have no reason to lie."

EARLY ON FRIDAY MORNING, THE DAY AFTER HOOVER'S funeral, I telephoned Mark Felt to tell him that I wanted to visit the director's office again, and in particular I wanted to meet and talk with Helen Gandy. I asked Mark to check with her to determine whether this would be a good time for me to visit. I did not want to hurt this gallant lady, who had dedicated her life to the nation and to the FBI. Some would say to Hoover, too. I had heard that unless Miss Gandy looked kindly upon me, she could sound the death knell on my tour of duty before it began. Other rumors called her the real power behind J. Edgar Hoover and that she would not tolerate anyone following him and succeeding.

So it was with some degree of apprehension that I returned to the director's office on this Friday morning. Perhaps there were only a few moist eyes in the Bureau, as Evans and Novak had written in their column, but Miss Gandy's would be among them. I had been informed that she was heartbroken and grieving heavily. I would have been quite surprised at any other reaction. Actually, I felt like a "plebe" midshipman coming around to report to an admiral for the first time.

Mark met me again in the director's reception room. Six feet tall, he had silver-gray hair, wore steel-rimmed reading glasses, was impeccably dressed and trim in appearance. His manners were suave and gra-

Pat Gray and Mark Felt at the Justice Department.

cious, his voice soft, and his attitude one of complete cooperation. On his handsome face there lurked none of the telltale signs of jealousy or envy that one might expect of a thirty-year career FBI official, hand-picked by Hoover as his principal deputy behind the ailing Clyde Tol-son and now forced by fate to serve a rank outsider, and an amateur at that. With Tolson's resignation he was in the pole position to assume the number-two job in the FBI provided that this new acting director did not go into orbit and select some unknown from the ranks of the FBI or from the political ranks. Mark and I never formally discussed his destiny and I don't know if he ever really concerned himself in those first few days about his role in the FBI after Hoover. There was a job to be done, a transition to be made, and a change of command had in fact occurred. I believed him to be a professional and I did not dwell on the succession to the throne of the FBI. As soon as it was appropriate, I promoted him to acting associate director and left it at that.

> It did not cross my mind that the President would appoint an outsider to replace Hoover. Had I known this, I would not have been hopeful about the future. There were many trained executives in the FBI who would have effectively handled the job of Director. My own record was good and I allowed myself to think I had an excellent chance.
>
> —W. Mark Felt
> *The FBI Pyramid From the Inside*, 1979
>
> Felt gives himself away here.
>
> —Handwritten by Pat Gray on the same page,
> date unknown

Mark and I walked up the same corridor we had traveled on Wednesday afternoon. Only now the pictures, testimonials, and memorabilia were all coming down. Men in neat gray smocks were busily removing them from the walls and packing them into boxes.

We stopped just before we got to the director's conference room. The door to the right was open, revealing a large office with two huge desks taking up most of the space. Steel filing cabinets lined one wall and many drawers were open. Packing boxes were on the floor. A woman was working at one of the cabinets and looked up as Mark and I entered. She knew who I was and I knew at a glance that this was the executive assistant to the director of the FBI. Mark introduced us. I took her hand and told her how very sad my wife and I were and that we knew the extent of her deep grief. Just a trace of a tear appeared in her eye and then this gentle lady set about making me feel at ease.

Helen Gandy was petite and feminine, her hair white, her face pretty, and her complexion perfect with no wrinkles showing, even though she was seventy-four years old. She had a beautiful smile and she turned it on me as she offered to show me about the office and help me meet some of the people. I could not picture her as the tyrant of the rumors and gossip that floated about Washington, but as I talked to her about the director and the FBI it was easy to feel her fierce sense of pride and loyalty.

As we walked through the offices she chatted with me quietly about the work of each of the people we met. They would, with two exceptions, stay on with me. Miss Gandy told me that she planned to retire. I had expected this, of course. Our visit drew to a close, and I had the feeling that Helen Gandy had heard about my remarks to the top executives of the FBI on Wednesday and approved of them. I sensed that she believed that her Bureau and Edgar Hoover's Bureau was in good hands. As we shook hands at the door, she told me to come back as often as I wished during the moving process, and offered her complete cooperation and assistance.

In the next week, I had the opportunity to visit and chat with Helen Gandy on several occasions, but just briefly. After Miss Gandy retired I did not hear from her, nor did I see her. How she evaluated my efforts as acting director of the FBI, I thought then, was a secret that she probably intended to keep to herself. Perhaps someday she would tell me she knew that I had tried so very hard to earn my badge as a special agent of the FBI. At least, I was sure, she would know from her own sources that I waged a relentless battle to prevent Hoover's critics from harming him in death or their beloved FBI in life.

On none of my visits with Helen Gandy did she and I discuss Hoover's files. My understanding was that she was removing Hoover's personal files now that he no longer occupied his government office, standard practice in Washington at that time.

My first discussion regarding FBI files didn't occur until I met with Mark Felt and Assistant Director Ed Miller in my Civil Division office the following Wednesday, May 10. We discussed many items at that meeting, and the subject of files came up only because the syndicated columnist Jack Anderson had recently published columns about "secret files" and "political dossiers" maintained by the FBI. Felt and

Miller told me that the Bureau maintained general files and investigative files, but not "secret" files.

I knew that Mark Felt had files in his office that he had taken from Hoover's office. I did not know these were called OC (Official Confidential) files until I learned of this designation in newspaper articles after I left the Bureau. I never looked at these files. I had more than enough to do to take the time to rummage through them. Nine months later, in February 1973, as I was preparing for my confirmation hearings to become permanent director, Mark suggested that we could review them if I got confirmed by the Senate and he also suggested that they be destroyed after such review. That review, of course, was never conducted.

In 1975, two years after I left the FBI and a year after Nixon's resignation, Helen Gandy and John Mohr were called before a congressional subcommittee looking into the destruction of Hoover's files. To my great dismay, they both lied about me under oath. Mohr claimed to Congressman Toby Moffett of Connecticut that the argument he and I had in his office over who would control Hoover's funeral arrangements was instead caused by my demanding to see the "secret" files.

Mr. MOFFETT. Your impression was that Mr. Gray was looking for secret files that would embarrass the administration?

Mr. MOHR. Yes.

Mr. MOFFETT. What led to that conclusion?

Mr. MOHR. Nothing he said specifically, but his overall comments and his own attitude. We got to the point where I told him in no uncertain terms that there were no secret files. I will not cuss here, but I think I did cuss at him a little bit. I think the secretaries even heard me out there talking to him. Let me finish. At that point he sat down in his chair and he said, "Look Mr. Mohr, I am a hardheaded Irishman and nobody pushes me around." I looked him right in the eye and said, "Look Mr. Gray, I am a hardheaded Dutchman and nobody pushes me around." With that, he left.

Mr. MOFFETT. That was it?

Mr. MOHR. That afternoon he was made Acting Director of the FBI.

Then, when it was her turn to testify, dear, sweet, elderly Miss Gandy told Congressman Paul McCloskey of California that she had destroyed no files without my personal approval.

> Mr. McCLOSKEY. So, did you ask Mr. Gray for permission to destroy Mr. Hoover's records?
> Miss GANDY. I did.
> Mr. McCLOSKEY. And did he give you that permission?
> Miss GANDY. Mr. Gray came into our office and asked about the files.
> Mr. McCLOSKEY. And what day was that approximately?
> Miss GANDY. It could have been after Mr. Hoover's funeral, whatever date that was.
> McCLOSKEY. But it was after Mr. Gray took over?
> Miss GANDY. Yes.
> Mr. McCLOSKEY. And as of that point in time, had you destroyed any of the personal records?
> Miss GANDY. No.
> . . .
> Mr. McCLOSKEY. How long after his death was it when you first commenced to destroy any part of his personal files?
> Miss GANDY. As soon as Mr. Gray gave his approval. I did not make any notes about dates and times.
> . . .
> Mr. MOFFETT. I want to go to the matter of Mr. Gray for the moment, if I might. There seems to be a contradiction between what Mr. Gray has told this subcommittee in conversations with the staff. I understand there is a letter to follow from him. There is a contradiction between that and what you said. Mr. Gray told the staff that he never looked at a single file. He knew that you were going through the files but he never knew what disposition was being made. Are you saying that that is not true?
> Miss GANDY. Do you think I should answer that?
> Mr. MOFFETT. I would like very much for you to answer that.
> Miss GANDY. Is it necessary that I answer it?
> Mr. MOFFETT. I would hope that you would see fit to answer.
> Miss GANDY. I have told the truth.

Mr. MOFFETT. And your testimony is that he did in fact look at the files?

Miss GANDY. You heard it.

Mr. MOFFETT. And he did know the disposition?

Miss GANDY. You heard it. I have no reason to lie.

They were both lying, but it was their word against mine. The week before the public hearings, Ted Jacobs, a staff lawyer for the subcommittee, called me at my law office in Connecticut to tell me that Gandy was going to testify this way. I told him it wasn't true. He said that Mark Felt, who had been with me in Helen Gandy's office, had confirmed my side of the story and Ted asked that I write a letter to the subcommittee detailing what I knew. I sent the letter that day.

The letter I wrote to Ted Jacobs was included verbatim in the subcommittee's final report. So was the false testimony of Mohr and Gandy. Four years later, as I fought off still another set of accusations, my attorneys obtained a copy of this memo from Clarence Kelley, who became director of the FBI in July 1973.

Memo   August 16, 1974

From: Director, FBI

To: Mr. Leon Jaworski, Special Prosecutor

With reference to destruction of personal correspondence files formerly maintained in Mr. Hoover's office, it was generally known that Mr. Hoover's personal files were destroyed after his death. However, during the investigation conducted in June 1974 to determine how a wiretap was placed on Morton Halperin three days before it was authorized by the Attorney General, former Assistant to the Director J. P. Mohr and Miss Helen Gandy, former Administrative Assistant to Mr. Hoover, confirmed that personal correspondence of Mr. Hoover was destroyed on the day of his death. During this same investigation exhaustive search

> was made for memos, letters, etc., relating to
> W. C. Sullivan. However, nothing was located of
> pertinence. Similar search was made in October
> 1971 with negative results.

Here, never shown by the FBI to the subcommittee looking into precisely this activity, was proof that Hoover's files were destroyed well before the dates Gandy claimed to the subcommittee and that both she and Mohr knew it a year and a half before they testified. They lied to that congressional subcommittee to protect J. Edgar Hoover. It was an ingrained habit with Hoover's handpicked top echelon, and I am now firmly convinced that they lied to each other and conned each other as much as they could.

The word *con* was a favorite in their idiomatic language. When I was acting director I often heard it used as follows: "So and so [a special agent of the FBI] is a great con man." Early in my tenure I treated it with a grain of salt and passed it off as just another remark. I was just not psychologically attuned to accept a derogatory remark as an actual fact. Idealistically, I believed in the Hoover legend of the FBI and I just knew that no member of the FBI would lie or "con" another.

What drivel now! My three young assistants, David Kinley, Mack Armstrong, and Barbara Herwig, were right. All three sensed long before I did that the entrenched top level of the FBI resented my appointment. "It's us against them, boss," they began telling me shortly after we arrived from the Justice Department. I didn't know what they were talking about. In fact, I thought they were wrong. I thought I knew it all, and I did not listen to them. I thought I had returned to another gentleman's organization in the service of our country. How much wiser I am now, and the discoveries, such as Gandy's and Mohr's lies about the destruction of Hoover's personal files, enlarge that wisdom.

David, Mack, and Barbara had all come with me from the Civil Division. All three were lawyers and good ones. Dave had been with me the longest, since my days at HEW when Bob Finch had hired me as his executive assistant, much to Dave's annoyance: Bob had told Dave he was going to get that job. Instead Dave ended up working for me, chafing at the bit as he learned my ironclad rule that a day wasn't done until all its assigned tasks were finished. "The doctrine of completed staff work," we called it. He was a Harvard Law School graduate, quiet, well mannered, competent, and smart. He wasn't afraid to work, either, and later became a deputy assistant secretary in that department. I lured him to the Civil Division as my executive assistant, and then to the Bureau in the same capacity. He was absolutely invaluable.

Daniel Mack Armstrong III had been a classmate of Dave Kinley's at Harvard Law School and was serving as an assistant United States attorney in the Eastern District of New York when he joined us in the Civil Division. Mack was soft-spoken, articulate, and thorough in his work. He brought to us the experiences of a young lawyer in the busy office of a United States attorney, and he was able to add a great deal to our work in the Civil Division because of this experience. Mack received many special assignments from me, all of them tough. He turned in an outstanding performance on every occasion and worked extremely well with other attorneys.

Barbara Lynn Herwig was a graduate of the University of California's Boalt Hall School of Law and an outspoken advocate of women's rights. Barbara was serving in the Appellate Section of the Civil Division at the time I asked her to join my personal staff. She was just beginning to work her way into the world of appellate advocacy under Morton Hollander, chief of the Appellate Section. Mort was recognized as an authority in appellate advocacy and was a most considerate and skilled mentor, idolized by the attorneys who worked with him in this specialized field of the law.

Although Barbara worked awfully hard in her efforts to proclaim that she was a "woman's lib" champion, I refused to knuckle under to her repeated admonitions that I treat her as just another attorney. She was furious, I know, when I held a door for her, or extended other traditional courtesies that gentlemen have extended to ladies for centuries. We all teased her unmercifully and took great delight in referring to her as "Ms." Nevertheless, Barbara was loved and respected by us and quickly became a valued member of my personal staff. She was very intelligent and able to handle the toughest assignments in a most capable and lawyerlike manner.

Later, as I looked back at the newspaper and magazine articles written in those first few days after Hoover's death, I could sense the great tensions that existed among the FBI, the White House, Congress, and the press, as all parties looked apprehensively toward the first power transition in the Bureau's history. But I didn't feel the tensions at the time, the way Nixon clearly had when he told Bea and me in the Oval Office that he wanted to avoid naming a permanent director right away. On the other hand, I did expect Congress to launch an investigation of the FBI with or without the benefit of a nominee to trigger the event.

In those early days, however, my thoughts were not of Congress, politics, or the press. My thoughts were of the FBI as an institution of government in a society of free people. I was convinced that these superb professionals would react well to professional leadership and competent administration of the affairs of the Bureau. There was no doubt in my mind that I was returning to the service of our country with a dedicated group of men and women.

It would take me a long time to learn that the FBI of J. Edgar Hoover was not as perfect as I had imagined it to be. Like Bill Ruckelshaus and Clarence Kelley, the two directors who followed me, I didn't know how to ask the right questions.

> When I was police chief in Kansas City, I gave an order and I knew it would be obeyed. I give an order here and I'm never sure what will happen. . . . I know that I was deceived. I think they should have told me, at least not make me stand out on a limb with this knowledge they had and should have imparted to me.
>
> —Clarence M. Kelley
> Director, FBI, August 1976

"Thirteen avenues of inquiry."

WHEN I BECAME ACTING DIRECTOR, I MADE A KEY DECISION. I decided that I would not be a mere caretaker, making no waves and taking no actions. Instead I was determined to make not only the needed day-to-day decisions but also those that were necessary for the FBI's continued long-term effectiveness and efficiency.

From the outset I recognized that the essential function of the FBI director was decision making, and in order to be able to do that, I needed a self-directed crash course in the functions and responsibilities of the Bureau. On Tuesday, May 9, I began a series of meetings and conferences with John Mohr, Mark Felt, and others at the FBI, as well as with Henry Petersen in the Justice Department, since his Criminal Division worked most closely with the Bureau. Out of those meetings and my own background study I distilled thirteen avenues of inquiry dealing with such topics as organized crime, subversion, narcotics traffic, and espionage. Also among the thirteen avenues were women as agents and changes in grooming and appearance standards. I asked for position papers to be written on each of the avenues, a process that would lead to my formation of the Office of Planning and Evaluation, whose primary purpose would be to continue this process of self-evaluation nonstop.

As the position papers came in, I realized that studying them, an arduous and informative task in itself, was not going to be enough to get me to where I could effectively direct a bureau of 20,000 employees spanning every state and territory of the country. I needed to get out and see the fifty-nine field offices, and they needed to see me. I determined to do it.

The first problem was one of logistics and security. In a time of frequent hijackings, should I fly commercial? Hijacking attempts in the United States had been increasing exponentially since 1968, and by May 1972 they were occurring at the rate of one every two weeks, most of them involving criminal extortion, spurred on by the infamous D. B. Cooper hijacking of the previous November, when Cooper parachuted out the open cabin door of a Boeing 727 in flight over Oregon, taking with him a ransom payout of $200,000. The prospect of the acting director of the FBI getting hijacked along with the four briefcases of sensitive documents I routinely carried with me on any trip was a good argument for never flying commercial, as was the fact that I would waste a lot of valuable time transiting through commercial airports waiting for connecting flights. But contracting with the Military Airlift Command to arrange my Bureau travel on an air force passenger jet was expensive. So we compromised. When it was efficient I flew commercial, and when it wasn't, I flew with the air force.

One of my first visits, on May 12, was to the New York field office, the Bureau's largest. As the entire staff gathered around the open clerical room (the largest space in the office), some at their desks and many others standing, I spoke extemporaneously.

"In the Washington field office," I told them, "I made the statement that I had been doing a certain thing for just about a week and I had asked several top officials in the Bureau what I had been doing differently. Much to my amazement they were not as discerning as I had hoped, and they were a little embarrassed when I finally said on not one single day had I worn a white shirt." That was greeted with much laughter and loud applause. I told them why I thought that was important.

"This is not to demean and denigrate the memory of Edgar Hoover, but Pat Gray is not Edgar Hoover. I'm married and I have four sons. I have two grandchildren. I was brought up in the navy and I'm just different. It's one of the most magnificent experiences to be with a submarine crew in action—people in shorts and sandals. Nobody knows who the captain is by his uniform or his insignia. Nobody knows who the executive officer is, or the first lieutenant. However, everybody knows what to do, because if each one doesn't do his job, everybody will get very, very wet, and they may not come home."

I finished by saying that although I now carried FBI badge number 2 (Hoover's badge number 1 had been retired), I had not yet earned it. I intended to earn it, and with it their respect. "The only thing I can say to you," I concluded, "is that my performance will be the benchmark that you should use to measure me. I will measure you in the same manner." They gave me a standing ovation.

Back at FBI headquarters my meetings with the senior executives were more restrained and businesslike. With John Mohr and Mark Felt I discussed the current qualifications for becoming a special agent: a law degree was self-sufficient, but any other degree required either proficiency in a foreign language or varying degrees of specific experience. At the time, about 75 percent of new agents coming into the FBI had served in Vietnam. Women were still excluded, but on May 9 I reiterated to John and Mark what I would soon tell Sandy Ungar of the *Washington Post*: that rule was going to have to change.

On May 10, Ed Miller, the assistant director in charge of the Domestic Intelligence Division, briefed Mark and me on plans for ensuring the safety of the upcoming national political conventions, the Democrats in July and the Republicans in August. After the "Days of Rage" at the 1968 Democratic Convention in Chicago, activist demonstrations were expected again this time, but our sources predicted that this time the Republicans would draw more "power and fire," as Miller put it. Fifty thousand or more were expected at the Republican Convention in Miami.

"The Miami office is well positioned," Miller reported. "The Cubans down there are right wing and could act as a deterrent to left-wing violence. We will have excellent live informant coverage in the radical groups at the conventions. Of our 2,100 informants in the security field, eight percent are targeted for the Republican convention."

"Why so many?" I asked.

"Because many of these outwardly political groups are sheltering terrorists and revolutionaries," answered Miller. "The Vietnam Vets Against the War are very anti-government and terroristic."

We then discussed the relative value of informants compared to technical surveillance: wiretaps, microphones, and mail coverage. I was in favor of more informants. "I just believe we have young kids out there who would help," I said.

"Yes," answered Mark, "but we've got to look at the risks. They would be untrained and these are some violent groups."

"We could use considerably more tech coverage," said Miller. "We've got twenty-nine wiretaps on now, eight in the domestic field. I could use sixty-five taps, thirty-three microphones, and seventy mail covers. All could possibly be convention-oriented."

When I took the question to Henry Petersen a few days later, he was dismissive. "Pat," he said, "I've never seen a national security wiretap request that was justifiable on its face." That reaction helped reinforce my own preference for increased live informant and undercover special agent activity in the domestic terrorism arena. I ordered an increase.

That same week, we received through the Organized Crime Section of the Justice Department several unsubstantiated allegations implying possible financial misconduct by Wesley Grapp, the special agent in charge (SAC) of the Los Angeles field office. This was the second largest field office of the FBI and Grapp held direct authority over 500 special agents and 300 clerical personnel. A twenty-five-year veteran, Grapp was recognized by all of the street agents as one of the toughest and meanest of the SACs. In Hoover's time, it had not been uncommon for street agents to be sent to Grapp's field office as a disciplinary measure, an unpleasant turn known as being "Grapped upon." If there was an archetype of the "Hoover hard-liner" outside of Washington, it was Wesley Grapp.

I immediately sent Assistant Director Joe Ponder and one of his inspectors to Los Angeles to investigate. During their investigation, Wes

Grapp volunteered some of his personal papers and the inspectors passed these along to me with their report. The report itself was inconclusive and I returned Grapp's papers to him and told him that I was satisfied that the allegations were unfounded, that I hadn't even bothered to read the papers he had volunteered, that I trusted him, and that the matter was closed. It was back to business as usual in the Los Angeles field office.

By May 12 the issue of women as special agents had been decided. In a meeting of the Executive Conference, several of the old-guard assistant directors had stressed their firm objection, but I had told them that there was no choice. Even though my personal opinion matched theirs—that the job was too physically demanding for women—both the applicable law and a presidential executive order clearly mandated the decision. I told Dave Kinley to send out a press release announcing that, except for the physical standards of height and weight, women applicants for the position of special agent will be treated *exactly* the same as male applicants. "Equal opportunity across the board will be the key," I said.

On May 16, my staff and I moved into J. Edgar Hoover's vacated offices. I ordered that new pictures be hung in the hallway where Hoover's had been, and I asked Dave to see that my official photo be sent out to the field offices. "But Mr. Hoover's photos are *not* to be discarded," I ordered. "His are to be hung in a place of honor in field offices with a suitable inscription underneath. Commence preparation of suitable inscription."

I had been on the job for two weeks. All in all, things seemed to be going well.

seven

"My men just can't figure this one out."

On Friday, June 16, six weeks after becoming acting director, I flew to California to visit the Los Angeles, San Francisco, and Sacramento field offices. I had been invited to give the commencement address at Pepperdine Law School in Santa Ana the next day. In the Bureau car on the way to the Newporter Inn for lunch after the speech on Saturday was Wes Grapp, whom I had met in person only the day before at the Los Angeles field office and who accompanied me to the graduation exercises. Grapp told me that word had come from Washington that there had been a break-in at the Democratic National Committee headquarters at the Watergate office complex. Details were sketchy. I asked if I could make a secure call from the Newporter Inn or should I make the call from the Santa Ana resident agency, one of the FBI's many small offices maintained outside the fifty-nine major cities that had field offices. Grapp said that a secure call could be made from the inn.

I called Mark Felt in Washington, but all he could tell me was that it was either a burglary or a bombing attempt. They had found a listening device. When I called the next day for an update, he had more details. Some of the burglars had connections to the Committee to Re-Elect the President, and one of them was James W. McCord, chief of security for the committee. Some were Cubans and all had brand-new $100 bills on them. One of them remained unidentified.

Gray's handwritten note of a telephone call with Mark Felt. June 18, 1972.

"Are you absolutely certain that we have jurisdiction?" I asked.

"I'm sure of it," he answered.

"Just check it and be absolutely certain," I ordered. "And then investigate it to the hilt with no holds barred."

Bea and I had spent that Saturday night at the Newporter Inn. Our original plan had been to spend the night in Palm Springs, but our escorting special agents told us it was awfully hot in the desert, so after lunch we asked the public relations lady at the Newporter Inn if at that late hour she could find accommodations for us. She did, and as we went up to our room, one of the special agents pointed out the hotel's villas and told us that John Mitchell and his wife, Martha, were in one of them. Though much was later made of this coincidence, Bea and I never saw them that weekend.

But we did bump into Fred LaRue, the forty-three-year-old Mississippi oilman and special adviser to Mitchell, who was there with the former attorney general and with Bob Mardian, a former assistant attorney general now working with Mitchell on Nixon's reelection committee, although we didn't see him. Bea and I were out by the swimming pool on Sunday and Fred noticed us there. He came over, sat down, and chatted for ten or fifteen minutes. Bea left and Fred and I talked for a few more minutes.

"That Watergate thing is a hell of a thing," he said.

"You bet it is, Fred," I answered. "We're going to investigate the hell out of it."

That was all either of us said about it.

Much later I learned that Fred, later called the "bagman" for his role in raising $300,000 to pay off the burglars, had been at a meeting in Key Biscayne with Mitchell, Jeb Magruder, and others three months earlier when the plan to bug the Watergate building was approved. At the time of our poolside encounter, LaRue had already been advised by Magruder that their plan had gone sour. He would later plead guilty to conspiracy and would serve four months of a three-year sentence in federal prison.

In those days my Catholic faith, like my belief in the fundamental integrity of the presidency, was still strong. Both in Washington and on the road, I went to early-morning mass before work. That Monday, June 19, I tried to call Mark Felt at 6:30 West Coast time, but twice the FBI operator connected me with the Washington field office instead of FBI headquarters. I left a message for Mark to call me, and I went to church.

Earlier that morning I had returned a call from Dick Kleindienst and told him that the FBI would vigorously pursue all leads. He agreed. When I got back to the Newporter Inn after church, Dick called again.

"Sometime today or tomorrow," he said, "the president is going to want to talk to me. Is there anyone at the FBI who can come to brief me this afternoon?"

"Yes," I answered, "Mark Felt."

A few minutes later, Mark called.

"We don't have too much this morning," he reported. Then, reading from a prepared summary, he gave me the details. The five men arrested early on Saturday morning had burglary tools, cash, and eavesdropping equipment in their possession. All were charged with burglary under the District of Columbia code. One of them had in his possession a personal check made out by E. Howard Hunt, who may have been a consultant in the White House, I was told. Hunt had been employed by the CIA until April 1970. In 1971, the FBI had conducted an investigation of him for a sensitive post at the White House.

"Our own investigation under the Interception of Communications statute is continuing," Mark said at the end of his reading from the summary.

"Are we in *solidly*?" I asked. I wanted to be sure that the statute, which was federal law and would therefore bring in the FBI, was adequate to keep us in the lead of the investigation.

"Yes," Mark answered. He then said he had a letterhead memorandum ready to send to the attorney general and to Bob Haldeman at the White House. A letterhead memorandum was a formal summary on official stationery written for dissemination outside the Bureau.

"Why?" I asked him.

"It's our standard operating practice," he told me. "Under Hoover we did it consistently."

"Don't send it," I told him. "We don't yet know what we've got a hold of. Before we begin writing memos to anybody about this investigation, we better be a little bit more sure of our ground."

"Just a minute," he interrupted. "Carol has something." Carol Tschudy was Mark's secretary. "She's saying it's important."

She was right. On Friday the Supreme Court had outlawed national security wiretaps on domestic subversives. I knew from my earlier domestic intelligence briefing with Ed Miller and Mark that we had several such warrantless domestic taps and microphones in place, so I told Mark to meet with Dick Kleindienst and then to get written instructions on which ones to cancel. I also told Mark to brief Dick on the status of the Watergate investigation. "After you give the attorney general the facts, discuss with him who should get our written summary and pass along to him my personal view that our approach to this case should be 'no holds barred.' "

At his meeting with Mark that afternoon in Washington, Dick ordered that four telephone taps and two hidden microphones be removed from the Black Panther and Weather Underground targets but to leave in place the one directed at the Communist Party, USA. On "that other case," as Mark put it in his phone message to me afterward, Dick told Mark that he agreed with an aggressive investigation of the whole matter.

On Tuesday, during my visit to the Sacramento field office, I sent out my first written order on Watergate, issued to ten field offices simultaneously.

> This will confirm instructions to appropriate offices that all logical investigation is to receive immediate attention under the personal attention of SACs by as many SAs as are needed to ensure that absolute, thorough, immediate, imaginative investigation is conducted in this case. All leads are to be set out by telephone or teletype as appropriate. Bureau is to be aware of all leads.

Bea and I got back to Washington that Tuesday night. On Wednesday morning, June 21, John Ehrlichman called.

"Pat," Ehrlichman said, "John Dean is going to be handling an inquiry into this thing for the White House. He's expecting your call." Dean was the White House counsel, the top lawyer on the president's staff. At just thirty-three years old, he had risen to a position of high authority and responsibility.

"I'll call him," I answered. "But as far as the FBI is concerned, we're treating this as a major special with all our normal procedures in effect. It's going to be an aggressive and thorough investigation and I expect we will be interviewing people at the White House. We'll need to set up procedural safeguards against leaks."

"Take those up with Dean," he said. "It's his inquiry. From now on you're to deal directly with him on this."

At 11:30 that morning, Dean came to my office. After a general discussion about the sensitivity of the case and the need to avoid leaks in an election year, he got down to specifics.

"I've been given the responsibility to handle this inquiry for the White House. Therefore I will sit in on any interviews of White House staff personnel."

"In what capacity, John?"

"In my official capacity as counsel to the president," he answered.

"Will you be reporting directly to him, or through Haldeman or Ehrlichman?" I asked.

"Directly to the president," he answered. He then said he wanted to schedule all White House interviews directly through me or Mark Felt, and that he would be sitting in on them.

"Well, John," I said, "I know more and more people are insisting that their attorneys sit in on FBI interviews these days. But I have to tell you that it's not our preference or our normal practice."

Dean was insistent: no FBI interviews of White House personnel without him sitting in. It didn't seem onerous, just cumbersome. At that point, the only White House staffer we in the FBI wanted to interview was Charles W. Colson, Nixon's special counsel, who had hired Howard Hunt. For at least another six months, none of us in the FBI had any inkling that the Watergate conspiracy ran anywhere near the senior people in the White House. That the president wanted to conduct his own parallel inquiry into possible illegal activity by people whose names appeared on the White House organization chart didn't seem odd to me, it seemed prudent. Dean's requirement that he or one of his staff attorneys sit in seemed reasonable. I agreed to his demand and passed it along to Mark Felt. Later, when we interviewed people from the Democratic National Committee, the victims of this burglary, their lawyers insisted on being present as well.

By Thursday, June 22, five days after the break-in, our agents from several field offices had traced the $100 bills found on the burglars to the Miami bank account of Bernard Barker, one of the arrested burglars, and from there the agents learned that four cashier's checks totaling $89,000 had been cashed through Barker's account. They also learned that an additional $25,000, drawn on the account of one Kenneth

Dahlberg, had also been cashed there. All but the Dahlberg check had been made out to a Manuel Ogarrio. In addition to this money trail, the agents discovered that some of the arrested burglars had CIA connections. Some had in fact been employed by the Agency.

That afternoon I held the first of what would be a continuing series of conferences with Mark Felt; Charlie Bates, the assistant director in charge of the General Investigative Division; and Bob Kunkel, the special agent in charge of the Washington field office. I needed these conferences in order to keep up with the investigation, since I had from the outset of my tenure assigned the day-to-day operation of the Bureau to Mark Felt and the 8,500 law enforcement professionals working for him, the way a navy captain assigns the running of his ship to his executive officer and the way J. Edgar Hoover had at the FBI for many years. Later, when it became apparent that the White House was involved, I would turn control of the investigation over to Mark, recusing myself because of my assumed relationship with Nixon and my position as a presidential appointee. But at this point, when none of us in the FBI even suspected that the trail led right to the Oval Office, I was still fully engaged.

In this early meeting we brainstormed theories of the case and its seemingly disconnected parts. CIA connections had appeared immediately, but they could have been incidental. Was it a CIA money chain, where the CIA would be burying money to be used later in some of its clandestine activities? Was this a political operation? A political money-laundering operation? A Cuban right-wing operation? Might it be a double-agent operation, since the tapes had been removed from the doors at the Watergate and then put back on? We just didn't know, but after that second meeting I called Richard Helms, the director of central intelligence, to alert him that we might be poking into a CIA operation.

"We've been meeting on this every day," he said. "My men just can't figure this one out. There is no CIA involvement."

At 6:30 that evening, just after I spoke to Helms, Dean came to my

5:00 PM C w C. Bates 6/22/72

1. Miami rpts photog. made to 7×10 prints for Barker + Fiorini - photog says photos were of onion skins of ltrs signed by Larry O'Brien.

2.

5:37 PM TCT Dick Helms

To tell him of our that that we may be poking in a CIA operation + to verify or deny.

He said he had been meeting on this every day with his men - they know the people - they cannot figure out this one - there is no CIA involvement.

EX. 4

Gray's handwritten note of a conference with Charlie Bates and a telephone call to Richard Helms, the director of central intelligence. June 22, 1972.

office. He told me he wanted to schedule FBI interviews of White House staff through me or through Mark Felt. I told him that this would be impractical and time-consuming. He backed down and agreed to let the White House interviews be scheduled through the Washington field office like all the others. He then asked me about the case in general and I gave him a rundown of our early theories: a CIA covert operation of some sort, since some of those involved had past Agency connections; a money chain, either political or CIA; a pure political operation; a Cuban right-wing operation; or some combination of the above. I told him that we had discovered Barker's bank account, which had led to Dahlberg's $25,000 check and the four Mexican drafts totaling $89,000.

"Have you narrowed your theories down?" he asked.

"No," I told him. Almost in passing, I mentioned that I had talked to Dick Helms.

eight

"Not even the president of the United States."

I WENT TO SEVEN O'CLOCK MASS ON FRIDAY MORNING, JUNE 23, and then straight to the office. My first phone call was from John Dean.

"Pat," he said, "there are rumors all over town that the FBI has been ordered to close out the Watergate investigation in twenty-four to forty-eight hours. Supposedly the leaks are coming from the FBI. What do you know about them?"

"They're not true," I answered. "That's what I know about them. And they're not coming from the FBI, I can assure you."

"The stories are coming from somewhere, Pat. They're also saying the Bureau's been ordered to hold up on White House interviews and to drag its feet on the investigation."

"They're not true, John. You know that. No such orders have been given to me and we've already started interviewing people in the White House."

It was to be a continuing theme of my many conversations with Dean as the investigation proceeded. Nothing, it seemed, was more important than the quelling of the incessant leaks, many of them false, that kept appearing in the newspapers and, later, in the weekly magazines. This leak, I learned much later from Dick Kleindienst, seems to have come from a telephone call that John Ehrlichman made to Henry Petersen, whose Criminal Division would oversee the investigation, on Sunday, the day after the burglary.

"That's it," Ehrlichman had told Henry. "You have the burglars. Close it out in the next twenty-four to forty-eight hours."

"Screw you," Henry replied. "We're not going to."

This is a perfect example of how a grain of leaked truth—John Ehrlichman's call to Henry Petersen—got contorted into a lie (that the U.S. attorneys had gone along with Ehrlichman's demand and ordered us to hold up interviews and close out the case) and then appeared unattributed in the press. Of course, the only part that the general public could see was the unattributed falsehood. This was to happen over and over again in Watergate.

A couple of hours after Dean's call, I met again with Charlie Bates to get an update. He assured me that the investigation was proceeding at full speed and that we had numerous leads that still tracked in a number of directions. So far none of our theories about a possible motive for the break-in and bugging had been ruled out, including a CIA connection. Even though Dick Helms had told me that the Agency had no direct involvement, that didn't mean there wasn't some peripheral connection between some of the men arrested and the Agency itself. After my meeting with Charlie, I called Dean back to pass along his summary of where things stood.

Dean listened to my update and then said, "Pat, there's a possibility that CIA aspects exist in the money chain you're following."

"We've thought about that, John," I answered. "But Dick Helms has told me the Agency has no involvement in this."

Dean thanked me and hung up. It was then close to lunchtime.

What I didn't know—and wouldn't learn until the rest of the country did, too—was that Dean and his fellow White House conspirators were in the process of hatching the plot that would eventually drive Nixon from office two years later. It was June 23, 1972, the day of the infamous "smoking gun" conversations.

June 23, 1972   *Oval Office, 10:04–11:39 a.m.*

HALDEMAN: Now, on the investigation, you know, the Democratic break-in thing, we're back to the—in the, the problem area because the FBI is not under control, because Gray doesn't exactly know how to control them, and they have, their investigation is now leading into some productive areas, because they've been able to trace the money, not through the money itself, but through the bank, you know, sources—the banker himself. And, and it goes in some directions we don't want it to go . . . Mitchell came up with yesterday, and John Dean analyzed very carefully last night and concludes, concurs now with Mitchell's recommendation that the only way to solve this, and we're set up beautifully to do it, ah, in that and that . . . the way to handle this now is for us to have [CIA deputy director Vernon] Walters call Pat Gray and just say, "Stay the hell out of this . . . this is ah, business here we don't want you to go any further on it." That's not an unusual development . . .

PRESIDENT: Um huh.

HALDEMAN: . . . and, uh, that would take care of it.

PRESIDENT: What about Pat Gray, ah, you mean he doesn't want to?

HALDEMAN: Pat does want to. He doesn't know how to, and he doesn't have, he doesn't have any basis for doing it. Given this, he will then have the basis. He'll call Mark Felt in, and the two of them . . . and Mark Felt wants to cooperate because . . .

PRESIDENT: Yeah.

HALDEMAN: he's ambitious . . .

PRESIDENT: Yeah.

HALDEMAN: Ah, he'll call him in and say, "We've got the signal from across the river to, to put the hold on this." And that will fit rather well because the FBI agents who are working the case, at this point, feel that's what it is. This is CIA.

PRESIDENT: But they've traced the money to 'em.

HALDEMAN: Well they have, they've traced to a name, but they haven't gotten to the guy yet.

PRESIDENT: Would it be somebody here?

HALDEMAN: Ken Dahlberg.

> PRESIDENT: Who the hell is Ken Dahlberg?
> HALDEMAN: He's, ah, he gave $25,000 in Minnesota and ah, the check went directly in to this, to this guy Barker.

There were three separate "smoking gun" conversations that day. In this first one, Haldeman not only sealed the fate of his boss when the tape became public, but he lied about me, too. I never tried to "control" the FBI in this or any other investigation and he knew it. As this tape and its subsequent events amply demonstrated, the opposite was true: Haldeman, Dean, and the others tried mightily to control me and the FBI. Their tactics were devious and brutal, enough to bring me to my knees but not the FBI itself. The battle, begun here with a sneak attack directed at me personally by men I trusted without question, would last for years. None of us would walk away unwounded, and all because we admired and worked for Richard Nixon, who not only junked his own presidency, but junked the careers of so many other people, many of whom had to go to jail.

At 1:30 Dean called me back. "Pat," he said, "General Vernon A. Walters, deputy director of the CIA, will be coming over to see you this afternoon. He has something to tell you."

I said I would meet with him, and a short time later Walters's secretary called to find out how soon he could come over.

While that call came in, a thirty-five-year-old White House fellow was sitting outside my office waiting for an interview to see whether or not he would be assigned to the FBI. He was Lieutenant Colonel Colin L. Powell. The job eventually went to another White House fellow, Major John C. Fryer, who became an important part of my personal staff. John went on to a distinguished air force career and became superintendent of schools in Jacksonville, Florida. Powell, of course, retired with four stars and became secretary of state.

At 2:15 a nervous-sounding Dean called me again, asking if the Walters meeting had been set up yet. When I told him it was about to take place, Dean asked that I call him immediately afterward. Fifteen minutes later, Walters came to my office.

Lieutenant General Vernon "Dick" Walters was a brilliant and charming fifty-five-year-old man. Fluent in many languages, he had been in the car with Nixon when it was stoned by a violent mob in Caracas, Venezuela, in 1958 and had been a close confidant and secret operative for Henry Kissinger in the Paris Peace Talks, but he was as new to his current job as I was to mine. Nixon had appointed him deputy director of the CIA on May 2, the day before I took over the FBI. Though I had not met him before, he and I got along well from the outset. After a few pleasantries, Dick got to the reason he was here.

"If the investigation gets pushed further south of the border," he said, "it could trespass onto some of our covert projects. Since you've got these five men under arrest, it will be best to taper the matter off here."

He then asked me if I was aware of the written agreement between our two agencies not to uncover each other's sources. I was well aware of it and agreed with its logical premise, though I had not actually read the document itself. I told him we would abide by the agreement and proceed very cautiously.

After Walters left, I called John Dean and told him the substance of our conversation. After that I called Charlie Bates and told him to continue tracing the path of the Mexican money chain through the banks but to hold up any interview of Manuel Ogarrio, the individual to whom four of the checks, totaling $89,000, had been made out. If there was indeed a CIA connection in Mexico, I surmised, Ogarrio would have to be it.

It was only a matter of time, I knew, before the press would begin harrying me about Watergate. It started sooner than I expected. At six that evening Marge Neenan called me at home to say that Sandy Smith of *Time* magazine had called. "He has information," Marge said, "about your personal actions in the Watergate case."

"What kind of information? Did he say?"

"That you refused an agent's request to authorize checking of Colson's toll calls and home calls."

"Baloney," I said. "What else did he say?"

Gray's notes of calls from his secretary, Marge Neenan (left), and to Sandy Smith of *Time* magazine. June 23, 1972.

"That you said you would wrap up this investigation in twenty-four to forty-eight hours."

"Give me his phone number, Marge."

This was outrageous. I called Smith. The first question he asked was whether I had met with John Mitchell last weekend in California and, if so, did we discuss Watergate. I told him we were both there but had not met.

"Why didn't you check Colson's phone calls?" he then asked. "My editors want to know this because you did check Hunt's."

"Sandy," I said, "you know I can't and won't discuss why we do or don't do anything in an active investigation. But I will tell you that I refused no request on Colson's calls because that request has never come up. We checked with Colson simply to get Hunt's call records and found that there weren't any in the White House. As for wrapping it up in forty-eight hours, I said nothing of the kind. I have instructed that this case receive immediate priority attention, and it is."

Smith then asked me why I had held up an electronic sweep of the Democratic headquarters to see if any other bugs were in place. I told him that I had held up a sweep of both the Democratic and Republican national headquarters until we had all the facts we needed, and that both sweeps had now been ordered.

I kept my tone cordial and businesslike with Smith, but inside I was seething: these were supposed to be closely held internal details. "Someone in the FBI is talking about the details of the investigation," I wrote on my note of the call. I picked up the phone and called Charlie Bates.

"Charlie," I said after telling him the details of my call to Smith, "someone is leaking from inside the FBI. I want you to have every agent from the Washington field office who has anything to do with this case in my office at eleven o'clock tomorrow morning. I don't care if it is a Saturday. This is going to stop now!"

The next morning Charlie called me at home to tell me that Sandy Smith had left a message for him. Charlie wanted to know if it was okay to call Smith back to see what he wanted. I said sure. At 10:30, as I was getting ready for the meeting with the case agents, Charlie called to report on his conversation with Smith.

What Smith told Charlie was that though there were some editors and reporters at *Time* who did not like the FBI, he, Smith, was not one of them. His editors had received some derogatory information about Pat Gray's performance in the Watergate case, and the source of the information was probably a member of Democratic National Committee chairman Larry O'Brien's staff. Smith then repeated to Charlie the same assertions he had asked me about the night before, and then added that there was a rumor being spread around town by Larry O'Brien that they can't trust the FBI and that the FBI will whitewash the whole case to protect Nixon.

At eleven I walked into my large conference room where Charlie Bates, Bob Kunkel, and twenty-seven agents from the Washington field office were waiting for me. I was in no mood for niceties. After laying out what I had heard from Sandy Smith and explaining how serious this sort of leak was, I demanded that the individual who leaked this stuff to Smith be man enough to step forward now and accept his discipline. When none did, I lit into them collectively.

"I will not put up with this," I said. "There is no excuse for it, and I want it stopped right now. What we need in the FBI are dedicated professionals, not a bunch of little old ladies in tennis shoes. There is no place in the FBI for flap-jaw special agents, and if I catch one in the act of leaking to the press or anywhere else, that agent will be brought before me and dismissed immediately. Now go out there, do your jobs, and keep your mouths zipped."

As soon as the agents dispersed, Charlie, Bob, and I stayed in my office to go over the case again. At the end of the meeting I told Charlie to bring me his copies of everything he had on the case to date. I knew that Smith's rumors were wrong, but I wanted to see for myself if anything in our files said anything like the information Smith had obtained.

I went home after the meeting still angry and disgusted. After reading Charlie's copies I decided I needed to see more detailed information if the source of Smith's misinformation was going to be narrowed down. I called Charlie and told him to deliver everything the WFO had, in any form, to me at my Harbor Square apartment by noon the next day.

Later that evening, Sandy Smith called Charlie back. The *Time* article would be cut to a minimum, he said, and there would be no mention of "the forty-eight-hour matter." Smith told Charlie that he had tried to eliminate "the Mitchell-Gray thing" entirely but his editors were insistent that it stay. The short article ran the next week and said that both John Mitchell and I were in California at the same time. "Both have denied meeting," said the article.

Though the article had been trimmed of the falsehoods, Smith had learned details of our investigation somewhere. But there was no way to narrow down his source. As to the false rumors, either Smith was making them up or someone was feeding him lies. Much later I would begin to suspect Charlie Bates of being one of the falsehood peddlers, but not then, so early in the case. All I got for my demand from Charlie on this Saturday in June was a fairly complete set of internal documents on the Watergate case.

Leaks or no leaks, there was no letup in the investigation itself. Over the weekend our agents located Kenneth Dahlberg, the Minneapolis man from whose account the fifth Miami check, for $25,000, had been cashed. He was at a wedding in Buffalo, New York. Dahlberg refused to be interviewed, on advice of his counsel, whom he would not even name. "It appears to me," Charlie Bates wrote in a memo, "that Dahlberg is under wraps not to talk to us."

On Monday I paid a scheduled visit to the Cleveland and Cincinnati field offices. Back at my desk on Tuesday, I met with Mark Felt and Charlie Bates. Again we went over all the leads and our still-hazy theories of what lay behind the break-in. We all still assumed that Congress would soon initiate its general inquiry into FBI operations now that Hoover was dead. All three of us knew that I would be called to testify, and we couldn't afford to have the FBI accused of not pursuing Watergate to the very end, even for a legitimate reason like the CIA link. We had to proceed as best we could. We had to know more about the Mexican money chain, even though our interagency agreement required us to step cautiously around any potential CIA assets. The investigation was slowed, but not stopped. There was still Kenneth Dahlberg in Minnesota.

In the middle of our meeting John Dean called. While Mark and Charlie listened, I told him of Dahlberg's stonewalling. "If he continues," I told Dean, "he'll be called before the grand jury where he'll have to testify. We want to talk to him now. We're not going to leave any stone unturned, John. You know I might get called before Congress and will be asked about this. It's very important that we continue our aggressive investigation."

Dahlberg was avoiding us. Ogarrio, on the other hand, was in Mexico City ready to be interviewed any time. The only thing stopping it was his possible CIA connection. I decided to call Dick Helms again.

"Dick," I said. "We need some specifics. Is there any CIA interest in Manuel Ogarrio?"

"I'll have to get back to you on that," he answered.

"Can you do it by tomorrow afternoon? I can have Mark Felt, my acting associate director, along with my assistant director in charge of the General Investigative Division join us for a meeting here to iron all this out."

Helms told me he would get right back to me and he did, a few hours later. "Pat," he said, "the CIA has no interest in Ogarrio. And Dick Walters and I can meet you and your people at 2:30 tomorrow afternoon."

At 10:30 the next morning, John Dean called. Again it was about leaks. This time he was upset about stories circulating about the materials that Dean had turned over to the FBI from E. Howard Hunt's White House office. Again I told him that the leaks had to be coming from somewhere else. He then wanted to be sure we were still holding off interviewing Ogarrio and Dahlberg, and I told him that Helms and Walters were coming to my office that afternoon to discuss exactly that.

Twenty minutes later John Ehrlichman called me.

"Cancel your meeting with Helms," was the first thing he said.

"For what reason?" I asked right back.

"It's not necessary," he snapped. "There is no reason at all to hold that meeting."

"Well, then," I wanted to know, "who is going to make the decisions as to who is to be interviewed and who isn't?"

"You do." He hung up. This was classic Ehrlichman—blunt and abrupt. I didn't like him, but this was an order. I called Dick Helms and canceled our meeting. He didn't ask why. Instead, he gave me two more names not to interview—Karl Wagner and John Caswell. These two names were new to me.

"They're active CIA agents," he told me. "Their names have to be kept secret."

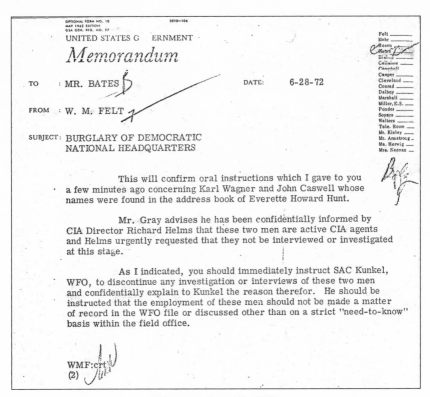

FBI memo. June 28, 1972.

I issued those orders, but it was too late to stop the Caswell interview. Our agents were contacting every name in Howard Hunt's phone
book and they had already gotten to him. We hadn't gotten to Wagner
and therefore never interviewed him. It didn't seem important at the
time. Nor did it even occur to me that Helms might be telling me a lie.
Nowhere in my entire upbringing, from childhood through the navy
and into the highest levels of government service, had I ever been given
any reason to suspect that in a private conversation the director of central intelligence would be anything less than brutally honest with the
acting director of the FBI. In the Defense Department's dealings with
Congress and the executive branch, we had always relied on the "presumption of regularity" working in both directions. The system would
fail if we weren't all acting in the country's best interests, if we couldn't
rely on a full set of common data underlying the things we argued

about before coming to an agreed position. We may have disagreed, and we might even have disliked one another, but we didn't lie to one another. The high public trust we all held simply didn't allow for it.

I didn't allow for it here, either. It didn't even occur to me as a possibility. Seven years later I would learn the truth, that Helms was hiding a key piece of evidence from me. The CIA had been supplying Howard Hunt and G. Gordon Liddy, the Watergate burglary mastermind whom we hadn't identified yet, with technical assistance and equipment long before the break-in.

> At this point [August 1971] low-level officers in the CIA began to wonder, and to ask their superiors, just what Hunt was up to. . . . A protest was lodged with [Deputy Director Robert] Cushman's executive assistant, Karl Wagner, who told [the Technical Services Division] to refuse any further Hunt requests, and then sent Cushman a memo protesting the involvement of the unknown Liddy and Hunt's frequent demands for help, and raising the "question of [the material's] frequent use in domestic clandestine activity."
>
> —Thomas Powers
> *The Man Who Kept the Secrets: Richard Helms and the CIA, 1979*
>
> This is why Helms asked me not to have FBI interview Wagner and gave me a false tale as to his reasons.
>
> —Handwritten by Pat Gray on the same page, date unknown

In our telephone call, and again later in the investigation when he held back physical evidence, Helms committed obstruction of justice. But at this point, in June 1972, I was still a believer in the system. I took him at his word.

Up until this episode, I had had very little direct interaction with the CIA. In my last job in the navy, as special assistant to Tom Gates, the secretary of defense under Dwight Eisenhower, I regularly participated in intelligence briefings that included the top-secret footage of Russian military facilities taken by the clandestine U-2 flights over Soviet airspace flown out of Turkey and Pakistan by the CIA. I knew that the CIA, like the Department of Defense, operated on a strict "need to know" basis where the left hand was not supposed to know what the right hand was doing. Suspecting that these mixed signals from Helms and Walters might be a result of this compartmentalization, I called in Mark and Charlie that afternoon.

"Could this be the case?" I asked them. Both agreed that it was possible, but only if the White House itself had placed something under the highest classification of national security.

"What I recommend," said Charlie, "is that we not back off without forcing the CIA to reveal completely its interest here."

"The FBI's reputation is at stake here, boss," said Mark. "I agree with Charlie."

"So do I," I said. "If the CIA's assets become too big a barrier in Mexico, let me know and I'll get back to Helms and tell him we can't hold this thing back without valid and overriding considerations. I'll tell him I can't do that for anybody, not even the White House. Not even the president of the United States. I'd resign if I were ordered to hold back without a valid reason."

nine

"These should never see the light of day."

For a week since getting back to my desk on June 21, I had worked nearly full-time on the Watergate investigation. Before a long weekend of travel to the West Coast, I had one more appointment. John Ehrlichman wanted to see me at the White House.

At 6:30 p.m. on Wednesday, June 28, I walked into Ehrlichman's outer office, and one of his secretaries told me to go right on into his private office. I opened the door and was surprised to see John Dean standing there with Ehrlichman. They were talking just a few feet in from the door, to the right of the coffee table. After the usual greetings, Ehrlichman, as always, got right to the point.

"John has something that he wants to turn over to you."

I then noticed that Dean had in his hands two white manila file folders.

"These contain copies of sensitive and classified national security papers that Howard Hunt was working on," Dean said.

"Why are you giving them to me?" I asked. "Do you want them in the Watergate case files?"

"No," he said emphatically. "These are national security documents. These should never see the light of day."

"Then why give them to me?"

"Because they are such political dynamite their very existence can't even be acknowledged," he explained. "To prevent questions about them, I need to be able to say that I gave all Hunt's files to the FBI. That's what I'm doing here. They have nothing to do with Watergate. They shouldn't be allowed to obfuscate those issues."

To me the clear implication of these remarks was that these files were to be destroyed. I certainly interpreted this to be an order to do exactly that as it came from the counsel to the president of the United States issued in the presence of the man to whom Nixon had directed me to report. There was no doubt in my mind.

"All right," I said, "let's put these in envelopes."

Dean stepped briefly into the outer office to obtain two large brown envelopes into which he inserted the files and handed them to me. The files themselves were one-eighth-inch to one-quarter-inch thick. One appeared to be thicker than the other. Nothing further was said about them. Dean then left and I stayed with Ehrlichman for five to ten minutes to discuss a topic that was clearly more important to him than these extraneous papers: leaks to the press. Then I left and went directly home.

Bea and I were leaving for a visit to the San Diego field office the next morning. I had no shredder in the small apartment where we were living and had no control over the trash that went out from there, so I put the envelopes on a shelf in the closet under my shirts, where they sat for two or three weeks until I remembered they were there and took them into the office.

In the director's office, there were two red wastebaskets under my desk that had been there on the day I took over. No one had explained to me that they were "burn" baskets, that their contents were taken out every night by the maintenance people and carefully destroyed. Had I known what the red baskets were for, I would have tossed the White House files inside. Not knowing what else to do with them, I placed them in my personal safe.

On Sunday, July 2, after my return from California, Dean called me at home in Harbor Square and asked to meet. I suggested we do that in my office, but he said he preferred not to because if he were noticed, the press was sure to report that the president's counsel had been in the Justice Department building on a Sunday.

"Come over here, then," I suggested. "We can walk around the grounds."

That afternoon Dean came to Harbor Square and we did walk around a bit before sitting down on a park bench. In his book *Blind Ambition*, Dean recalls that it was at this meeting that he first asked me to provide FBI teletypes and investigative reports on the Watergate case, but I think that request came from him later in the week by telephone. What I do distinctly remember was what he said at the outset of our walk:

"It's a hell of a note, isn't it?" he said. "When the counsel to the president and the acting director of the FBI have to meet on a park bench because of the leaks and publicity surrounding this Watergate case."

ten

"Mr. President, I have something that I want to speak to you about."

BACK AT MY DESK ON MONDAY, JULY 3, I CALLED MARK FELT, Charlie Bates, and Bob Kunkel to my office for a ninety-minute meeting to go over the entire Watergate investigation to date. The break-in had happened just over two weeks ago and we still had not narrowed down our theories, even though we had made substantial investigative progress.

We started with a rundown of what we had learned so far. In addition to tracking the $100 bills back to Ogarrio and Dahlberg, we had learned more about the higher connections of the five arrested burglars, James McCord and the four Cubans. Of the greatest interest to us was E. Howard Hunt, who by now had been positively identified as having been in the Watergate Hotel the night of the burglary. Our agents had interviewed Charles Colson, special counsel to the president, who said that Hunt had been a consultant on his staff at the White House until March 29 and could not explain why Hunt still had a White House office. Among the materials from Hunt's White House safe turned over to us by John Dean was electronic eavesdropping gear identical to those we had already identified as having been purchased by McCord in Philadelphia.

Two leads from the personal telephone book of one of the Cubans were promising. One was the office number of Kathleen Chenow, a former secretary to David Young at the White House. Chenow was now living in England. The other number was that of George Gordon

Liddy, a former FBI supervisor now working for the Committee to Re-Elect the President. Prior to working for CREEP, Liddy was reported to have shared a White House Domestic Council office with David Young. Both men were under the direct supervision of John Ehrlichman. On June 29, after Liddy had told our agents that he would not talk about the case, he was fired from CREEP.

Another set of questions revolved around Alfred Baldwin, who had been an FBI agent for two years starting in 1963. He was the lookout posted in the Watergate Hotel across from the break-in site, and there were conflicting reports that he had once been hired as a bodyguard for Martha Mitchell. The investigating agents requested permission to interview John Mitchell to resolve the question, and I gave it to them.

We were also trying to locate an unidentified man who had been seen with Hunt at various times by several witnesses. While we brainstormed, I drew a set of overlapping circles to indicate where the leads pointed:

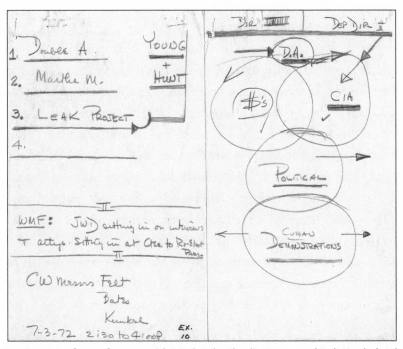

Gray's notes of a conference with Mark Felt, Charlie Bates, and Bob Kunkel. July 3, 1972.

We had begun to track the money, we knew that some of those involved had both CIA and Cuban anti-Castro connections, and we knew that E. Howard Hunt and David Young had both worked in the White House. On top of those four overlapping circles, we also wondered if Frank Sturgis, one of those arrested, might be a double agent at work here since the columnist Jack Anderson had gone in person to his bail hearing and had offered to post the bail himself, though we hadn't developed anything further along that line. We also thought, given the constant complaints from Dean and Ehrlichman about leaks, both to me and to Mark Felt, that perhaps this Democratic headquarters bugging incident was an anti-leak project. And on top of it all, we had the director and the deputy director of the CIA talking to us directly about the Agency's links, or lack thereof, to the burglary and the Mexican money chain.

In the middle of our meeting, John Dean called me, wanting to make sure we were still holding back on interviewing Ogarrio and Dahlberg. I told him we were, but that we were meeting at that very moment on the whole topic and I would call him back later. Dean's call sparked a discussion among the four of us. None of us liked having him sit in on our interviews of White House personnel and having other attorneys present whenever we talked to CREEP staffers. At that early date neither I nor any one of my top three Watergate agents, from Felt on down, was suspicious of Dean's motives. That wouldn't come for another eight months. The problem was more general—people being interviewed by the FBI are more reticent when a lawyer is sitting beside them. But we all knew that there was nothing we could do about it. The White House rules had been laid down for us and we had to follow them if we wanted to do any interviewing. Henry Petersen and his U.S. attorneys were well aware of it and had agreed to accept the restrictions. Since June 23 their grand jury had been interviewing many of these same people, and in the grand jury room there were no White House lawyers present.

By Wednesday I had decided that as far as the CIA was concerned, enough was enough. I called Dick Walters at about 6:00 p.m. and said

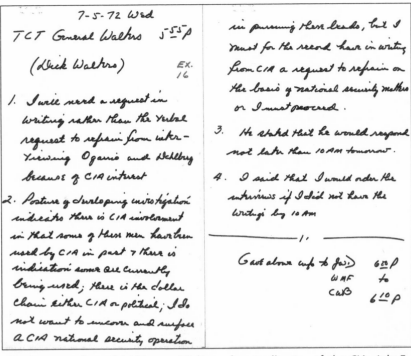

Gray's notes of a call to Vernon Walters, deputy director of the CIA. July 5, 1972.

that our investigative need to interview both Ogarrio and Dahlberg was pressing. In order for us to continue to refrain from interviewing them, I would need a written, not verbal, request from the CIA, and if I didn't get it by ten the next morning I was going to authorize the interviews. He said he would respond by my deadline.

At 10:05 a.m. on Thursday, Dick arrived at my office with a three-page memorandum on blank paper, marked "SECRET." For two and a half pages it reiterated information that the CIA had given the FBI in memos dated June 20, June 21, and June 27 outlining the Agency's prior dealings with Hunt, McCord, and the Cuban Americans who had been arrested at the Watergate and naming several of the Agency's covert support private companies, including the Mullen Company that had employed E. Howard Hunt. I scanned it rapidly looking for the writing I had requested on Ogarrio and Dahlberg. It wasn't there. Instead, the next-to-last paragraph on the last page merely stated that

Dick Helms had talked to me on the phone about Ogarrio and Dahlberg, and the memo then said that the Agency had had no "operational contacts" with Ogarrio and "the last recorded contact of the Agency with Mr. Dahlberg was in May 1961."

I had said that the FBI would proceed without a written confirmation asking us to hold back. What I got was a three-page classified document *not* asking us to hold back. It seemed pointless.

But of course it wasn't. Almost a year later, after I had resigned and began to learn of the CIA's complicity in using the names of Ogarrio and Dahlberg to try to inhibit the FBI's investigation, the purpose of all the reiteration at the front of this memo would become clear: Helms and Walters had allowed the CIA to be used by the White House in a domestic political cover-up, something they certainly wanted to keep secret, especially from me. But there is nothing "secret" about the fact that the CIA has no dealings with a person. In order to keep this admission of no interest in Ogarrio and Dahlberg a secret, therefore, the memo had to contain some real ones. So they gratuitously added them here and classified the document "SECRET. Warning Notice: Sensitive Intelligence Sources and Methods Involved." The sole purpose of all the reiteration was to keep their damning admission of complicity a secret.

After I read Dick's memo, both of us engaged in a general discussion of the credibility and position of our respective institutions in our society. Neither of us was happy with the way some in the Nixon White House seemed to be trying to manipulate us in his name. Dick leaned back in the red leather chair in my office and put his hands behind his head.

"You know, I've come into an inheritance," he said. "I don't need to worry about my pension, and I'm not going to let these kids kick me around anymore."

He didn't say Dean's and Ehrlichman's names, but I knew who he had to be talking about. They were the ones who had been calling me about this. Dick got up and, as we stood together just before he left, he said, "Maybe one of us ought to call the president and let him know what his people are doing to him."

"You know him better than I do," I said. "You should be the one to make that call."

"No," he answered, "I think you should because these are people the FBI wants to interview." We shook hands and he left.

As soon as he was gone I called Charlie Bates and told him that we had received the CIA writing and that it was not pertinent. "Order the immediate interviews of Ogarrio and Dahlberg," I said.

Then I sat there, alone in my office, and mulled over the conversation Dick Walters and I had just had. It had left me confused, uncertain, and uneasy. For more than a week an important part of the Watergate investigation had been delayed, and for no clear reason. More and more, I became convinced that the president should be informed. But I had never called the president before. I had never even talked to him without someone else present. The closest I had come to having a private conversation was when Bea and I had visited with him in the Oval Office on the day of Hoover's funeral, and even then the White House photographer had been there for part of it. On the day he had appointed me there were five of us in the room in the Executive Office Building, and again there had been a photographer. The thought of making the call was frankly intimidating. To me the president of the United States was an awesome figure. I simply didn't have the guts to break protocol, pick up the phone, and call him directly. What I needed instead was a conduit.

I decided to call Clark MacGregor, whom I knew. He had been the head of the Office of Legislation for the president, and was a mature, experienced political figure. Though he had just been appointed Nixon's campaign director to replace John Mitchell, I still thought of him as a senior White House adviser. I asked Ron Thompson in my adjacent telephone room to call MacGregor. When Ron told me that MacGregor's secretary said he was in California with the presidential party, I asked Ron to call the California White House immediately.

I was so agitated by this difficult decision that it didn't even occur to me that it was well before eight in the morning there. It took a few minutes for Clark to call me back at 7:51 his time. I don't even know if he was at work yet.

"Clark," I said, "Dick Walters and I are uneasy and concerned because of the confusion and uncertainty in determining whether or not there is CIA interest in people the FBI wishes to interview. We both feel that people on the White House staff are careless and indifferent in their use of both the CIA and the FBI. This can be injurious to both our agencies and to the president."

"I see," said Clark.

"Clark, would you please pass this on to the president."

"I'll take care of it," he said.

Thirty-seven minutes later Nixon called me. I hadn't expected that at all. The day before, the FBI had thwarted an aircraft hijacking. Nixon's first words were, "I want to congratulate you and ask you to convey my congratulations to your agents in San Francisco who just yesterday so successfully terminated the hijacking by the two Yugoslav hijackers."

"Thank you very much, Mr. President," I answered. "I am pleased to hear this and I know that the agents will be pleased to hear it, too, and I will convey it to them." Then, nervous and worried that I might lose the chance, I just blurted it out.

"Mr. President, there's something I want to speak to you about. Dick Walters and I feel that people on your staff are trying to mortally wound you by using the CIA and the FBI and by confusing the question of CIA interest in or not in people the FBI wishes to interview. I've just talked to Clark MacGregor and asked him to speak to you about this."

There was a perceptible pause. Then Nixon said, "Pat, you just continue your aggressive and thorough investigation." That was the end of the call.

The next day, July 7, Kenneth Dahlberg gave us a sworn statement. He said that he had combined several cash contributions to the

Nixon campaign into one $25,000 cashier's check, which he had then given to Maurice Stans, the former secretary of commerce who was now the chairman of the campaign finance committee. How the check got into the hands of Bernard Barker, one of the burglars, who had cashed it in Miami, Dahlberg had no idea, since he didn't even know who Barker was. Our agents then decided to interview Stans.

Manuel Ogarrio turned out to be a reputable attorney in Mexico City who had caused the $89,000 in Mexican bank drafts to be drawn for the benefit of long-standing clients whom he declined to identify. We then set about trying to identify them.

On July 12, Dick Walters came back to my office to pass along some additional details the CIA had found on its dealings with Howard Hunt. I accepted his documents and passed them along to the investigating special agents. I then asked him if he had spoken to Nixon since our last meeting.

"Not on this topic," he said. "Why?"

I then related my call from Nixon, and told Dick that I had warned the president that his underlings might mortally wound him if they were allowed to keep it up. I told Dick that I had seen this behavior in the navy, where we called it "wearing the captain's stripes." In fact, back in 1968 while I was still in my private law practice and before I was asked to join the administration, I had written Nixon a letter warning him of exactly that possibility and urging the new president-elect to keep a tight rein on his subordinates.

"I agree," said Walters. "He needs to be protected from his self-appointed protectors. They're going to harm him while trying to cover their own mistakes. Or harm you and me, too, if they keep it up."

"I'll resign before I let that happen to the FBI, Dick."

"So would I. Maintaining our agencies' integrity is the best service we can render him."

"Then our views coincide."

That was the end of the so-called CIA interference in Watergate. From July 6, the day I spoke to Nixon, no more attempts were made by anyone in the CIA, the White House, or anywhere else to slow the FBI's investigation. As time passed I began to wonder if Dick Walters and I hadn't been a pair of alarmists.

The July 6 and July 12 Walters memos had detailed the CIA's assistance to several of the White House "plumbers." Both memos went straight from me to Mark Felt and Charlie Bates, and then into the FBI files. There, for anyone with a more suspicious mind than ours at the time, was a possible "smoking gun" pointing directly at the CIA. Yet the memos never leaked.

That same week John Dean called me at the FBI, asking for the documents he and I had discussed on the park bench near my apartment. My first concern was for their security. "These are my director's copies. They've got to be kept safeguarded at all times," I said. "Have you got a proper safe to keep them in?"

"Yes, I do," Dean answered. "But if it will make you more comfortable, I can come and read them in your office."

"That wouldn't be practicable, John. We've got six volumes of teletypes on this case already. But if you really do require them in the conduct of your inquiry for the president, I'll loan you my personal set. You can come and get them directly from me."

"Thanks, Pat. I'll send my assistant, Fred Fielding, to get them."

"No. You'll have to come over and get them yourself."

"Okay. Do you mind if I use the rear door?"

I told him that would be fine. When he came to get the six volumes of teletypes and the other written reports I had, I once again reminded him how sensitive they were and how important it would be to safeguard them. He told me he understood. As I handed them to him in a brown leather, government-issue lockable briefcase, I asked him again:

"You're using these as part of your report directly to the president, is that right? Not to Haldeman or Ehrlichman."

"Directly to the president," he answered.

Two weeks later, on July 19, the attorney general's office wanted another letterhead memorandum (LHM) summarizing the case.

I hadn't been comfortable sending the first one to Bob Haldeman as well as the attorney general, but Mark Felt assured me it had been standard practice under Hoover to keep the White House informed. "Ordinarily we would send LHMs to the AG and the White House," he said.

It may have been Hoover's practice, but he hadn't been appointed by the man currently occupying the White House. "Let me think about it," I said. "If George McGovern was president I would do it, but here I need to be more arm's length."

I directed Mark to ask Assistant Director Dwight Dalbey, the FBI's chief legal officer, for an opinion on the legal basis for the FBI providing information like this to the White House. "Anything else on Watergate?" I asked.

"Yes," said Mark. "Silbert says the case will not be completed before the grand jury for another three to four months."

"I just can't believe that."

"It's true. He met with Kunkel last night and talked about a trial in late fall."

"This is just ridiculous," I said. "We will be completed long before that, won't we?"

"Yes. I think we will be in good shape in thirty days to close this case."

The next day, Dwight's opinion came back and it was unequivocal.

To: Mr. Felt   Date: 7/20/72
From: D. J. Dalbey
Subject: DISSEMINATION OF INFORMATION
THE WHITE HOUSE
CRIMINAL CASES

You advised me that the Acting Director desires an opinion on the legal basis for dissemination by the FBI to the White House of information concerning a criminal case being investigated. More specifically, if I understand the situation, he means a case being investigated as a criminal case for prosecution involving a violation of Title 18, United States Code, and which does, or may, implicate Federal employees as subjects. Our reply is limited to such a situation.

We conclude that the FBI has no authority, or duty, to initiate dissemination of information to the White House concerning the criminal investigation in progress. Note that we use the word "initiate." We did not consider the matter of disseminating such information to the White House on specific White House request. In this latter situation we assume that since the President is the top boss of the Executive Branch he can obtain from that branch any information that he wishes. This is a different matter, legally and otherwise, from the one in which we would on our own decision initiate dissemination of the information. . . .

This discussion raises the question of the legality of dissemination to the White House in the past. It is my understanding under Mr. Hoover we disseminated information on criminal cases to the White House when, as, and if Mr. Hoover directed we do so, and this was done on Mr. Hoover's instructions without reference to the matter of whether we did or did not have the authority. The practice apparently had the sanction, grudgingly or otherwise, of the Attorney General and apparently was at least condoned by the White House. This is not to say either that it was right or it was wrong. Our only position is that from a strict legal standpoint, there was no specific authority for it. The authority and the obligation of the FBI are to keep the Attorney General fully informed and leave the rest to him.

Here was my answer on Dean's request for FBI reports. Clearly it was a "specific White House request." I had no choice but to provide to Dean anything from our files that he asked for in the president's name. My initial response had been correct, and I would have to continue giving him any reports he wanted.

Here, too, was my answer on dissemination of the letterhead memorandum, as Dwight made very clear. We could not and should not voluntarily send anything to the White House, or anywhere else, only to the attorney general. I underlined the last sentence and wrote, "Do so in this particular case and in all future cases."

As I had said from the beginning, Hoover's methods were not going to be mine. The day after I got this opinion we sent the letterhead memorandum up the chain of command to the deputy attorney general and to Assistant Attorney General Henry Petersen. If the White House were to get a copy of this one, and I assumed they would, it would come from the attorney general's office, not from the FBI.

On Wednesday, July 26, Dean called to ask for another batch of reports, and two days later he came to my office and picked up seventy-three investigative reports, which he would hold until mid-September.

Not all of the information went from the FBI to Dean. Some came the other way. A day or two before we were to interview Donald Segretti, the young California lawyer who was later to be identified with many of the Nixon presidential campaign's "dirty tricks," Dean called me and asked if that name meant anything to me. I said it did not.

"Well, he just called here," said Dean. "He's in a panic because the FBI wants to talk to him. He says he knows nothing about the Watergate burglary. Why do your agents want to interview him?"

"I have no idea, John," I answered. "Probably the Watergate. I've never heard of him and I don't know what led us to him. The best thing for him to do is just tell the truth to the agents."

"Of course," said Dean. "I agree."

Three and a half months later, in October, Donald Segretti's name would become familiar not only to me but to anyone reading a newspaper. At this stage, however, I took little note; his name was just one of dozens on the Washington field office's interview list. We in the FBI had our own investigation to direct, not the internal one that Dean was conducting for the White House. If only we had known what he really was doing.

> Making sure that the FBI did not surprise us was a key to protecting the White House. When I learned, for instance, that agents wanted to interview the vacationing Kathleen Chenow, secretary of the Plumbers' Unit, about Howard Hunt's activities in the White House, I dispatched Fielding to England to get her. Fred brought Ms. Chenow back within twenty-four hours. Thus we could say we were actively "cooperating" with the investigation by producing the witness at our own expense. But we were in fact afraid she might reveal damaging information if an FBI agent caught her by surprise. I got to her first and took advantage of the opportunity to advise her not to testify about "national security" matters, such as the Ellsberg break-in.
>
> —John Dean
> *Blind Ambition,* 1976

Dean "got to her first" not by outracing the FBI agents as he intimates here but by lying to me. On June 28, in the midst of his attempts to get the CIA to block the FBI's investigation into the Mexican money chain, Dean called me and told me that in addition to Ogarrio and Dahlberg, the FBI should refrain from interviewing Chenow on "national security" grounds as well. As he admits here, there were no national security grounds. Dean was lying to me, and the resultant short delay created his "opportunity."

Chenow was interviewed by the FBI on July 3. She told us that she had made arrangements to install a White House private line for Howard Hunt to be used primarily by him as an answering service. Beyond that detail, she claimed to know nothing about the burglary, nor did she recognize any of the burglars' names. Her boss, David Young, a special White House staff assistant, was interviewed the same day, with John Dean sitting in. Young told us nothing of substance.

eleven

"Intensive investigation continuing."

SINCE THE FIRST WEEK AFTER THE BREAK-IN, I HAD RECEIVED
daily summaries of the progress of the Watergate burglary investigation. These single-page reports always ended with the same sentence:
"Intensive investigation continuing." It was an understatement.

By the first week in July we had positively identified the man seen
frequently with Howard Hunt. It was, as our agents had come to suspect, G. Gordon Liddy, the former FBI agent and CREEP staffer who
would turn out to be the mastermind of the burglary. He declined to
be interviewed and was called before the grand jury.

Also that week, Penny Gleason, a security officer for CREEP who
had been on switchboard duty the morning after the break-in, told us
that McCord's wife had called Rob Odle, the director of administration for CREEP, after which Gleason heard Odle tell his secretary, "Get
Assistant Attorney General Santarelli on the phone." It was suggested
by the Washington field office agents that I contact Dick Kleindienst to
arrange an interview with Santarelli, whose wife was the director of
personnel for CREEP.

I knew Donald Santarelli as a rising young star in the Justice Department. His actual title was associate deputy attorney general, a detail I rather pointedly noted on my reply when I said I would arrange

the interview. When contacted, he denied having received a call from Odle that morning and said the only conversation he had had with Odle about any of this was when Odle later asked him about a recommendation for a replacement for McCord. Anything else he knew about the case, said Santarelli, he read in the newspapers. As far as I know, we never interviewed his wife. Later in the year, Santarelli would leave the Justice Department to take over the Law Enforcement Assistance Administration.

Penny Gleason also told us that she had heard from the CREEP bookkeeper that Maurice Stans, the committee's finance chairman, had instructed that any records the FBI wanted were not to be sent to us through Rob Odle because "something might happen to them." On July 5, we interviewed both John Mitchell and Maurice Stans. Neither provided any pertinent information.

On July 12 we were ready to arrest both Hunt and Liddy, but assistant U.S. attorneys Earl Silbert and Don Campbell told Bob Kunkel of the Washington field office not to do so. It would be better for their case, they said, to avoid the resultant preliminary hearing where Hunt's and Liddy's attorneys would be allowed to see the evidence we had so far gathered against their clients. At that same meeting, Silbert told Kunkel that he was both impressed and overwhelmed by the quantity and quality of the investigative reports the FBI was delivering. He should have been. So was I.

We made progress on the money chain. Bernard Barker took the Fifth Amendment at his bail bond hearing on July 14 when asked to identify who had given him the four Mexican checks totaling $89,000, but Maurice Stans, when we reinterviewed him the next day, said that he had given the $25,000 Dahlberg check to Hugh Sloan Jr., who supervised funds received by CREEP. Stans said that he knew nothing more about the check, and that Sloan had resigned from the committee prior to the break-in. We went looking for Sloan.

By the time we talked to Sloan two days later, he said he would not be interviewed until he spoke to his attorney, but when our agents immediately contacted his lawyer, he said Sloan had just replaced him. That same day, July 17, our agents tried to interview Bob Mardian, the former assistant attorney general who now worked for CREEP. Mardian invoked attorney-client privilege, saying he had recently counseled Stans, Liddy, and Sloan.

On July 21, agents interviewed Jeb Magruder, the president's deputy campaign manager, who said that he had hired G. Gordon Liddy and had authorized Hugh Sloan to give Liddy up to $250,000 to handle convention sites and "problems." Magruder said he had specifically ordered Liddy not to do anything illegal or embarrassing to CREEP. The agents also interviewed John Ehrlichman at the White House, who said that he had met Hunt and Liddy on just one occasion, when the two were working on a "leak program." Ehrlichman denied any knowledge of any illegal activity by CREEP.

Also that day, agents interviewed Fred LaRue, the Mississippian who had chatted with Bea and me at the Newporter Inn swimming pool on the weekend of the burglary. LaRue told the agents that he was the one who had hired Alfred Baldwin (the Watergate lookout) on McCord's recommendation, and he also said that he was the one who had fired Liddy on Bob Mardian's recommendation.

By the end of the month, we had made progress tracing the four Mexican checks to the Texas Finance Committee to Re-Elect the President. Its chairman, the Houston oilman Robert Allen, sent us back to Maurice Stans, who then provided more details on July 28. He gave more detail about the overall funding of CREEP and acknowledged that Manuel Ogarrio may have gotten the funds from a Texas campaign contributor, but declined to elaborate without talking to his lawyer. At that point the agents served him with a subpoena to appear before the grand jury.

On August 24, another Houston oilman, Roy Winchester of Pennzoil, told agents that in April a Mexican he believed to be Manuel Ogarrio came to his office and gave him four checks valued at "over $80,000," which Winchester then hand-delivered to Hugh Sloan in Washington.

Back in June, the name Donald Segretti had come to the FBI's attention as a name in Howard Hunt's address book. A check of the calls he made from his Los Angeles home showed that he had called both the White House and the Robert Mullen Company, the CIA-linked corporation for which Hunt also worked. Agents from the Alexandria, Virginia, field office quickly discovered that Segretti had no CIA connection. We in the FBI had no record of him in our files. We then wanted to interview Robert Bennett, the president of the Mullen Company (and later a U.S. senator from Utah), about Segretti, but again the prosecutors preferred to use the grand jury instead.

On August 28, agents interviewed White House staffers Dwight Chapin and Gordon Strachan about Segretti's activities. Chapin admitted he gave Segretti the job of harassing Democratic candidates, but said that Segretti chose his own tactics without guidance from either of the White House men. As usual, John Dean sat in on the joint interview.

The Segretti investigation led us to Herbert W. Kalmbach, a Los Angeles attorney and close personal friend of Nixon. Earl Silbert asked that Kalmbach be interviewed about payments he reportedly made to Segretti, and due to Kalmbach's closeness to the president, the agents first asked for my approval, which I immediately gave. Kalmbach told the Los Angeles agents that Dwight Chapin had instructed him to pay Segretti's salary and expenses out of campaign funds, and that he had done so to the tune of $30,000 to $40,000.

By September, as the grand jury indictments loomed, press reports of varying accuracy sprouted, some of them obviously drawn from supposedly secret grand jury testimony. On September 2, Earl Silbert asked the FBI to make an electronic sweep of his offices and the grand jury room itself. The sweeps were negative, though our follow-up investigation discovered that the private court-reporting firm was producing an extra copy of its official testimony transcripts. Advised of this potential leak source, the firm reverted to its previous method and tightened its trash-disposal methods. We never determined whether this was a source.

The indictments came down on September 15. The original five burglars, along with Howard Hunt and Gordon Liddy, were charged with multiple counts of conspiracy, burglary, interception of communications, and unlawful possession of intercepting devices. All seven pleaded innocent and Chief Judge John Sirica of the U.S. District Court assigned the case to himself.

twelve

"That's a crock and you know it."

I NOW KNOW THAT MANY OF THE HIGH OFFICIALS IN THE FBI deeply resented my appointment as acting director. J. Edgar Hoover clearly had not singled out any one of these men to be his successor. The result of this egocentric failure on the part of the late director was to leave a claque of ambitious men straining mightily to hold the reins of power. Though I wasn't aware of their animosity at the beginning, I did know that, as in any command situation, I had to take the first presented opportunity to establish dominance. Such an opportunity, an unpleasant one, arrived at the end of the summer, just before the Watergate indictments came down. New allegations concerning Los Angeles SAC Wesley Grapp appeared at FBI headquarters. Letters, both signed and anonymous, now quoted Grapp as saying publicly that he ran his own shop regardless of what the new acting director said, and to prove it he continued to enforce the old dress and grooming standards in direct contravention of my specific orders.

At the same time, we were informed that local newspapers in Los Angeles were dredging up the earlier financial allegations, now alleging through unnamed sources that Grapp had taken out several large unsecured loans from banks and individuals, apparently trading on his position in the FBI to collateralize these loans. Mark Felt told me that Sandy Smith of *Time* magazine had come in to see Charlie Bates to say that his editors had instructed him to check out Grapp's loans. Smith, who knew how to trade a favor for a future tidbit, told Bates that he intended to stall.

As I had with the initial allegations against Grapp, I sent in a team from the Investigation Division, whose job was to perform internal inquiries within the Bureau, and, when their report dealing with both sets of complaints came back to me, I referred the financial findings to the Justice Department for an opinion on possible criminal violations while I turned my attention to Grapp's alleged public insubordination. The Justice Department found nothing illegal or improper in Grapp's financial dealings, but the same could not be said for the FBI's inquiry into his insubordination.

The inspection team had determined that Grapp had indeed continued to insist on the old standards, and that he had in fact publicly abused one of his employees over a mustache. It was clear from the inspection report that he was guilty of insubordination. I called him to Washington to confront him directly.

When I told the senior executives at FBI headquarters what I was going to do, they were appalled. Hoover hadn't done things that way. Send Grapp a letter telling him of the disciplinary action you are going to take, they said. Do it long distance, they said. No, I replied. I wanted to give this senior special agent in charge a chance to face me in person and to hear it from me in person. At that point I was met by a unanimous statement from these men that none of them would sit in on my meeting with Grapp. Several, including Mark Felt, said that before the meeting I should have Grapp frisked. Frisked! It was my turn to be appalled. No, they said, he's a dangerous man, this Wesley Grapp. I told them that under no circumstances would I subject a special agent in charge to such treatment. I told them that the meeting was going to take place, and I directed Dwight Dalbey, a very wise and strong individual, to sit in on the meeting.

On Friday, August 25, Wes Grapp came into my office for his meeting. Here was a picture-book FBI agent. He stood two inches taller than me, erect, perfectly groomed in the old white-shirt style. His hair was jet black, neatly trimmed and combed straight back, with just a trace of gray showing around the edges; there was composure in his piercing blue eyes. An imposing man, he had what we in the navy called "command presence." As special agent in charge of the hundreds of agents in the Los Angeles field office, he carried the additional title of assistant director, a rank carried only by his counterpart in New York.

With microphones in place, I sat down at the head of my conference table and had Wes sit on my right. Behind us, in a chair with his equipment, was the sound technician, and in the far corner of the room, sitting on a small sofa with orders from me to simply be there and remain silent, was Dwight Dalbey.

I detailed the allegations against him and pointed out to him how thoroughly I had reviewed all the material, including his written response to the charges. At the end of this I laid it on the line for him.

"I have examined the total record," I said, "and I have concluded that there is absolutely no way for the good of the service of the Federal Bureau of Investigation that you can continue as a special agent in charge of the Los Angeles field office—just no way that you can remain there."

I looked him in the eye. He looked back and said nothing.

"I want to make sure," I said, "that we have all the cards out here on the table. I want to make sure that you view this situation as seriously as I do. In fairness to you, you should consider a request for retirement. I cannot dictate that, of course, but I want you to consider it, because the action I am prepared to take today is to suspend you for twenty-five days without pay, to place you on probation, to censure you, and to transfer you to the El Paso field office as the special agent in charge. And now I'm willing to listen to anything that you have to say to me."

Grapp started off politely enough. "I feel like the old story about Abraham Lincoln," he said. "Walking through the cemetery at night, he kicked his toe against a tombstone and he said, 'It hurts too much to laugh, and I'm too old to cry.'"

I didn't take the bait. I didn't laugh, or even smile.

"I would assume," he said, "that you have construed this to be insubordination on my part—"

"I *have* construed it to be insubordination."

"Nothing," said Wes, "could be further from the truth." He went on to tell me about how similar our backgrounds were, in upbringing, training, the navy. He told me that I had made a fine speech out in Los Angeles, and he thought that some of his people had overreacted to it. Then he tried to turn the tables on me.

"Now what do we mean by 'overreacted'?" he asked. "Somebody told me that one day you asked for a hot plate so you could have some tea, and you didn't want a full-sized stove brought in for that purpose. Or another example is that one day you asked for some plywood, or whatever, for the wall and when you came back from lunch the whole room was covered with plywood, according to the story."

"Neither of which are true," I said. I had heard these rumors, but they were so off the mark I hadn't pursued them.

"I don't know, sir. I'm merely talking about overreaction."

"But neither of which are true. They're rumors."

"But very easily *could* be true," said Wes.

He was grasping at a straw here, and he knew it. He dropped that line of attack and then went into a lengthy defense of his actions, all of which I had read and heard before.

"Wes," I said, "this is a matter of principle. We're talking about the kind of mutual trust and affection that's got to exist between the SAC and the acting director."

Grapp's composure slipped a little. He was more agitated in his chair as he launched into another lengthy defense of his actions. This time, however, he did admit to "two mistakes." I knew all about the incidents, of course, and though they would not have merited this kind of disciplinary action, they did illustrate the problem. The first "mistake" was when Grapp found himself in the public elevator of the building where the Los Angeles field office was located with an employee who had a mustache. Grapp chewed him out, and ended up asking him, in front of other people, "Why do you cultivate under your nose what grows wild on your ass?"

The other incident was more serious, as it broke the chain of command, something that every officer in the military and every special agent in the FBI is taught from the very beginning not to do. Grapp had come into the office one day to find several agents looking unoccupied. He stormed up to them and demanded to know their names. This was a direct violation of long-standing command procedure, but I think he thought he could bluff it past me. I told him that he should have dealt with these agents through the supervisors.

"Not in every case," he said. "It isn't as strict as in the military."

"It is *stricter* than the military," I said. "The FBI has got higher traditions and standards than the military, and I can tell you that. The line is right to your top men. You know it, Wes, and I know it."

Grapp knew he was beaten here. He changed tactics.

"Well," he said, "let's get back to the top men. One man who I had implicit trust in—and you did, too—was keeping book on me the same as he did on Martha and John Mitchell, and the same as he has on you."

I looked him right in the eye. Now it was my turn to lean forward in my chair.

"I don't buy the book," I said. "I don't buy the record keeping. I'm not out to get any SAC, but if I find people who are doing that they are going fast. Just as fast as I can run them out."

"I'm glad of that," Wes said. "If I may finish my story, he's kept book on you and the cost of the airplane out there. He came to me with it. That you had wasted $4,000 of the taxpayers' money so you could give your wife a free trip. I told him it was none of his damn business."

Now I got angry. "Tell him to step up and say it to me, Wesley Grapp. Don't you bring it to me. Tell that man to get up here and say it to me." I knew he was accusing Chester St. Vincent, one of the special agents in his office. My own staff had reported the rumor to me.

"He won't come here."

"Well, then, don't you bring it."

"All right."

"And," I said, "if you say something again about Chester St. Vincent that can't be substantiated, let me warn you that one of the matters at issue here in this present case right now is false official statement, a violation of Title 18 of the United States Code."

That was the end of that threat at this meeting. "Wes," I said, "you can take whatever time you need to clear your personal effects out of your office in L.A. as SAC, but your suspension is effective Monday."

"You're *suspending* me?" He hadn't heard it, or hadn't believed it, when I had told him at the top of the meeting.

"That's correct. From duty, without pay."

He was very quiet now and took my letter and read it. He sat there, and I could tell that he had finished reading, that he was thinking of something to say. At last he spoke.

"The Los Angeles office—I did not intend to mention it—has told me consistently from the first week after Mr. Hoover's death that there was a contract for me—"

"That's a crock and you know it," I said. If his Mafioso-style "contract killing" rumor was designed to intimidate me, it had the opposite effect. "I've heard this from other SACs and the next time I hear it from one, I'm going to dismiss him. I told Neil Welch that up in Detroit. I will not tolerate this kind of rumormongering in the Federal Bureau of Investigation. You're men, not little old ladies in tennis shoes, and I'm sick and tired of this gossip."

Grapp had played his last card. "I'm exceedingly sorry, sir," he said finally.

"I am, too," I said. "I hate like hell to have to come to this, but I've got the FBI to worry about, too."

"You have a heavy responsibility," said Grapp.

"So do you. I want you to go to El Paso and do a good job. Good luck to you, Wes. Good-bye."

We stood and walked to the door together. We shook hands, and Grapp left. I turned back to Dalbey, who had sat quietly through the entire proceeding, said, "Thank you, Dwight," and then I walked into my private office.

I knew that I had to put in a strong man to replace Grapp. Joe Jamieson, the special agent in charge in Philadelphia, was just the man, and I called him immediately.

"Joe," I said, "I'm promoting you to assistant director in charge of the Los Angeles field office. The situation there is serious. How soon can you be there?"

"I'll be there in twenty-four hours, sir."

This was on Friday. The following Thursday I received a memo from Los Angeles. It was signed by Jamieson, and it read:

TO: ACTING DIRECTOR, FBI
FROM: SAC, LOS ANGELES
RE: WESLEY G. GRAPP
SPECIAL AGENT IN CHARGE
RECORDING DEVICE

On 8/29/72 Mr. EWING G. LAYHEW, Supervisor of Squad 18, Los Angeles Division, informed me that at the request of SAC WESLEY G. GRAPP, a recording device had been installed in the SAC's office by he [sic] and SA ROBERT F. JACOBS. According to LAYHEW, this installation occurred several years ago and had the capability of recording telephone conversations as well as conversations taking place in the SAC's office.

I requested that LAYHEW and JACOBS come to my office and show me the installation. LAYHEW looked in a drawer in a cabinet to the left of the desk and advised that the Sony recorder and switch box placed in the drawer was missing. SA JACOBS then pulled out the two top drawers on the right side of the desk and looked in and advised that the microphone was still there. JACOBS borrowed my knife, cut the microphone, a "Minimite," loose and gave it to me. A Sony recorder was subsequently located in the top drawer of a two-drawer Mosler safe in a closet off the conference room, back of the SAC's office. Also in the drawer was other Bureau property charged out to SAC GRAPP including his FBI Handbook.

This was too much, the final and last straw in the Grapp case. As if to magnify his total disregard for FBI rules that got in his way, Grapp had taken this recorder and placed it on top of his *FBI Handbook*.

Part I, page 1, of the *Handbook* reads, "A Special Agent shall not engage in entrapment or any other improper, illegal or unethical tactics in procuring information or evidence . . . shall not install secret phone systems or microphone plants without Bureau authorization."

I rescinded my order transferring Grapp to El Paso as special agent in charge. I ordered him demoted to special agent and transferred to Minneapolis.

Wesley Grapp did what I knew he would do. He retired from the FBI.

thirteen

"Contact with an anonymous source."

ON SEPTEMBER 5, A GROUP OF TERRORISTS FROM THE PALES-
tinian militant group Al Fatah, calling themselves "Black September,"
raided the athletes' compound at the Olympic Games in Munich, West
Germany, and took members of the Israeli team as hostages, demanding the release of hundreds of terrorists jailed in Israel and in West
Germany. The Israeli government refused to negotiate and in the ensu-
ing series of gun battles eleven Israeli athletes, five of the terrorists, and
a West German police officer were killed.

Within days of the massacre, Mark Felt called me in Seattle. "We
have a follow-up from Tel Aviv," he said. "The embassy called CIA and
said they have info that Al Fatah will try an attack on an eastern airport
in the U.S."

"Do we know which one?"

"No."

"Then let's gear up and be ready at all the major ones. What else?"

"We've got the same story from a Black Panther informer in L.A.
Ed Miller wants to apply for a tech on the Cleaver faction."

"Do it."

The Cleaver faction of the Black Panther Party was the 150-member
violent wing that had split from Huey Newton's less-violent 400-
member organization in 1971. Eldridge Cleaver, who had fled to Cuba

in 1968 after a gun battle with the police in Oakland, California, was now in Algeria, running his so-called International Section. The CIA had previously passed along information to us that he and his faction were in active contact with Al Fatah and other Arab extremist groups.

Early the next morning, terrorism broke out on another close-to-home front. I got a call from Henry Petersen. Bea and I were still in our hotel room in Portland, Oregon, for a field office visit later that day.

"Pat," said Henry, "I've just been talking to Dick Kleindienst. There's been a terrorist attack on St. Croix. Eight white tourists staying at a plush resort have been killed by a group of five to seven black men armed with automatic weapons. Now they're holding out in a stronghold on the island. Governor Evans has some difficult decisions to make. The Coast Guard has offered him a helicopter and the Marshals Service has bulletproof vests available."

"Has he given any thought to using marines or other U.S. troops?"

"No. We think local constabulary guided by your FBI people can do the job and that's what we've told him."

"What's our jurisdiction, Henry?" St. Croix was a U.S. territory in the Caribbean and subject to American laws and protection, but I wanted specific statutory authority before I ordered in my special agents.

"It's pretty clear," said Henry. "Deprivation of civil rights."

I called Mark Felt and told him to handle it. We sent in a dozen special agents, but because the FBI had so few black agents, we didn't have the trained manpower to work the front lines and go undercover to help root out the perpetrators. Eventually five local men were arrested by local authorities and convicted of the murders, which apparently had happened as part of an armed robbery turned violent. All were given multiple life sentences.

On Tuesday, September 12, I came back to my office after a week of travel to field offices in Alaska, Washington, Oregon, and Montana. After a long day of catch-up, I met at five that afternoon for a briefing with my staff. One of the items Dave Kinley reported on was a request

THE WHITE HOUSE

WASHINGTON

September 1, 1972

MEMORANDUM FOR: THE DEPUTY ATTORNEY GENERAL

SUBJECT: INFORMATION FOR CAMPAIGN TRIPS:
                                    EVENTS AND ISSUES

In order for John Ehrlichman to give the President maximum support
during campaign trips over the next several weeks, the following
information is required for each of the states listed at Tab A.

(1) Identification of the substantive issue problem areas in the
     criminal justice field for that particular state. Please limit
     yourself to problems of sufficient magnitude that the President
     or John Ehrlichman might be expected to be aware of them.
     Brevity is the key, and often all that is necessary is to flag a
     sensitive problem so it can be avoided or more extensive pre-
     paration can be undertaken should we choose to speak about it.

(2) A list of events relating to the criminal justice area that would
     be good for John Ehrlichman to consider doing. For each suggested
     event, the following items should be indicated:

     (A) Purpose of the event.
     (B) The nature of the group or institution involved.
     (C) The content of the event.
     (D) Names of specific people who can be contacted
          for the purpose of setting it up (together with
          titles, addresses, telephone numbers, etc.).
     (E) All trade-off factors to be considered in scheduling
          the event.

Portion of White House memo. September 1, 1972.

that had come in on Friday from Ralph Erickson, who had replaced
me as deputy attorney general, asking for an immediate answer to
some questions from the White House. Dave said that because it was
an expedited request, he had passed it along to Thomas Bishop, assistant director of the Crime Records Division, which handled this sort of
thing. Bishop had approved the request and so had Mark Felt, so Dave
had then initialed his own approval and authorized a teletype in my
name that was sent to twenty-one field offices. It sought answers for
Ralph to pass back to the White House. It wasn't unusual for the White
House to ask the FBI for general and statistical information on criminal

activity, nor was it rare for such a request to demand an immediate response. I was confident that Dave had done the right thing, especially since both Felt and Bishop had approved it, but I asked to see the White House memo anyway.

The subject was "Information for Campaign Trips: Events and Issues." It began, "In order for John Ehrlichman to give the President maximum support during campaign trips over the next several weeks, the following information is required. . . ."

I hit the roof. "This is a political request!" I said. "No way we should have passed it along."

Nor no way the White House should have asked us to do this in the first place, but that was outside my control. The FBI should not have acceded to this improper request, but now it was too late. A teletype had gone out to the field under my name and all twenty-one offices had promptly replied by Monday morning. Tom Bishop's Crime Records Division had then prepared a summary and passed it back to the White House through the deputy attorney general's office. I proceeded to chew out Dave and everyone else involved in the decision, making them all aware of the mistake they had made. Then, with that lesson learned, we all turned back to our more pressing problems. As far as I was concerned, the matter was closed. It certainly wouldn't happen again.

In mid-September, Ed Miller called me in my office with an urgent request. Information had just come to us that our worst fears were real: dozens of Al Fatah assassins were already here planning to send letter bombs to the home addresses of Israeli diplomats and their families living in the United States and Canada. The head of the Arab Education League in Dallas, a Dr. Wadi, had a list of their names in his office safe. Miller wanted me to give my assent to a surreptitious entry so we could get our hands on the list. Without a prior court order that would be illegal. My instant reaction was to say yes. These thugs wanted to kill innocent women and children. I didn't even consider the legality—this was a gut response. I wanted that list.

"Can we do it?" was the first question I asked. As far as I knew, we hadn't done a "black bag job," as they were called, since Hoover had forbidden them six years earlier. People both inside the Bureau and from other agencies had urged me to reinstate the capability for use in nondomestic operations, but when I asked them about it both Felt and Miller told me it would take months to get it back as an operational program.

"Wadi's out of the country. His office is empty. Dallas assures me they can do it without getting caught," Miller said.

After Miller answered a few more detailed questions, my mind was made up.

"Do it," I said.

Though I did worry about the hue and cry if we got caught, I never had second thoughts about the decision. Those letter bombs would be sent to Israeli diplomats at home where they could be opened by their children.

The Dallas agents performed flawlessly, and we got the list of names and addresses. Some were in Canada. Those names we passed on to the Royal Canadian Mounted Police, and the rest we went after ourselves. We got all of ours and harassed them out of the country by knocking on their doors and saying we wanted to fingerprint them. Though it was clearly illegal, the niceties of due process weren't applied; nobody in the intelligence community, the Justice Department, or the White House was willing to risk the time that might allow one of them to slip free and commit the atrocity he was here for.

(Four years later, as my lawyer Steve Sachs and I fought our way through the myriad prosecutors and grand juries of the Watergate cover-up investigation, I told this story to Philip Heymann, an associate special prosecutor, in response to a question. The incident was peripheral to Watergate, and Steve had never heard about it. Heymann was sympathetic. "Mr. Gray," he said, "I would have done the same thing. We will never prosecute you for that." Outside Heymann's office, Steve shook his head. "Gray," he said, "the next time you confess to a crime I think I'd like to hear about it first." Then he laughed. "Look on the bright side," he said. "You may get indicted, but I can get you B'nai B'rith Man of the Year.")

Sometime later the sources came alive again with the eastern airport attack story. O'Hare Airport in Chicago was the target and the incident was supposedly going to happen that day. The Chicago field office went into high gear. Within fifty minutes, 120 FBI agents were deployed all over the airport, not knowing what to expect but ready for anything.

The attack never happened. Whether the intelligence was faulty or the attackers were deterred by the speedy arrival of the FBI, we never learned. Later, in a lengthy debrief we analyzed our response. Certainly the traveling public at the airport never knew they had been surrounded and intermixed with heavily armed FBI agents ready to do battle with violent terrorists intent on mass murder. That was a plus. Our response time was fair. On the negative side, most of our agents had no body armor and some had only their sidearms as weapons. Communication was spotty since our radios and walkie-talkies weren't all on the same frequency. In the future we would have to be better equipped.

That summer became a time of great unease among all the responsible agencies in the federal government. International terrorism was a new and fast-growing phenomenon. In May the Lod Airport massacre in Tel Aviv had been carried out by the Japanese Red Army Brigade on behalf of radical Palestinians. American Weatherman radicals had traveled to China and Cuba. Eldridge Cleaver was operating out of Algeria and now black terrorists had machine-gunned white tourists in the Caribbean. None of us understood exactly how, or even if, all this hung together, but we all knew that we would have to deal with the events themselves. The Munich Olympics massacre had been horrific and none of us harbored any illusions that the United States was immune from something similar. Or worse. Clearly, what the Wadi assassins had in mind fell into that category.

Shortly after the Wadi incident, I got a call from Geoff Shepard, Ehrlichman's assistant, who had passed along the campaign information request that had caused me to hit the ceiling. He and Fred Fielding, John Dean's assistant, were now the point men in establishing a high-level interagency committee to coordinate our response to international terrorism. The result, formed at the end of the month, was the

President's Cabinet Committee on Terrorism, chaired by the secretary of state and including the secretary of defense, the directors of the CIA, the FBI, the National Security Agency, and several other members, including John Ehrlichman.

At the very first meeting at the end of September, Ehrlichman let it be known that the White House wanted the full responsibility for combating foreign terrorists inside the United States to rest with the FBI, not with the State Department. He needn't have worried. Everybody at that meeting washed their hands like Pontius Pilate and said, "You do it, FBI. You storm the embassies. You protect the hostages. You go out and get the logistic support you need." Nobody there, the secretary of defense or the rest of them, wanted to take the responsibility for combating these Al Fatah guerrillas and the other types that were coming in.

The FBI, which is supposed to be an investigatory agency and not a police force, got handed the task of adding a paramilitary capability to its already burdensome caseload. Five months later, at the Sioux Reservation town of Wounded Knee, South Dakota, the flaws in this "plan" became brutally apparent.

As September came to a close, no one inside the FBI doubted that we had all been stretched to our maximum capabilities. Between Watergate and the search for murderous terrorists already inside the country, the workload had been intense, and it should have come as no surprise to me that not all of our agents would rise fully to the challenges we all faced. Some of them faltered, and to my great disappointment one of them was Bob Kunkel.

In May, antiwar protests had broken out in the District of Columbia, as had happened for the past several years. This time the confrontations between police and marchers had turned nasty. Mixed in with the nonviolent sign carriers were several malevolent groups, among them a very confrontational group of several hundred people called the Attica Brigade. The metropolitan police had thousands of officers, uniformed and undercover, in place to try to control the demonstration, but the Attica Brigade got away from them. Throwing rocks and other objects, they broke windows in several government

Grounded plainclothes policeman (left) grabs demonstrator by the leg; then (center) rises, gun in hand, to face crowd; finally (at right) he is led away from the scene of confrontation by a fellow law enforcement officer.
By Elizabeth Dietz—The Washington Post

The incident at the antiwar demonstration in Washington that led to Bob Kunkel's transfer. May 22, 1972.

buildings, including the Justice Department, and even struck police chief Jerry Wilson hard enough to draw blood. In the midst of the melee, an undercover police officer went down and was set upon by the Attica Brigade rioters. While a *Washington Post* photographer took pictures, he was rescued by other officers.

As it was first reported to me, there was no FBI involvement in the episode. But Mack Armstrong kept saying I wasn't getting the full story, that his friend Special Agent Oliver "Buck" Revell kept telling him that undercover FBI people had been part of it and the new acting director was not getting the truth. When my repeated queries to my assistant directors kept returning the same story, I ordered in the Inspection Division. Its formal inquiry uncovered the truth: there were FBI agents in the published pictures. One of our undercover agents in the "ragamuffin squad" had gone to the rescue of the undercover police officer and had been taken down and lost his weapon, thereby prompting his backup, three other FBI undercover agents, to draw their weapons to rescue him. Nobody got hurt, and two hundred Attica Brigade members got arrested, but the truth, apparently, had been too "embarrassing" to relate to me. In Hoover's time as director, "Don't Embarrass the Bureau" had been such a firm unwritten rule that to make a truthful report about an incident like this was a surefire way for any special agent, up to and including a SAC, to get himself demoted, transferred, or both.

The SAC who kept sending the covering lie up the chain of command to me was Bob Kunkel. When the final report got to my desk in September, I called Bob in and told him I was transferring him to St. Louis. I also disciplined the supervisor of the undercover squad, who had also filed false reports about the incident, suspending him without pay for six weeks. I wanted everyone in the FBI to know that it was the lie, not the embarrassing episode, that would draw a serious rebuke from me.

At the same time I was transferring Bob Kunkel, Charlie Bates learned that I was bringing Bob Gebhardt in from San Francisco to head the Identification Division. Charlie telephoned me to press his own case to be returned to San Francisco. He had a strong desire to return to the field, he told me, because he hated the paperwork and lack of action at FBI headquarters. He also asked if he could take his title of assistant director back to the field with him so that he would be assistant director in charge of the San Francisco field office instead of special agent in charge. I told him I would consider it.

A few days later I told him that I would transfer him back to San Francisco, but that he would go as special agent in charge, not as assistant director. This irked him and he tried to persuade me to change my decision, but I held firm. San Francisco was not as big or as complex an operation as New York City or Los Angeles, which were headed by assistant directors, and I would not be persuaded. In my planning, Chicago was the next field office to be headed by an assistant director. Charlie left, and I could tell that he was pleased to be going to San Francisco, but quite displeased that he could not go as assistant director in charge.

Although the May protests in the District of Columbia precipitated Bob Kunkel's disciplinary transfer, the marches themselves weren't a big concern to the FBI, nor were most of the participants. It was the violent and subversive fringe that we were after: the Cleaver faction of the Black Panther Party, who were collaborating with Al Fatah, and the Weatherman fugitives.

The Weathermen found their origins in the Students for a Democratic Society campus organization and in the famous "Days of Rage" at the 1968 Democratic National Convention. They preached the destruction of the American form of government and backed up their preachings with a bomb or two here and there on a fairly regular basis. In the process they cared not if innocent lives were endangered or even lost. All were fugitives from justice. All had successfully evaded capture. At the time that I became acting director, twenty-six Weathermen were on our fugitives list, sixteen of them for more than two years.

The Domestic Intelligence Division, under Assistant Director Ed Miller, was charged with finding them, and I was appalled to learn when I came on board that not one had been caught. I immediately ordered them "hunted to exhaustion," a phrase we had used in submarine war tactics. Dogged pursuit of an elusive enemy was what I had in mind. What I did not have in mind was the use of illegal means to accomplish that. And what I didn't know—and wouldn't learn until long after I was out of the Bureau—was that Mark Felt and Ed Miller were doing exactly that: approving illegal surreptitious entries behind my back.

Surreptitious entries were, and still are, an important FBI tool. Placing a microphone inside the offices of a suspected terrorist or mobster usually requires that someone enters the premises and physically installs the device. When done in conjunction with a valid court order, this is a time-tested and legal intrusion by the government into the privacy of the individual under investigation. (It's important to note that it's the Federal Bureau of *Investigation*: the Bureau is an investigatory agency, not a national police force. Its primary function is to gather evidence to be used by federal prosecutors.)

During the 1950s and 1960s, the FBI used black bag jobs fairly regularly. In the early days, even a telephone wiretap required a surreptitious entry in order to "tap" the local number to be monitored, though by the time I arrived on the scene wiretaps were being set up via leased lines from the telephone company, which allowed us to intercept calls at the company switchboard and record them far from the premises in question.

But black bag jobs have a separate, and less clearly legal, attribute. While inside the premises, special agents can observe things that are there, including correspondence. Letters and postcards can reveal the return addresses of senders, and those senders might be persons of interest to the FBI. The temptation to "bag" the private residence of an innocent cousin of a dangerous radical or a known spy, looking for nothing more than an address or a phone number, was great, and for a long time the FBI succumbed to it routinely. But in 1966 Hoover had a change of heart—some in the Bureau called it "cold feet"—and he forbade the practice. What he didn't know was that it went on anyway. Mark Felt and Ed Miller continued to approve the illegal bag jobs, keeping the paperwork out of the regular system and referring to each approval as "contact with an anonymous source." They didn't tell Hoover, and when I arrived they didn't tell me, either.

It didn't occur to me to ask. When I ordered the surreptitious entry in the Wadi case, I thought I was reviving—for this extraordinary circumstance only—an abandoned tactic that I had been assured was known only to a few older agents who had been trained to carry them out prior to the Hoover ban. I did not know that the black bag jobs were still being performed, without approval from Hoover or from me. As for the Weatherman fugitives, what I had in mind when I ordered them hunted to exhaustion was a greater use of shoe leather and undercover agents. When I came to the Bureau I found special agents in dungarees and long hair and when I left we still had them. I did authorize the use of carefully selected young special agents to penetrate "the underground," including the Weathermen. They were to try to penetrate as members, to live with these people, to sleep with these people, to make love to the women if necessary, and to smoke marijuana if necessary. At no time did I authorize anyone to burglarize. I can recall many discussions as to how long we ought to leave a fine, clean-cut, well-trained special agent of the FBI in such a lifestyle before it would be too late to bring him out and retrain and restore him. We never did reach a decision on this.

Actually, I didn't get many reports that one of our agents had succeeded in penetrating "the underground" to the extent that he was living and operating within it. One agent in San Francisco, I believe, got as far as living in a "pad," but I don't think he actually penetrated the underground. In my year in the FBI, we never caught one of the Weathermen.

fourteen

"Now why the hell would he do that?"

With the September 15 indictments in place and a trial looming, the Watergate investigation and prosecution was on track as far as the Justice Department was concerned. Henry Petersen and his three U.S. attorneys, Earl Silbert, Seymour Glanzer, and Donald Campbell, had narrowly focused the FBI's investigation on the federal Interception of Oral Communications statute. Henry was a career prosecutor and the highest-ranking Democrat in the Justice Department, but he had stated from the outset that he was not going to "turn this into a fishing expedition."

By the end of September the FBI had completed most of its initial work, and the product was impressive. In June and July we had interviewed fifty-eight people from the Committee to Re-Elect the President, many of them repeatedly. At the White House our agents had interviewed eleven staffers up to and including John Ehrlichman, and in August and September three more. We had traced the cash used to fund the burglars, identified G. Gordon Liddy and E. Howard Hunt as their White House handlers, and passed leads indicating possible campaign law violations to the Justice Department for further action. The U.S. attorneys had now turned to the grand jury for testimony and the FBI for supporting detail as they prepared for the trial, which would begin in January. It was all going according to plan.

The investigation plan had been in place from the beginning, based on standard procedure in any conspiracy case: Prosecute those caught while searching vigorously for their motives and accomplices, then throw the book at the ones you identify and offer leniency to any one of them who will identify the rest. The plan worked. James McCord would indeed break and start talking, but not until the following March.

We always knew that McCord held some of the keys. Very early in the Watergate investigation, during our June 28 skull session, Charlie Bates mentioned that Donald Guthrie, a special agent in our Birmingham, Alabama, office, was a close friend of McCord, who was himself a former FBI agent. Charlie suggested that McCord might talk to Guthrie since the two families were close. I said I would have to think that over because McCord was already represented by an attorney and we could get ourselves into another ethical wrangle if we tried to step around that relationship. I said "another" because we had already had a problem when one of our agents had tried to interview one of the arrested burglars in the Washington jail. I considered Charlie's suggestion for a couple of days, then told him to go ahead and talk to Guthrie. Charlie then reported to me that Guthrie thought he could make contact through McCord's wife and would be glad to do it, both as an agent of the FBI and as a friend of McCord. Again I considered it but finally determined that any attempt by us to go around McCord's attorney could too easily backfire and bring real heat upon us in the FBI.

In retrospect, I think this approach may have worked and might have broken the case much earlier. But it would have been highly unethical. Instead, we followed the prosecutors' strategy of first obtaining convictions of the suspects and then prevailing upon them to talk. I knew that sooner or later the true story would have to come out, and it did. In March, faced with a harsh prison sentence, McCord began to talk. To me, keeping the FBI on the ethical high road was well worth that nine-month wait.

But it was not well worth it to everyone else. Those six months between the September indictments and the March confession, not particularly excessive in a behind-the-scenes criminal case, would prove to be far too long for the primary audience in any national political case: the press. It was an election year, this was a political case, and I was a Nixon appointee. Now that the indictments were in, the news media went into overdrive, but their focus wasn't entirely on Watergate. Much of it was on the FBI as an institution and on me as an individual.

The FBI had been using and had been used by the press long before I got there. Top Bureau officials each had their pet reporters and vice versa. Sandy Smith of *Time* was cozy with Mark Felt and Charlie Bates; the syndicated columnist Robert Novak got much of his fodder from William C. Sullivan, who had been fired by Hoover in 1971 after a well-publicized dispute; and Jeremiah O'Leary of the *Washington Star* had numerous sources. So did the columnist Jack Anderson. Every one of them had multiple overlapping motivations.

With a trial now in the offing, the press began trying to ferret out the details of what might come out in court. Duty-bound to prevent the taint of prejudicial pretrial publicity, both the prosecutors and the FBI tried mightily to stem the leaks. It was like damage control on the *Titanic*.

Looking for both leaks and new leads, we at the FBI tracked all the newspaper stories. Their batting average was not good. On October 1, Jeremiah O'Leary and Patrick Collins wrote a front-page piece in the *Washington Star* stating that FBI agents were investigating a report that the Watergate security guards had been paid off. We were not. After several more press accounts of varying accuracy, John Sirica, the judge presiding over the upcoming trial, issued an amended gag order on October 6, enjoining any parties to the case from making any statements outside the official proceedings. This, of course, included the FBI. The order was only partly successful. With the presidential election just a month away, Washington was awash in rumor, speculation, and intrigue, much of it appearing unfiltered in national newspapers, usually attributed to unnamed sources.

On October 10, the *Washington Post* ran a front-page story by Carl Bernstein and Bob Woodward that began, "FBI agents have established that the Watergate bugging incident stemmed from a massive campaign

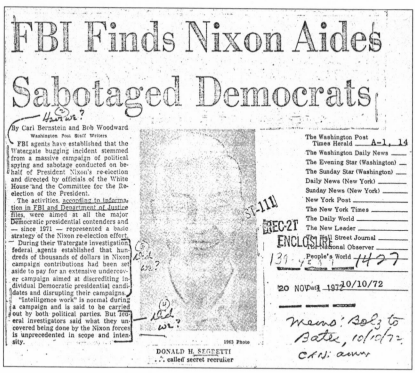

Portion of FBI document with Gray's handwritten notes.

of political spying and sabotage conducted on behalf of President Nixon's re-election and directed by officials of the White House and the Committee for the Re-election of the President." The lengthy piece named Donald Segretti in particular as being involved in these alleged activities and said that the information for the article had come from "information in FBI and Department of Justice files." I asked Dwight Dalbey, our senior legal officer, to review the newspaper allegations and our own files to determine if there was any possible violation of federal law by Segretti, whom we had interviewed three times in June and who had been served a subpoena in August to appear before the grand jury. Two days later Dalbey responded, "We should not be surprised to learn that Segretti has violated some Federal laws, but the known facts are too few to permit a conclusion at this time."

We then asked Henry Petersen whether we should pursue the Segretti allegations beyond what we had already learned. On October 18, I

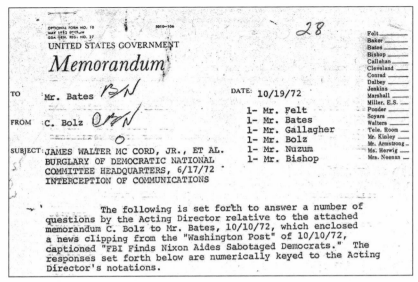

Portion of FBI memo. October 19, 1972.

got Henry's answer from Charlie Bolz in our Accounting and Fraud Section, who had put the question to Henry.

"Mr. Petersen advised he was fully aware of the extent of the FBI's investigation of Segretti and he is also aware of the allegations as to Segretti's political harassment activities and attempts to recruit personnel to assist in such, as set forth in recent news articles. Mr. Petersen stated he does not believe Segretti's activities are in violation of any Federal statutes and, accordingly, he can see no basis for requesting any additional investigation of Segretti by the FBI at this time."

But I also had questions about the October 10 article's claims that much of the information in the story had come from our own files. I marked up our file copy of the article with ten specific questions and gave it to Charlie Bates.

The detailed memo I got back a week later was careful to differentiate what we in the FBI had learned in our interviews from what the prosecutors had learned in secret grand jury testimony. It was also careful to point out what claims in the article were either conjecture or simply false.

Segretti had come to our attention because Howard Hunt's telephone records showed that Hunt had called him in California. When we interviewed him, he refused to tell us very much, including who paid him. So he was then called before the grand jury on August 22, where he was more forthcoming, admitting that he had been hired by Dwight Chapin of the White House and paid by Herbert Kalmbach, Nixon's personal California lawyer and the associate chairman of CREEP. Chapin and Kalmbach had then confirmed this when interviewed by our agents immediately after Segretti's testimony. As for the lead sentence of the article, which claimed that the FBI had established that the Watergate bugging "stemmed from a massive campaign of political spying and sabotage conducted on behalf of President Nixon's re-election and directed by officials of the White House," the internal memo I got said, "The foregoing is pure conjecture on the part of the news reporters."

The nine-page memo did point to some areas of agreement between the article and what was in our files, but the vast proportion of the memo pointed to discrepancies between what the article claimed was in the FBI files and what actually was there. In response to my ten specific questions about claims made by the article, the most frequent answer was either "We developed no such information" or "The foregoing statement is absolutely false."

C. Bolz to Mr. Bates
RE: JAMES WALTER MC CORD, JR.

        (8) The attached news article states "According to
FBI reports, at least 50 undercover Nixon operatives traveled
throughout the country trying to disrupt and spy on Democratic
campaigns."

        COMMENT: The foregoing statement is absolutely
false. The FBI's investigation of the Watergate incident, other
than learning of Segretti's activities, did not develop any
information as to other individuals ("Nixon operatives") who
traveled throughout the country trying to disrupt and spy on
Democratic campaigns.

Portion of FBI memo. October 19, 1972.

Two days after this article appeared, John Dean called me to complain about the apparent FBI leaks in it. I told him I was looking into it, and then he asked me for any additional teletypes and investigative reports I had. That evening his assistant, Fred Fielding, came to my office and picked them up. It was the last of the three batches I made available to him.

The next morning, I left for another series of field office visits. Over the weekend, the *Washington Post* claimed that in August, during the Republican National Convention in Miami, Segretti had been shown his FBI interview reports by White House people less than twenty-four hours after he gave the interviews to the FBI. We in the Bureau knew this claim was totally false, because our reports were of interviews he had given us back in June; the report of his August grand jury subpoena service hadn't been dictated and typed until after the convention. On Monday, Sandy Smith in *Time* magazine reported that Gordon Strachan, a White House aide, said that he had helped hire Segretti. Smith's report was accurate. That same day I spoke with Mark Felt by telephone from the Salt Lake City field office.

"Sandy Smith talked to Charlie Bates," said Mark. "He says his source is someone in the Department of Justice and it's the same as Bernstein and Woodward's."

Though we in the FBI never learned who that source was, others were certain they knew. Starting in October, Dick Kleindienst kept telling me that I should fire Mark Felt. "He's leaking, Pat, and we know it," he told me at least five times. Finally I went to Mark and asked him if it was true. He vehemently denied it.

"You can transfer me if you don't believe me," he said. "But those allegations are not true. You have my word on it."

But Dick kept insisting that I fire Mark, that he was getting his information about Mark's leaks from an unimpeachable source, the same one who was passing it along to the White House.

October 19, 1972   *Executive Office Building, 1:48–4:09 p.m.*

NIXON: You know, materials are leaked out of the FBI. Why the hell can't Gray tell us what the hell has left? You know what I mean?

HALDEMAN: We know what's left.

NIXON: We read about it.

HALDEMAN: We know what's left and we know what's leaked and we know who leaked it.

NIXON: Is it somebody in the FBI?

HALDEMAN: Yes, sir.

NIXON: What'd you find out?

HALDEMAN: Through a full circle through the—

NIXON: Department?

HALDEMAN: —the place where it's come from. The FBI doesn't know who it is. Gray doesn't know who it is, but we do know. And it's very high up.

NIXON: Somebody next to Gray?

HALDEMAN: Mark Felt.

NIXON: Now why the hell would he do that?

HALDEMAN: It's hard to figure. Then again, you can't say anything about this, because we'll screw up our source, and the real concern is Mitchell is the only one that knows this. And he feels very strongly that we should—we'd better not do anything because—

NIXON: Do anything? Never!

HALDEMAN: If we move on him, then he'll go out and unload everything. He knows everything that's to be known in the FBI.

NIXON: Sure.

HALDEMAN: He has access to absolutely everything. Ehrlichman doesn't know this yet. I just got this information. I'm going to tell him, but I don't have to tell him the source.

NIXON: Don't tell him. Don't tell him the source.

HALDEMAN: I'm not going to, but if we tell him the fact. Suggest that he—without saying that we know that—tell Pat Gray. He doesn't know anything about this, but he knows the fact that Pat should not have confidence in Mark Felt anymore. So, I think Pat ought to know that.

. . .

NIXON: How did we stumble onto Felt?

HALDEMAN: Through an official in a publication who knows where a reporter in the publication is getting his stuff. In other words we learned it from the reporter.

NIXON: Why is he telling us?

HALDEMAN: Because he has stronger ties here than he does to the publication . . . It's a legal guy.

NIXON: The *Post*?

HALDEMAN: A legal guy.

. . .

NIXON: Who made the contact?

HALDEMAN: He made the contact here, with a guy at the Justice Department.

NIXON: Why did he do it?

HALDEMAN: Because he knows what the problem is. He's deeply concerned about it . . . So he has told the guy at Justice, who he knows, what the route is . . . The guy at Justice told John Dean. He has not told anybody else, including Kleindienst or Pat Gray, because he's afraid that either of them might react in such a way as to do more harm than good.

NIXON: So say nothing.

Four days after this conversation between Nixon and Haldeman, Charles Colson called me. I had known Colson, one of Nixon's closest advisers, for several years.

"You sound far away," he said after the White House operator put him on the line. "Where are you?"

"In Connecticut."

"I'm sorry," he said. "I didn't want them to chase you to Connecticut." Colson was genial, but he got quickly to the point. "I've been getting reports that there are leaks in the FBI from the old guard and from those who are mad at you for politicizing the FBI."

"Chuck, you know I'm not doing any politicizing. Where are you getting this?"

"Sandy Smith is the conduit," he answered. "What do you know about that?"

"Well, I do know he has some contacts in the FBI. Quite a few, as a matter of fact, and we have warned our people plenty on this." Colson had nothing more to add to the conversation, and neither did I.

On October 25 Bernstein and Woodward ran a front-page story in the *Washington Post* claiming that Hugh Sloan's grand jury testimony had tied John Mitchell and Bob Haldeman to the use of campaign funds to finance illegal activities. But Sloan had said nothing of the sort. In the flap that ensued, Bernstein tried to cover his tracks by claiming that Angelo Lano, the case agent from the Washington field office, had been his source and had corroborated the story prior to publication. Lano was furious and filled out a sworn affidavit to the contrary that we used in a detailed report that we forwarded over my signature to the attorney general. As recounted in the FBI report, Woodward and Bernstein were called before the U.S. attorneys, who decried their tactics and reminded them that all officials in the case were bound by Judge Sirica's order.

As the election got closer, the articles got even more pointed. Not all were off base. In its weekly edition out on Sunday, October 29, *Time* very accurately reported that Dwight Chapin, Nixon's appointments secretary, had admitted to FBI agents that he had hired Donald Segretti to disrupt the Democratic campaign. *Time* went on to say, "Chapin has also told the FBI that Segretti's payment was set by Nixon's personal attorney, California lawyer Herbert Kalmbach. . . . Kalmbach, too, admitted to FBI agents that the money he paid Segretti came from cash kept by the Committee for the Reelection of the President in the office of its finance chairman, Maurice H. Stans."

Though his information was two months old (Chapin had told us that on August 28), Sandy Smith was far ahead of his competition. Bernstein and Woodward ran it on Monday in the *Washington Post* under the headline, "Magazine Says Nixon Aide Admits Disruption Effort." Later that morning, while I was at the Richmond, Virginia, field office I got a call from Mark Felt.

"I just had a conference with the attorney general," he said. "The president is on the ceiling about this leak, and Kleindienst thinks it's someone who's after you. His advice is that you should be here in Washington between now and election time as much as possible."

The election was a week away but my field office visit schedule was prearranged. Those personal visits by the director, which Hoover had rarely made, seemed much more important to me than staying in Washington to help the president's reelection campaign. I flew to the San Juan, Puerto Rico, office that afternoon and didn't get back to Washington until Tuesday night.

On Wednesday I met in my office with Sandy Smith but could learn nothing of his source for the story that had bounced the president off the ceiling. That afternoon I went to a regular staff meeting at Dick Kleindienst's office, and afterward he asked me to meet with him in private.

"Pat, you just have to fire Mark Felt," he said. "He is the leaker here."

"No, Dick, I'm not going to fire him," I said. "But this time I want to know. Where's all this coming from?"

"It's coming from John Mitchell. He's heard it directly from the source."

"Who's the source? I need to know that."

Dick agreed. "It's Roswell Gilpatric," he said. "He's now outside general counsel to *Time* magazine."

I knew who Roswell Gilpatric was. A deep Kennedy insider, he had been John F. Kennedy's deputy secretary of defense and a prime mover in forming the Defense Intelligence Agency in response to the Bay of Pigs failure and the Cuban missile crisis. But why would a Kennedy man report this to John Mitchell?

"He knows John," said Dick. "And he thinks what Felt's doing is abhorrent. So when he learned the source from *Time*'s reporter, he passed it along."

Sandy Smith was *Time*'s reporter and I had just met with him, trying to correct some of the inaccuracies in his reporting without revealing anything that had not yet been made public by the prosecution. If his source was Mark Felt, or anyone else high in the FBI, the stories would at least be accurate. One last time I confronted Mark with Dick's demand, but I did not reveal any of the details Dick had given me. They had been passed to me in confidence and they have stayed that way until now. (Mitchell, Kleindienst, Smith, and Gilpatric are all dead.) When Mark once again vehemently denied the accusation, I put the matter away. Choosing between the personal word of the number-two man in the FBI, a man sworn to uphold the law, and the frequent unreliability of a reporter, I chose the former without a second thought.

As the election approached, there was one more political blowup, this one with lasting effects for the FBI. On October 24, Bob Woodward had called both Mark Felt and Tom Bishop to say that he knew about a "directive" issued by the FBI "last summer" that dealt with investigating candidates for Congress. Though neither Mark nor Tom would comment to Woodward, both were well aware of what the reporter was asking about. Since 1950, the FBI had routinely gathered public information and gleaned its own files for background information on nonincumbents running for Congress, trying to learn in advance whether the candidate would be friendly or hostile to the Bureau, should he or she win the election. Called Congressional Relations, the program was run by Tom Bishop's Crime Records Division and so far no one in the Bureau had told me about it.

The next morning, Mark called me in Key Biscayne as I was getting ready to go to the Miami field office, first to tell me that contrary to the big *Washington Post* story out that day, the FBI had not talked to Bob Haldeman, and then to brief me on Woodward's blind inquiry into the Congressional Relations program. As soon as I heard the outline of the program from Mark, including the 1971 Congressional Assassination Statute (which made it a federal crime to attempt to kill, kidnap, or assault a member of Congress and gave the FBI specific authority to investigate any such attempts) that was used to justify it, I ordered him to stop the practice.

Tom Bishop didn't want to give up the program, but it was too late. One of our agents in Elyria, Ohio, had gone past his instructions and had openly inquired about a local candidate, identifying himself as an FBI agent in the process. The local paper picked up the story and soon it hit the national wires. Bishop immediately drafted a self-destruct-type internal memo on plain bond paper to Mark with a full defense of the

Gray's note of a telephone call from Mark Felt. October 25, 1972.

program. At the end Bishop wrote, "If Mr. Gray desires, of course, the program can be and will be discontinued. I do not, however, feel that it would be in the best interests of the Bureau to announce its discontinuance by a national press release which, although factual, might give some people the incorrect impression that the FBI has been conducting investigations on Congressional candidates."

Mark Felt passed Bishop's blank memo along to me with his recommendation that the program be canceled but agreeing with Bishop's desire not to issue a press release about it. I overruled them both on the press release. "We will tell the people exactly what we have been doing! Why? And that we are closing it as of this instant," I wrote on the bottom of the memo. The program was terminated the next day and the press release went out.

I then ordered a full internal review of the Crime Records Division, which resulted in its being disbanded and its members all reassigned to other divisions. I offered Tom Bishop the SAC job in Chicago and told him that he could keep his assistant director title because I was going to elevate the position to assistant director in charge to match

New York and Los Angeles. Instead, he submitted his retirement request and I accepted it. Though he would stay on until the end of January in order to get his full retirement benefits, Bishop had now become another of Hoover's "dukes" to leave the Bureau with a less-than-positive attitude toward the new acting director.

fifteen

"There is no hurry for the president to see you."

ON NOVEMBER 7, RICHARD NIXON WON HIS HISTORIC LAND-slide, carrying every state but Massachusetts and the District of Columbia over George McGovern. One of the first things he did after the election was to call a meeting of his entire cabinet, say a few words to them, and then leave the room while Bob Haldeman asked every secretary and other cabinet-level officer for his or her resignation. Though I wasn't at the meeting, I, too, was asked to submit mine. It wasn't accepted.

Two weeks after the election, while I was home in Connecticut, I suffered another flare-up of the gastrointestinal blockages that had reoccurred ever since my ruptured appendix on a submarine war patrol in World War II. This one was serious. On November 19 I went into the Lawrence and Memorial Hospital in New London for surgery and wasn't released until December 3. In the hospital I was given a suite of rooms where I continued to conduct FBI business long-distance. Dave Kinley traveled back and forth from Washington, keeping me well supplied with paperwork and the special agents of the New Haven office were there twenty-four hours a day to provide security, communications, and much-needed good fellowship.

When I got out of the hospital, the doctors ordered a month of convalescence. I worked out of our Stonington house for another week before going to Florida for two weeks and then back to Stonington for

Christmas and New Year's. Though I was itching to get back to work, it wasn't the worst of times to be away. The Watergate investigation was in a quiet phase waiting for the trial to start, and most of official Washington was equally silent. Congress was out of session, the Democrats having held their majority in both houses in spite of Nixon's huge presidential victory. The executive branch was at a near standstill as Nixon and Haldeman reappointed or replaced all of the senior leadership.

On December 9, as Bea and I were getting ready to go to Florida, I called Dick Kleindienst at nine in the morning. Word had come down that he had been asked to stay on as attorney general.

"Hi, Dick," I said when he answered a little groggily. "I just called to congratulate you. Did I awaken you?"

"No, I've been on the phone for quite a while," he answered. "More to the point, how are you doing, Pat?"

"I'm feeling fine. I'll be in Washington Monday morning and all day Tuesday, then down to Florida for a week. I could see you and the president on Tuesday."

"No need to do that. John Ehrlichman and I agree there is no hurry for the president to see you. It can be done after you return from Florida. I want to see you on Tuesday, but there's no hurry about seeing the president."

I did meet with Dick as Bea and I passed through Washington, but he had no word on Nixon's decision whether to nominate me as permanent director.

Back in Connecticut over the holidays, as I was just about fully recovered, I went out one afternoon to burn the Christmas trash in an incinerator we kept at the end of our gravel driveway. Between my illness, surgery, hospitalization, recovery, and family houseguests, it was just about my first moment to be alone. For the past several days I had been working through more FBI paperwork, getting ready to report back to my office on January 2, and in doing this I came across the manila envelopes from E. Howard Hunt's White House office, which John Dean and John Ehrlichman had given to me back in June. Here was a good chance to dispose of them securely, so I took them out with the wrapping paper to be burned.

The incinerator was next to the water well cover near our woodpile, all behind a stockade fence. It was a very private place, out of view of anyone in the house. I put the envelopes on the well cover while I got the fire going with the other trash. When the flames were roaring, I opened the envelopes and took out the files.

My longtime involvement in national security dealings at the very highest level had taught me one thing—the best way to avoid giving away a national secret is not to possess it in the first place. That's what "need to know" means, and I had been told by the president's top domestic adviser—my designated contact person for all presidential business—that I had no need to know what was in these folders. The president's counsel had assured me they had nothing to do with Watergate, and I believed him. I opened the first folder and read the top sheet of paper. It was a mimeograph copy of a State Department dispatch marked "Top Secret." I skimmed it just quickly enough to see that it had something to do with the Diem assassination in Vietnam, which had happened nine years earlier during the Kennedy administration. I riffled through the other sheets, saw that they were the same, then ripped them all in half and tossed them into the fire. I then opened the other folder and saw that they were onionskin copies of letters. These I did not read. I tore them in half and tossed them into the incinerator, then did the same with the two envelopes.

As far as I was concerned, that was the end of the matter.

"Who stands to gain by such tactics?"

On Tuesday, January 2, 1973, I finally got back to my desk at FBI headquarters. My recuperation from the November operation had been slow, but I was now fully recovered and eager to resume my normal schedule. I called Jack Hushen, the Justice Department press officer, to let him know he could issue a release saying I was back on duty, and then got to work.

Two months earlier, after I had issued the press release explaining why I had abolished Tom Bishop's Crime Records Division, Senator Sam Ervin, the chairman of the Senate Judiciary Committee's Subcommittee on Constitutional Rights, had sent me a long letter asking a series of specific questions about the prior activities of the now-defunct division. Unable to give the senator a timely reply because of my surgery and long recovery, I had asked my staff to prepare a set of answers to Ervin's questions while I was away. Now that I was back, I called in Tom Bishop, who was still riding a desk pending his retirement date of February 1, to go over those answers with me before I finalized them in a formal reply letter. It was the first time I had seen Bishop since before he had submitted his request for retirement while I was in the hospital in Connecticut.

At 3:30 that afternoon a very unhappy Tom Bishop came in to see me. He approved all the answers to Ervin, then angrily turned to the events that had led to his leaving the Bureau.

"Last November, the weekend after the press release," he said, "my wife woke me in tears saying there is a piece in the paper saying you are going to lose your job. Since then I've had my reputation ruined."

I tried to calm him by pointing out that he had been in no danger of losing his job and had in fact been offered the top job in Chicago at his current assistant director level. "And then," I said, "when the Bureau announced your retirement in December, that release included both your letter to me and my laudatory response to you."

He shook his head. "No. I've been hurt by it. That White House request for campaign help would never have been permitted by Mr. Hoover. It was a political request."

"Did you say that to the newspapers, too?" I retorted. "Because those are the same words."

Bishop denied that, but I had my doubts, as did the rest of my staff. When Bishop was interviewed by our internal inspectors immediately after the White House memo flap in September, he had said he saw nothing improper in the request and had only asked Mark Felt which FBI division should handle it. When I reminded him of that now, he backed down entirely.

"I didn't want to leave the FBI creating a lot of waves," he said. He then left my office.

That evening's edition of the *Washington Star* ran a front-page story by longtime FBI reporter Jeremiah O'Leary headlined, "'Purge' Indicated in FBI Shifts." The story began:

Eight senior officials of the FBI's abolished Crime Records Division have received terse written notices from the office of Acting Director L. Patrick Gray transferring them to jobs elsewhere in what some of them are calling "a purge of old J. Edgar Hoover hands," The Star News learned today.

O'Leary wasn't the only reporter in Washington now turning to Gray and the FBI, and the ones with good sources were turning to them without my knowledge.

January 5, 6, or 7, 1973   *White House Telephone*

JOHN EHRLICHMAN: John Ehrlichman, Bob.

ROBERT NOVAK: Hi, John. I just read your transcript on television.

EHRLICHMAN: Good heavens—speedy service from Merkle press.

NOVAK: John, I don't know if you can help me on this at all. I know you could if you want to help me on this. I get a lot of flack from the old boys network and the FBI against Gray. They're leaking all over hell—the press, the other people. Is this one of the reasons for the delay in Gray's nomination?

EHRLICHMAN: No, no. The reason is that the Senate Judiciary Committee has suggested that any FBI nomination be deferred until after the confirmation hearings on the bulk of the Justice Department package. And that's to be the 19th.

NOVAK: So you would think the nomination would come sometime after that?

EHRLICHMAN: Oh, definitely it would be after that.

NOVAK: Has a decision been made one way or the other?

EHRLICHMAN: No, it has not. You can say categorically that the President hasn't decided because he hasn't.

NOVAK: I see. Not quoting you or the White House or anybody, can you give me any background if you are concerned at all by this criticism of . . . Jerry O'Leary sort of a pipeline to the old gang.

EHRLICHMAN: Well, not concerned, Bob, with the merits, so to speak, concerned with the phenomenon, yes, plenty, because there's a real . . . there are all kinds of symptoms of a breakdown of the integrity of the system there.

NOVAK: Would you think that would adversely affect your consideration of Gray in that?

EHRLICHMAN: Well, it isn't my consideration, it's basically the President's and frankly I have not discussed this with the President for about a month. When the signal came that the thing wouldn't, the nomination wouldn't be appropriate until after Inauguration, he laid it aside.

NOVAK: So it's generally still an open question.

EHRLICHMAN: That's right, and I don't think he'll even pick it up again until after the Inaugural and then he'll go to work on it. And, frankly, Pat's illness was a convenient circumstance in a way in that it was a legitimate reason for laying it aside for the time being.

NOVAK: But in the consideration this phenomenon would have to be ground into the process?

EHRLICHMAN: Oh, I suppose so, although I think for my own part I'm coming to the conclusion that whoever goes in there is going to have to just really undertake a drastic review of the whole setup.

NOVAK: The consideration would have to be in some extent whether Pat can cut it.

EHRLICHMAN: Well, that would apply not only to Pat but everybody.

NOVAK: Right. Thank you, John.

. . .

Follow-up conversation with Ron Ziegler:

EHRLICHMAN: Novak wanted to talk about the FBI and whether or not the White House was concerned about all the leaks and the old boys bolting against Gray and so on and I said that the President had laid aside the FBI question until after the Inaugural.

ZIEGLER: Good.

EHRLICHMAN: That there would be no decision until then; that the Senate Judiciary Committee didn't want a nomination until after the Inaugural and that anybody who was selected was going to have to take a hard look at what are symptoms of the deterioration of the system within the FBI at the time that he took over, whoever it was.

ZIEGLER: This is the position I'm taking.

EHRLICHMAN: Good.

A few days after his conversation with Ehrlichman, who never disclosed it to me, Novak ran his column under the headline "J. Edgar Hoover's Legacy: A Political Snakepit at the FBI."

> An undercover campaign by the old-boy FBI network, past and present, against Acting Director L. Patrick Gray has fully disclosed to the White House the tainted legacy of J. Edgar Hoover's 40-year reign over the Federal Bureau of Investigation. . . .
>
> It is Gray's house-cleaning that triggered the campaign against him by the old Hoover hands. . . .
>
> THE RESULT: Present and former FBI men, pro-Hooverites and anti-Hooverites, are briefing newsmen and White House aides about Gray's iniquities. . . .
>
> The menace is clear. If Gray is nominated, the old boy network will slip derogatory information to the Senate judiciary committee. Liberal Democratic senators, eager to prove Gray has politicized the FBI serving Mr. Nixon's partisan interests, would be expected to cooperate.
>
> But at the very least, Gray seems innocent of such political charges. Close students of the FBI know that Hoover's famed reputation for being above and beyond politics was sheer mythology and that Gray is non-political by comparison.

That Monday, January 8, the weekly issue of *Time* came out with an article by Sandy Smith titled "Tattletale Gray." The week before, Smith had called Charlie Bolz, who had recently left the FBI, and asked Bolz to tell him why he had left. When Bolz told him it was for personal reasons having nothing to with Watergate, Smith then tried to pry Watergate information from him even after Bolz said he was still bound by Judge Sirica's gag order. Charlie was so upset by the call that he called a former Bureau colleague who then wrote an internal memo to Bob Gebhardt. It ended, "Smith said he was writing an article for Time. . . . He inferred it would be critical." That was an understatement. Virtually every claim in its 830 words was either a mischaracterization or a complete falsehood.

Nothing has damaged morale at the bureau as much as one of Gray's own innovations—the publicizing of his disciplinary actions. He terms it "airing the linen," but around the bureau these days the practice has earned him the nickname "Tattletale Gray." . . .

Gray claims he is getting rid of "Hooverites." . . .

But the nagging problem that will not go away is Gray's tie with President Nixon. Whatever Hoover's flaws, no one could accuse him of playing partisan politics; he intended the bureau to be above such doings and made that ideal stick during his reign. . . .

In September [Gray] ordered his agents to collect political intelligence for Nixon, and, within the bureau, defended his actions by simply shrugging: "Wouldn't you do that for the President?" . . .

Several agents complained that Gray's spot inspection of the Washington field office in search of the leaks was actually slowing down the Watergate investigation. Recently Gray transferred three FBI officials who pushed the Watergate investigation into the White House and presidential re-election committee. Two accepted the transfers. The third quit the bureau. Said one Washington agent: "I've been around here a long time, and no one has ever questioned my integrity. Now, because the White House is upset, my integrity has been challenged twice in one week."

—Sandy Smith
"Tattletale Gray," *Time*, January 15, 1973

I was so incensed by the piece that I sent a ten-page, point-by-point rebuttal to John Ehrlichman. "I have never stated or claimed that I am getting rid of Hooverites," I told Ehrlichman. "In fact, I have specifically stated and been quoted in the press to the contrary. . . . I have never used the term 'airing the linen.' . . . I have never made any such statement ['Wouldn't you do that for the President?'], within the Bureau or anywhere else. I have made no public comment whatever on this matter." As for the three officials who left, without putting any names in the memo I gave Ehrlichman the real reasons for the transfers of Bates and Kunkel, and for Bolz's resignation.

I said nothing to Ehrlichman about the "Washington agent" who complained to Smith about his integrity being challenged because the White House was "upset." What upset the White House, of course, was precisely what the agent was doing—demonstrating his lack of integrity by giving anonymous quotes to a reporter. Had I known who he was, I'd have done more than "challenge his integrity."

I then called Smith into my office, and when he refused to correct any of his published misstatements about me, I ordered him out of my office and told him never to come back. I was through with *Time*, though they were far from through with me.

Shortly after this flurry of press pieces appeared, I received an anonymous memo on plain white paper. "News Articles Attacking the Acting Director" was its title and it ran for nine single-spaced pages with sixteen pages of underlined clippings attached. When I first got the memo, I was too busy to read it and put it away, only to rediscover it after I had left the FBI. Thus I never learned who actually wrote it, but I'm fairly certain it was Tom Smith of the Domestic Intelligence Division, a confidant and political ally of Mark Felt and Ed Miller. It also appears, both from its content and from some handwriting on it, that Mark Felt had a hand in its preparation. Here's how it starts:

> Over the past few weeks there has been a spate of news articles which appear to be obviously designed to raise doubts in the mind of the public as to the capability of L. Patrick Gray to become the permanent head of the FBI. As the days pass with no announcement or indication from the President that Mr. Gray will be nominated to permanently

head the FBI, the frequency and viciousness of the articles have stepped up. This would seem to indicate the possibility that the articles have been written for the express purpose of causing the President to alter his decision in the matter, and failing that to raise questions which might result in a negative attitude during Senate confirmation hearings. The question is, Who stands to gain by such tactics? Why would newsmen, many of whom were hypercritical of J. Edgar Hoover and his policies, now use the same slanted news to attack Mr. Hoover's successor?

A careful analysis of some of the news articles results in a great deal of enlightenment on the subject. Analysis, coupled with considerable inside information relating to individuals and situations in the Bureau, permits the drawing of a conclusion that one individual, assisted by a small clique of well-placed followers, feels that he has a lot to gain by discrediting L. Patrick Gray. That individual is William C. Sullivan, former Assistant to the Director who was forced into retirement in 1971 following a bitter clash with J. Edgar Hoover.

The memo then proceeded to blame articles and columns from various publications, including the recent two by O'Leary and Novak, on leaks and misinformation provided by Bill Sullivan, who, according to the memo, "obviously sold a bill of goods to Evans and Novak. Jeremiah O'Leary has apparently succumbed to the same line." It also attacked Bob Mardian, who had brought Sullivan back into government as head of a newly created unit of the Justice Department, the National Narcotics Information Center. As a transparent attempt to unseat a candidate for the job I now held, this document had no equal. Not only did it take aim at Bill Sullivan, it also exposed the shooter. The memo did not mention Sandy Smith, nor did it mention

Bob Woodward. Both of them, as we all now know, were getting their leaks from Mark Felt.

Bill Sullivan: I had formed my opinion of this very nervous man in two long briefings I had requested from him the previous July and October. Sullivan had been sitting in my office on July 6 when Nixon returned my call to San Clemente to warn him of the concerns Dick Walters and I shared over the attempt to misuse our two agencies by lower-ranking White House officials. As soon as Sullivan heard that it was the president on the line, he got up without a word, then returned when Marge Neenan told him the call had ended. Well trained by Hoover, Sullivan was a deep source of both fact and opinion, and after those two briefings I had come away with many pages of notes and a tendency to agree with Mark and the others who cautioned me against letting Hoover's fallen favorite back into the Bureau. But I had no reason to believe he was guilty of this anonymous memo's accusations.

On Wednesday, January 10, 1973, the trial of the seven Watergate burglary suspects commenced. Judge Sirica, who had issued his formal gag order shortly after the indictments in September to try to stem extrajudicial statements by both sides in the case, ordered the jury sequestered. After the opening statements, E. Howard Hunt offered to plead guilty to a partial list of the charges against him: conspiracy, burglary, and one count of wiretapping. Sirica ordered a recess while he considered the deal.

The next day, Sirica rejected Hunt's partial plea, after which Hunt then pled guilty on all counts. He posted a $100,000 bond and was released to await his sentence. The trial of the others then commenced. Assistant U.S. Attorney Earl Silbert told us in the FBI not to attempt any interviews of Hunt until further notice.

The following Tuesday, January 16, the four Cubans—Barker, Fiorini, Gonzales, and Martinez—pled guilty to all counts. Sirica quizzed them in open court: Were other government officials involved? Where did the money come from? Were any of them still working for the CIA? Their answers to all of the above were either "no" or "no knowledge."

That left James McCord and Gordon Liddy still on trial, which continued until closing arguments on January 29. The next day the jury found both men guilty on multiple counts.

Though the trial of the seven men initially charged in connection with the burglary itself was now over, the investigation into Watergate continued. In fact, it had never stopped.

In early December, while I was working from my Connecticut home after my operation, I had discussed with Dave Kinley the likelihood of getting Henry Petersen to reopen the investigation of Segretti and the possible campaign law violations he seemed to be involved in. Dave had then passed the ball to Mack and Barbara, who convened a series of December meetings with Bob Gebhardt, Charlie Bolz, and others at FBI headquarters. The result was a December 7 FBI memo to Henry Petersen asking whether the activities of Segretti, Dwight Chapin, and others warranted further investigation by the Bureau.

Henry held the memo until after the initial Watergate trial was concluded before responding on January 30, 1973. He now agreed that it was time to pursue the leads and asked us to reinterview Dwight Chapin. This time, with the stakes even higher because we were going to begin a possible criminal probe into the White House itself, I wanted to make sure that all our inquiries were maintained on a strict need-to-know basis. On February 2, I called Mark Felt and asked him to work out the necessary procedures with Bob Gebhardt. Mark suggested that the Chapin interview reports be kept in the SAC's personal safe and that an accountability sheet be maintained for each document. I thought this was a great idea and instructed Mark to follow this procedure in any sensitive interview from here on out.

With these strict new procedures in place, Angelo Lano interviewed Chapin on February 2. Chapin said he knew nothing about Segretti's specific activities and could not "expound on anything that would assist the Government in any aspect of this investigation." After reading Lano's report of the interview and comparing it to Chapin's previous statements, Henry Petersen and his prosecutors concluded that Chapin was holding back information and decided to continue investigating him. He would later be found guilty of lying to the grand jury and would serve eight months in prison.

As my daily summaries always said, the intensive investigation was continuing.

seventeen

"I think it's going to be a bloody confirmation."

ON THURSDAY, FEBRUARY 15, 1973, JANA HRUSKA, THE DAUGH-
ter of Senator Roman Hruska and the secretary to John Ehrlichman,
called my office at FBI headquarters to say that I was to meet with
Ehrlichman the following morning. That day I had flown to College
Station to speak with the students at Texas A&M, so I did not return
Ehrlichman's call right away.

By this late date, I was sure that Richard Nixon was going to name
someone else to be permanent director of the FBI. When he had
named me acting director the previous May he had said that he would
not name a permanent director until after the November election.
Furthermore, he had made it very clear to me that there was no commitment to name me to the post, although my name would be considered along with any others.

All during this time after the election there had been no word from
the White House regarding my status, even though Dick Kleindienst
had told me shortly after my return to Washington that he was backing
me for the position. I heard nothing from John Ehrlichman or Bob
Haldeman about my chances to be the president's nominee, nor did
I ask them. I had returned from my surgery, reported to the attorney
general, and to Ehrlichman and Haldeman, that I was back and fit for

duty, and that I hoped to be the president's nominee; as far as I was concerned, that was enough.

The days became weeks, the weeks became a month. I heard nothing. No evidence, no information, no rumors. So I began to prepare myself mentally for the inevitable: someone else was going to get the nomination, the nomination that I had worked day and night for nine months to earn for myself.

This was my frame of mind that Thursday evening when I returned John Ehrlichman's call. When I reached him, he told me that I should meet him in his office at the White House at 8:45 a.m., and then the two of us would go to the Oval Office to meet with the president at nine. I told John that I had a scheduled flight to Milwaukee with Bea that same morning at 10:30. "No problem," he said. "You'll make your plane." No hint as to the purpose of the meeting.

The following morning, Special Agent Tom Moten picked me up at the usual time—a few minutes after seven—and we drove to FBI headquarters. Tom had been Hoover's driver for years, and mine for the last nine months; we were together almost daily, early in the morning and late in the evening, and we had become close. I told him that we would be going over to the White House in about an hour and that I was to meet with the president and Ehrlichman.

He beamed. "That's great. Today must be the day."

"I don't know, Tom. I'm not even sure the president wants to talk about my nomination. He may just want to raise hell about all these press leaks that those White House people think are coming from the FBI."

"Oh, boss," Tom said, "the president's just got to do the right thing. You've earned it."

Since the flight to Milwaukee would come so quickly after the White House meeting, Tom went back to the apartment to get Bea while I got in an hour's work at my desk. Then, at 8:30, we drove to the White House.

When we arrived, Bea knew there was nothing to say, so she just squeezed my hand, and I got out of the car.

The officers of the Executive Protective Service at the desk just inside the door at the lower level of the White House knew me on sight, but they checked my credentials and their appointment list anyway before waving me on to the elevator. I arrived on Ehrlichman's floor and walked to his office. John was behind his desk and motioned me toward a sofa, then came over to sit down beside me.

"Pat," he said, getting right to the point, "I want to inquire about your health. Have you recovered fully from your operation?"

"Yes, I have, John," I answered. "I've been fit and back on the job with no problems since early January."

"Good, good," he said. "The president will be very interested in that, because he's going to tell you this morning that you are going to be his nominee as permanent director, if he thinks you are physically up to the job."

There it was. I was elated and could hardly trust myself to believe what I was hearing. But there it *was not* as well. What lay behind these words of concern for my health, six weeks after I had reported back, fully recovered? What other litmus test was masked here?

"That's great, John," I said emphatically. "I'm ready to go up on the Hill to do battle with the Senate Judiciary Committee."

"Congratulations, Pat," he said, getting up. "Let's go on up to see the president."

Ehrlichman led the way to the Oval Office, as I did not know how to get there from John's office. In fact, I had been in the Oval Office with Nixon only three times before, and two of those had been in 1970 when I had been a member of the president's Cabinet Committee on Education and had escorted state delegations of black and white leaders on short ceremonial visits to the White House. The other time had been the short private visit Bea and I had had with him right after Hoover's funeral.

As we entered, Nixon was seated at his desk. I don't know if others have gotten used to coming face-to-face with the president in the Oval Office, but even today I can feel the thrill and slight lump in my throat. He arose and motioned John to the chair on the right side of his desk, and me the chair on the left. There were no handshakes, just a short

"Hi, how are you?" and then Nixon sat down, followed by Ehrlichman, and then me.

The president got right to it. "Let me ask you," he said. "Just how is your health since you had your operation?"

I told him that it was good, and I started to tell him some of the details, but he cut me short.

"In other words," he said, "as far as your ability to work and everything, why, no questions need be raised. In other words, you'll put in the long hours and all."

I told him that this was true, that I had been doing this since the day after the operation in my hospital room.

And that was the end of his concern for my health. It took two minutes to dispose of it as a topic in a meeting that was to last for more than a half hour. A meeting that was quickly to turn into a Nixon monologue into which neither I nor Ehrlichman could get a whole sentence before Nixon would veer off on another tangent. It was to be the most disquieting half hour in my thirty years of government service.

"Let me ask you a couple of other things," he said, "having to do with whether we decide here . . ." At this point he hesitated for just a second, but it was enough to let me know the important point: they hadn't really decided to nominate me yet. Nixon quickly went on.

"As you probably are aware, if you were to be nominated—and I've talked to John Mitchell about this—you obviously open up, before a different committee than the Ervin Committee, the whole Watergate thing. Now the question is: Do you think you can handle it? What I mean is, the Watergate committee, even though it has these three wonderful jackasses on it, will be bad enough. Your committee would have Kennedy and Tunney on it, and they'd like to make quite a deal about the thing. What I'm getting at is this. I'm not concerned about the substance, about the facts coming out. All I'm thinking about is whether it's in the interest of everybody concerned to have the man who is to be nominated to be director of the Bureau to be badgered and so forth, and whether it's good for us to have that story told twice before two committees, and so forth. So why don't you give me your judgment on that. You must have thought about it."

"Oh, yes," I said. Indeed I had. Nixon was talking on the one hand about the Senate Select Committee on Presidential Campaign Activities, chaired by Sam Ervin of North Carolina, which had just been established to investigate the Watergate affair, and on the other hand about the Senate Judiciary Committee, chaired by Jim Eastland of Mississippi, which would conduct my confirmation hearings. The Judiciary Committee was populated by many powerful liberal senators such as Ted Kennedy of Massachusetts, John Tunney of California, Birch Bayh of Indiana, and Philip Hart of Michigan. Both committees were controlled by the Democrats and both were out to get the hated Nixon, if they could. These senators, as it later turned out, knew more about Watergate and the subsequent cover-up than did the FBI. So did the president. He knew it as we sat there, and he was concerned that I might not stand up to the pressure. Of course, he was not concerned for me, he was concerned for Nixon. He wanted to learn how much, if anything, I knew about the cover-up and if that knowledge could hurt him through my answers to the senators' questions. Neither of us could know on that date how well founded that fear was.

Before I could say anything more, Nixon went on about the Judiciary Committee. "Without being limited to Watergate," he said, "they would probably ask you about other things that the Bureau's done. Have you got into this domestic wiretapping? Incidentally, whatever you're hearing, it's time to start getting out the truth, which is that it's not the Robert Kennedy Justice Department where there were over a hundred [wiretaps] a year. It's been cut down to a very small amount. I would not be that defensive about it . . ."

This spurred Ehrlichman into action. He leaned over close to the president and they whispered back and forth animatedly. Looking back on it, and knowing what I know now, I'm sure that Ehrlichman must have been telling Nixon to lay off the domestic wiretap stuff because Gray doesn't know anything about the seventeen wiretaps that the administration had secretly placed on newsmen and White House staff personnel in 1969. Ehrlichman knew all about them because, as we all now know, he kept the files on those taps in his own safe after the taps were discontinued in 1971.

After their brief huddle, Ehrlichman leaned back and in a louder voice said, "Don't worry, he can tell a strong story." At the time I thought they were referring to the *Keith* decision of the U.S. Supreme Court, which in June 1972 had barred wiretapping of domestic groups unless there were certain degrees of foreign involvement. We had to lift several ongoing FBI wiretaps when the decision came down, and I ordered extensive legal research into the problem so that we could thereafter be in compliance with the new guidelines. I could indeed tell a strong story, the only story I knew then.

Nixon then tried to make it even stronger for me by tying the whole domestic wiretap issue to the terrorist threat. "If you're limited to tapping just these foreign governments, these foreign activities here, then you miss these violent groups," he said, leaning back in his chair. Then he pushed forward and seemed much more excited.

"Either one, either side, you know," he went on. "There's this violent Jewish committee that wants to kill the Arabs, and the Arabs want to kill the Jews, and Christ, they're . . . Hijacking is another thing. You've got to get into that. Some of that requires wiretapping. It's your responsibility to do this, and your authority. I just don't think that we should be defensive. First of all, we're doing less. Second, it's extremely necessary; we must not be denied the use of the weapon. The idea that we're wiretapping a lot of political groups is bullshit."

Here I agreed with the president. Terrorism and hijacking had been major problems for all of us. We were under immense pressure to stop the hijackings and prevent attacks within our borders, and at the same time we had been greatly restricted by the *Keith* decision. I wanted to tell the president what we were doing to strike a balance, but he simply wasn't interested. Before I could utter a word, he changed the subject back to the confirmation hearings.

"Let's get back to the fundamental part of it," he cut in. "You know the mood of the Congress. They're panicked, depressed, by Watergate and so forth. What should we do? Would it hurt or help for you to go up there and be mashed about that?"

"I think probably, Mr. President, that I'm the man in the best position to handle that thing."

Now I had his attention. "Why?" he said.

"Because I've consistently handled it from the outset," I told him. "And I handled all kinds of questions from all kinds of press people before Judge Sirica's order shut off the valve. I've been responsible for a great deal of decision making as far as the Federal Bureau of Investigation is concerned."

I went on to tell him that because the Ervin Committee had been convened to look into Watergate there would be considerably less heat on that topic from the Senate Judiciary Committee. "I think I'm going to take the expected heat from Kennedy, Bayh, Hart, Tunney—that group— but I don't think it's going to be nearly as severe as it would have been."

Little did I know how eager Kennedy and his cohorts were to get at Watergate. I think now that Nixon knew, and that in this meeting he just wanted to gauge my reaction and to see how strong my belief in our Watergate investigation was. It was strong and I told him so.

"Now, if you bring somebody else in," I said, "you can be attacked as ducking the issue, trying to put a new boy in so he can go up there and say, 'I didn't have anything to do with this. This happened on Gray's watch.' Then they'll want to get him back in there and let him talk about it. I think it's a thing that we ought to meet head-on."

Nixon still wasn't satisfied. He knew what kinds of questions they'd ask, and he was still uncertain of my answers, so he tried to put words in my mouth.

"What kind of a story could you tell when they say that you didn't go into it hard? You could say that we had a very intensive investigation, we ran down all the leads. Who'd you talk to? Yes, we questioned them at very great length, took sworn statements . . ."

Ehrlichman popped in again, very interested. "Did you swear in statements?"

"Yes, we did," I told him. I wasn't disturbed by the conversation at this point, because I had been giving regular reports to John Dean, and I still, at this late date, believed him when he said that he in turn was reporting directly to the president. So it wasn't surprising at all to me that Nixon knew more about the investigation than Ehrlichman did.

The president was starting to focus his questions now. "Why didn't you question Haldeman? What do you say to that?"

I had a ready answer here because I had asked the same question during the briefings I had been given on the case. "Perfectly good reason we didn't question Mr. Haldeman," I answered. "Because no agent, even the case agent right at the lowest level, felt that any trail led to Mr. Haldeman. He did not recommend that a lead be set out to interview Mr. Haldeman. The field supervisor did not. The circulation charts did not. The bureau supervisor did not—"

"But leads did lead to others?" Nixon interjected.

"It did lead to others," I said, "and we went after them."

"You questioned Mitchell, Stans, and so forth," said the president.

"Yes," I answered. "Stans three times, Mitchell once, Haldeman not at all. I'm not really afraid of that thing because I called those agents in at the end of that first week and gave them unshirted hell, and told them to go and to go with all the vim and vigor possible. Furthermore, I called Larry O'Brien that Saturday morning and I said, 'Mr. O'Brien, I hear that there's a rumor going around this town that the FBI is not pursuing this with vigor.' And he said, 'Oh no, no, no. Let me assure you that we are very happy with what you are doing.'"

Frankly, I had been pleased with the Democratic National Committee chairman's remarks, and I thought they would be of interest to Nixon. They apparently weren't. He went on to suggest that the senators might ask about morale in the Bureau, and I again started to give him a detailed answer, but again he wasn't interested in my answer. He wanted to move on, and the meeting took an unpleasant turn.

"You haven't been able to do anything—or have you?—about the leaks coming out of the Bureau," he stated. "The whole story, we've found, is coming out of the Bureau."

This angered me, as I had heard just about enough out of the White House on the subject of leaks. I had heard this line incessantly from Ehrlichman and Dean throughout the Watergate investigation, and I had rebutted it, in writing, to Ehrlichman. It truly was a sore point with me, because I just could not bring myself to believe that a special agent of the FBI would go to the press with a complaint instead of making it known to his own supervisors, or make it known directly to any one of the three assistant United States attorneys in charge of the investigation. Or they could have gotten the problem straight to me through any one of my young special assistants, and the agents all knew this. As a last resort they could have used an old Bureau tactic—the anonymous letter to the director. All of this I had told to Ehrlichman and Dean, since they had called me time and time again as the stories appeared in the press. Each time the leak was the fault of the Bureau, as far as they were concerned. Even then, I sensed that the president was pushing them to the phone; now it was even more obvious to me that Nixon must have raged more and more with every headline. Now I had a chance to tell the president directly.

"Well," I said, "I'm not completely ready to buy that, Mr. President. We have done something."

"Yeah," said Ehrlichman. "Pat and I talked about that, and he's convinced that it's not the Bureau—"

"That's not what our *Time* magazine guy says," interrupted Nixon. "He's got a direct channel to the Bureau."

"Well, he probably has," I said. "Sandy Smith used to talk to a lot of guys in the Bureau, but I won't talk to the S.O.B. anymore because three times we laid the cards out on the table—gave the same cards to *Time* and *Newsweek*—and each time they wrote differently. Three times. So I just said, 'No more to this clown,' and I won't deal with him."

The president shook his head, as if to indicate that I had misunderstood him. "This source is very high," he said.

I hadn't misunderstood him. I knew that he was talking about Roswell Gilpatric, the lawyer for Time, Inc., who had identified Mark Felt as the source of leaks to Sandy Smith. But Mark had vehemently denied it to me in our face-to-face meetings. I believed Mark, and that was that.

Today, I'm not so sure of my categorical acceptance of Mark Felt's assurances. Now I know that Hoover's hard-liners deeply resented my presence in the FBI and everything I sought to accomplish as acting director. I am convinced that they did everything they could, whenever they could, to sandbag me and to ensure that my tenure would be short. Several of them, Mark Felt included, hungered for Hoover's job; none could have it if I were confirmed as permanent director. Be that as it may, on that February day in the Oval Office I was in no mood to hear it even from the president.

But the president and Ehrlichman were in no mood to drop the subject, either. "There's no two ways about it," said Ehrlichman. "There is no question about their getting their information right off of the 703s—or whatever those forms are—the investigation summary forms."

"Three-oh-twos?" I said, surprised. An FD-302 is the detailed summary of an FBI interview written by the agent or agents who performed it, designed to be used confidentially during an investigation but subject to the discovery process in a later court proceeding and admissible as evidence. Prior to that, 302s are very closely held.

"Yeah," the president chimed in. "Because I would say that if these things were false, then it would be time to bring those questions to an end. But this is a case where they have true information, and I say well, damn it, it's somebody from the Bureau."

Then the president abruptly changed course.

"Do you think Petersen's office puts it out?" he asked me pointedly.

I had no way of answering that except to tell him that FD-302s went to people outside the Bureau, to the U.S. attorney's office, and select others in the Justice Department. I told him of our strong internal controls and accounting for them within the FBI. I also acknowledged that no system is foolproof, that they still could leak out of the Bureau. I didn't really believe it, but I had to acknowledge the possibility. Nixon was really on the attack now, and the FBI was his target. His demeanor had changed; he was becoming flushed and his hand and body movements were quicker as he shifted in his seat and leaned toward me aggressively.

"Well, let me ask you this," he said. "Did you follow through on the directive, which I understand was given, that everyone in the Bureau was to take a lie detector test to whether they played a part in the wiretapping of my plane in 1968? Has that been done?"

I didn't know what he was talking about. "No," I said, and glanced over at Ehrlichman. His face was as perplexed as I knew mine was. To the president I said, "No, that directive was not given out."

"Well, it's given now," snapped Nixon.

"Yes sir," I answered. What else could I say?

"Yeah," he said, looking me in the eye and nodding his head sharply. Then he turned to Ehrlichman.

"What happened there?" he demanded. "Who dropped the ball on that?"

Ehrlichman was flustered. He knitted his brows and shook his head. "I don't know . . . of it, Mr. President," he said tentatively.

"Well, that charge has been around. Whether it's true or not, I don't know," the president went on, getting more and more heated. "That has to be—the *Washington Star* has the straight story, but Johnson killed it in the *Star*—that has to be checked out, just for the integrity of the Bureau."

My mind was still rushing to take this all in. All I could relate it to were the Anna Chennault taps that President Lyndon Johnson had ordered through Deke DeLoach in 1968, but these had been wiretaps on the South Vietnamese embassy, and on Chennault herself. Anna Chennault was the widow of Claire Chennault, commander of World War II's famous "Flying Tigers." She had many connections with the South Vietnamese government and was thought by Johnson's people to be working with the Nixon-Agnew campaign to stall peace negotiations until after the 1968 election. At Johnson's direction, the FBI monitored her calls during the week leading up to the election, but nothing untoward was learned. There had been some monitoring of Spiro Agnew's toll call records as part of the same program, but nothing that I knew of on Nixon himself. All of this I had recently learned because John Dean had asked me to look into it for the president, and Mark Felt had produced the files for me. I tried to remind Nixon of this, telling him of the Dean request. He waved me off.

"But there was a wiretap. There was a tap for sure," he insisted.

"On your plane, sir?" I asked. I didn't get it. Then Nixon brought it into perspective.

"Hoover told me," he said in an exasperated tone, "that the Bureau tapped my plane in 1968. And he told Mitchell the same thing. Now, I want everyone in the Bureau who had anything to do with wiretapping at that time questioned and given a lie detector test. And not just because *I'm* telling you this, but because the allegation's been made, and the *Star*'s been running the story and we want to knock it down."

I looked at him for a moment, running this all through my mind. Nixon stared back.

"Don't you believe we should?" he demanded.

"Oh sure," I said. "But I didn't have any directive like that. All I had was some questions from John Dean about Bromley Smith, and Anna Chennault and company."

Finally the president backed off a bit. "I understand," he said. "I'm not making charges, but I do know that this has come up."

This was indeed something for me to think about. Hoover had reported to President Nixon that Lyndon Johnson had had Nixon's private plane bugged by the FBI during the '68 campaign! I had no immediate reason to doubt this; I couldn't imagine J. Edgar Hoover fabricating something like that for delivery to the president of the United States. Johnson had just died of a heart attack three weeks earlier, but I knew that he had had a direct phone line to Deke DeLoach and if the tapping had taken place, DeLoach would have ordered it. I said this to the president.

"Well, then," said Nixon, getting excited again, "DeLoach must be brought in and put on a lie detector also. He's retired, I know, but he's still got to take one anyway. Don't you agree, John? We've got to get to the bottom of this damn thing."

Nixon was back on his rampage. I couldn't interject a word.

"I'm not going to be in here," he went on, "denying it from here unless the director of the FBI tells me that it's been checked. The FBI cannot be above the law on this thing."

Or on anything else, I said to myself. I had to get him off of this lie detector discussion, because I had absolutely no intention of subjecting special agents of the FBI to such an outrage. This was a totally unjustifiable order, and I was not going to be part of such an operation. I never believed in leadership through intimidation, and I thought that if we could get past today's discussion there would be another, less impassioned meeting in which I could get the president to rescind this directive.

Out loud I merely said that we would look into the allegation. Ehrlichman, who had been quiet for some time, spoke up.

"Was Felt there in those days?" he wanted to know. I couldn't answer that, because I didn't know where Mark had been assigned in 1968.

"Who do you think should be the second man over there?" Nixon asked quickly.

"I think, Mr. President," I answered, "that my recommendation to you would be to continue Felt. But what I'm in the process of doing is to come up with an overall plan to submit to you, and you and I should discuss that plan."

Nixon blithely ignored the idea of an overall plan. Instead he returned the conversation to Mark Felt. "The problem you have with Felt," he said, "is that the lines lead very directly to him."

Ehrlichman picked this up, turned to me, and said, "You know we tried to trap him. We planted traps and waited to see if something would turn up."

I looked at Ehrlichman for a moment before the president made a suggestion:

"Well, why don't you get in the charge, then?"

"Well," agreed Ehrlichman, "maybe that's the only way to get to the bottom of it."

"Of course, he's not a newsman, on the other hand," said Nixon. "He's a lawyer for *Time*."

"That's right," said Ehrlichman.

This had gone far enough. "I know who he is, Mr. President," I said quietly. They both stopped and looked at me.

"I knew these allegations existed," I went on. "And I think that the one thing that I should say to you, Mr. President—in fact, I must say it to you—is that those people over there are like little old ladies in tennis shoes, and they've got some of the most vicious vendettas going on. Their gossip mill is churning all the time—"

"In the FBI?" the president broke in.

"In the FBI," I answered.

Nixon nodded. "It's eaves by eaves," he mused. "Each hating everybody else." He seemed to take some satisfaction in this. He understood the implication perfectly, and he showed it by jumping to his next question. "What about this fellow Sullivan?" he asked. "Good, bad, or indifferent? Would you bring him back?"

I was quick with my response: "I wouldn't bring him back. I wouldn't touch him."

"Why not?" asked Nixon, and he leaned attentively forward for my answer.

"His first words when he came back to Washington," I explained, "in response to questions from some of the people in the Domestic Intelligence Division as to why he was here, were two words: 'For revenge.' Bill Sullivan was a very disappointed man when Hoover put Deke DeLoach in that position of assistant to the director."

What I didn't tell Ehrlichman and the president was that Felt and Ed Miller, head of the Domestic Intelligence Division, had both told me that there would be a "mutiny" in the FBI if Bill Sullivan were reinstated. What Ehrlichman and the president didn't tell me was that it had been Sullivan who had taken the files on the Kissinger wiretaps from the FBI and delivered them to Bob Mardian, who had in turn given them to John Ehrlichman, the subject of their earlier whispered conversation.

This Bill Sullivan question was a delicate one, more delicate than I knew at the time, and Nixon and Ehrlichman could see that I was in-transigent in my decision to keep him out of the FBI. Nixon turned back to Mark Felt.

"Coming back through to Felt," he said. "It would be very, very difficult to have Felt in that position without having that charge cleared up. And incidentally, let me say this—this is also a directive. You should take a lie detector test on him."

I could not believe what I had just heard. Place a lie detector on the acting associate director of the FBI over *news leaks*? I stared at the president and tried desperately to say something coherent. The words did not come out.

Nixon stared back. "You're willing for him to take a lie detector test, aren't you?" he demanded.

I wasn't going to fight this. Not here; not today. "Sure," I said offhandedly. *No way*, I said to myself. And I guess I didn't hide my feelings very well, for the president came right back at me.

"Why shouldn't he?" Nixon was furious.

I tried to defuse the situation with a generalization. "Well, hell," I said, "I've taken one."

"Has he ever taken one?" Ehrlichman wanted to know.

"I don't know," I answered.

"Have him take one," the president ordered. "John, you prepare the questions: Has he talked to *Time* magazine? This, that, and the other thing. And he's to do it or he doesn't get the job. That's the way it has to be."

For a moment no one said anything. I wanted this topic to vanish, and the only way to do it seemed to let it alone. Then Nixon went on.

"You see," he said, "there's a lack of discipline over there at the present time. And that's part of the problem. The morale. That's part of the problem with the leaks."

"In the FBI, Mr. President?" I asked with disbelief in my voice. Neither morale nor discipline were lax in the FBI. I knew it and so did Ehrlichman. In my January rebuttal of the "Tattletale Gray" piece in *Time*, I had passed along to him the results of a survey I had asked for in December in which the heads of twenty-one field offices reported that morale among their agents was at least as high as ever or in some cases higher than ever in the history of the Bureau.

Had Ehrlichman even mentioned this report to the president? Apparently not, because Nixon was adamant. "Sure," he said. "This stuff didn't leak when Hoover was there. I've never known of a leak when Hoover was there. I could talk to him in this office about everything, and the reason was that they didn't love him—they feared him. They've got to fear the man at the top, and you've got to get that again."

Again I was quiet, just listening to this outburst. I had never led men by fear. Not during two wars, not in peacetime, not in HEW, in the Justice Department, or in private business. Certainly not in the FBI.

The president barely paused for breath. "And," he continued, "Hoover would lie-detect those guys. I know that he even did it to Lou Nichols once, because of charges that he leaked. You've got to play it exactly that way. You've got to be brutal, tough and respected, because we can't have any kind of relationship with the Bureau—which is necessary here, you know—unless we can trust it."

"That's right," added Ehrlichman. Lou Nichols, who had retired from the FBI in 1957, had been almost as close to Hoover as Clyde Tolson. The Oval Office meeting had now turned into a lecture. And there was nothing academic about it.

"I used to have," said Nixon, "and I would expect to have with the director in the future, a relationship with Hoover. He'd come in about once a month, for breakfast, or he'd come in here. He'd come in alone, not with the attorney general. I'd talk about things with him, and he'd raise hell about Helms and the CIA, and the State Department and so forth. Much of it was extremely valuable, and it never leaked out of here. So you knew that he was giving me the stuff that he had. And he talked to Ehrlichman, who was my contact. Ehrlichman will be in the future, because you've got to have one man who will not talk. I wouldn't think of having it go to anyone else."

Ehrlichman nodded. "I could use Dean," he volunteered. "But he's too busy on other things."

This was the same chain of command that I had been working under all along. When I was appointed acting director, Nixon had told me that I was to take my orders from Ehrlichman. John had in turn told me that my contact would be John Dean.

Nixon further clarified it. "The reason, Pat," he said, "is that the relationship of the director to the president is like the relationship of the chairman of the Joint Chiefs to the president and commander."

I don't know why Nixon tried to make this comparison, as he must have known that it simply wasn't true. In a conflict or war, the president as commander of the military can issue orders directly to his top generals, who in turn can report directly to him, bypassing the secretary of defense, but in the rest of the executive branch the procedure is different. The FBI director reports to the attorney general, not directly to the president. Perhaps he saw that I was deeply shocked by this tirade, that there was confusion and hesitation in my responses to his "directives" and he therefore wanted to reinforce his orders by relating them to my military background. In any case, without waiting for a reply from me, he escalated the one-sided meeting to philippic levels.

"Now, having said that," he rushed on, "we can't do it, we cannot do it, unless there's total communication, and total discipline, in that Bureau. And, hell, I think that if we pick up *Time* magazine and see that something's leaked out of the Bureau—I understand leaking out of the CIA, those goddamned cookie-pushers—but if it leaks out of the Bureau, then the whole damned place ought to be fired. Really, it should. Just move them all out into the field. I think you've got to do it like they did it in the war. You remember in World War II, the Germans, if they went through a town and one of their soldiers was hit by a sniper, they'd line up the whole goddamned town and say, 'Until you talk every one of you is going to be shot.' I really think that's what has to be done. I mean, I don't think you can be Mr. Nice Guy over there."

This was not the Nixon I thought I knew. Certainly it was not the man I had worked for and admired in 1960. Whatever was going on here, I knew that it was going to take much reflection on my part to sort it out later. Meanwhile, in the midst of this diatribe, I had to hold my position, take it all in and hold my temper. I decided to respond only when I could catch at specific things that Nixon said, answer them directly when I could and remain quiet when I couldn't. Here, an attack on what Nixon claimed was a lack of discipline in the FBI, was a place where I had to speak up. I started to tell the president that I hadn't been "Mr. Nice Guy," but he cut me right off again.

"The leaks *are*," he said. "They *are* occurring, and they're from someplace."

"That's right," I answered. "From someplace. But as to discipline, I have done things with regard to discipline that even Mr. Hoover was afraid to do. I took on Grapp and I met him face-to-face. And I threw him right out of the Federal Bureau of Investigation. These guys know they can't lie to me like they used to lie to Hoover."

The Grapp case was a good one to use here, because Nixon was familiar with it. Grapp had powerful friends, and after I fired him from his job as SAC of the Los Angeles field office, several of them, including Cardinal McIntyre and Henry Salvatore, a wealthy Nixon campaign contributor, had gone directly to the White House to intercede—unsuccessfully—on Grapp's behalf. But if I thought that this would alter Nixon's perspective, I was quickly shown otherwise.

"I'm not really referring to that kind of stuff," he said with a wave of his hand. "Frankly, I am referring to discipline of the highest sensitivity involving what may be political matters. Partisan political matters. For example, let's suppose something on the Pentagon Papers leaks out. Let's suppose that there's a leak to a certain member of the press. I've got to have a relationship here where you go out and do something and deny on a stack of Bibles."

Nixon was very intent here, leaning forward, biting out his words. His eyes demanded a reply from me.

"Right," I said.

Nixon didn't back off. He still faced me head-on, searching, I think, for a hint of hesitation on my part. Then he nodded his head again.

"Okay," he said. He seemed satisfied that I had understood him.

And I had, as long as he placed this burden on me in the context of national security investigations. As commander in chief this was clearly his responsibility, and that's the way I understood him that day in the Oval Office. But it's clear to me now that he was laying the groundwork for other, less straightforward requests in the future. The interrelationship of political and national security matters plays itself out in some of Washington's grayest areas, but I had no idea how dark were the corners preferred by Nixon. And Ehrlichman. Not in February 1973. The beginning of that education for me was still two months away.

"You've got to get that," the president went on, "because I don't have anyone else. I can't hire some asshole from the outside."

Ehrlichman came in to pick up on this new theme. "The relationship," he said, "is a self-serving one in a sense. Hoover used to call and say, 'We've picked up something here. Joe Kraft is talking to the North Vietnamese.' For example."

Nixon liked this example. Joseph Kraft was a well-known newspaper columnist and a former speechwriter for John F. Kennedy. "We knew," he said, "that Joe Kraft, when he was in Paris, that son of a bitch was talking to the North Vietnamese. So Hoover got us the information."

Ehrlichman was nodding his head rapidly. "Very helpful for us to know," he added.

I looked back and forth at the two of them as they spoke. The president watched my reaction.

"See what I mean?" he asked. "Not because of what he *wrote*, but because he was a goddamned *agent*. See? That's the kind of thing that we've just got to know."

This was all news to me, and I just took it in, saying nothing. Did they really mean that Joseph Kraft had been an enemy agent? Or was this more hyperbole?

"We live in a dangerous world," intoned the president, as if to answer my questions.

I shook my head. "Oh, I know that," I said, mildly irritated that he would say something like that to me.

"Now," said Nixon, "that's the sort of thing where you don't want to have that done by Felt or whoever is down the line. I mean you just—if you have to identify it—you say, 'Well, boys, we've got to do something to tap the North Vietnamese.' Or maybe you get the Israelis to do it."

"Yes, sir," I answered. I began to tell him my thoughts on our liaison with other agencies, but Nixon rushed on.

"Hoover, of course, was a great cops-and-robbers guy in through the whole era. He was overly suspicious, actually, but that helped a bit, because he got us information. Which was extremely helpful because, you see, these past four years have not been easy. We've had almost the entire bureaucracy, including many in Defense who were opposed to what we were doing in Vietnam, opposed to Cambodia, opposed to Laos, opposed to May eighth . . . It worked, and when the time for the December bombing came . . . And incidentally, most of the White House staff was against it. They didn't go out and yap about it but they were against it. I understand that. But when the whole media's against you, when the bureaucracy's against you, with the professors, the church people, and the rest, let alone the Congress . . . It's a hard damn fight. Now at the present time we've come through with that big issue rather well, and we have some allies from unexpected sources driving the goddamned media right up the wall. This POW thing . . ."

The president was wild, running his train of thought past his ability to articulate. He was starting to stutter, almost beyond coherence.

"Let me tell you," he sped on. "There were times—an-an-an-and Lyndon Johnson told me this same thing—when I felt that the only person in this goddamned government who was standing with me was Edgar Hoover. He was the only one."

Then he stopped, and he continued staring me in the eye. His rush of words had left flecks of spittle at the corners of his mouth, and his head shook slightly side to side from the tension in his neck muscles. I tried to calm him down.

"Well," I said, "I was sure standing there with you all the way through it." It seemed to work a little.

"I'm sure of that," he said, calmer. "I'm sure of that. Now what did I mean 'standing with me'? Now I don't mean just coming in and saying, 'Now look, Mr. President, you're doin' great.' "

"No, no," I answered.

"He would often do that. But the point is that he would break his ass if he saw something that was wrong, or being done—if somebody was pissing on us, I mean—leaks, that sort of thing. Not interfering with the rights of the press. Not interfering with the rights of the . . . you know, the . . . you know all that crap."

I assured him that I did. It wasn't "crap" to me, but he could call it anything he wanted to, as long as he didn't interfere with it. By now I had concluded that the best way to handle this meeting with the president was to let him ramble on while I murmured agreement; there seemed little danger in this as long as there were to be no more "directives."

"The thing is," Nixon went on, "in your case, you see, the difficulty with having someone who is, basically, as you are, a Nixon loyalist and a friend, first of all, is that they're going to raise all kinds of hell over that."

"Sure," I said. "I know it."

"Second, a Nixon loyalist and a friend feels generally—and I've found this to be true of half the cabinet—he's got to bend over backwards to prove that he's neutral."

The president looked at me pointedly. "We can't have that. Publicly, you must do that. Publicly. But privately what you've got to do is do like Hoover. Now the reason Hoover's relation with me was so close—even closer than with Johnson, though he saw Johnson more often—was that we started work in the Hiss case. He knew that he could trust me, I knew that I could trust him, and as a result he told me things. Like this wiretap he told me about."

The wiretap again. Was this the only thing that Hoover had told Nixon? He just couldn't stay away from this topic.

"Now understand," he went on. "My purpose in checking this wiretap business is not to put it out. I don't intend to put it out. But I damn well want to know who did it. See what I mean? I want to know who in the Bureau to use, and I want to know . . . See, then you may find that whoever's the guilty one may put out the story that he did it and . . . that will be useful. We'd like to know such things, that's the whole point. Not to just . . ."

Nixon trailed off. At this point I was mystified. I didn't quite get what he wanted, and I could not believe that this was the president. What was this? I had plenty of research ahead of me, to fathom this matter out. Was he leading up to suggesting that we do something similar for, rather than against, Nixon?

As these questions raced through my mind, Nixon watched my facial reactions closely, and then he abruptly leaned back.

"Of course, Johnson should not have done that," he said.

There. Something to grasp at in the conversation.

"No question about it," I agreed firmly.

"Absolutely should not have wiretapped either the plane or the phones. The phones were done for sure—even DeLoach has admitted that. But the planes he now denies. And Hoover told me that it was the plane, the cabin on my plane for the last two weeks of the campaign. They put it in on the basis of Madame Chennault or some goddamn thing. What the hell do you think happened then? Every damn political discussion we had went straight to Johnson. And you know what the hell he did with them—gave them to Humphrey."

Nixon paused here for effect. "That kind of a game is a hell of a game," he concluded.

And I had to agree. That kind of lawless activity, if it had occurred, would have to be uncovered. The president was so certain of what Hoover had told him that I was becoming convinced there was something to it.

"We could get positive evidence of that," I told him. "We could nail Deke on that because I'm sure, from what checking I've done on this other thing, that it came through Deke."

Finally the president seemed willing to let it drop. "Well," he said, "we just want to be sure. We want to know who did it, you know."

Here he turned to Ehrlichman, who had been quiet all through this tirade but who had been keenly watching me the whole time. Ehrlichman nodded his head slightly. The president turned back to me.

"Well," he said, much more relaxed now, "let me say this. The main point is that, as I said, I think it's going to be a bloody confirmation."

"Oh, I do, too," I agreed. I never expected anything else; every Nixon appointee had a brutal time whenever he appeared before any congressional committee.

"All right," he continued. "We just wanted you to know that if you do go through it, you've got to be prepared to take the heat and to get bloodied up. And if you do go through a bloody one, let's remember that you're probably going to be in for just four years."

"That's right," I answered. Again this was no news to me.

"And then they're going to throw you out," said the president. "So let's get in there and do some good for the country. As you know, I would never ask the director to do anything that was wrong, but I am certainly going to have to ask the director of the Bureau at times to do things that are going to protect the security of this country."

"No problem," I said. And it wouldn't be. Not with me, not with the security of the United States as a goal. I wondered why he was telling me this; it's a primary responsibility of the job, and I had been doing just that for nine months.

"You see," Nixon said, getting excited again, "this country, this bureaucracy—Pat, you know this—it's crawling with, Pat, at best, at best, unloyal people and at worst treasonable people. We have to get them, break them."

"Right," I said. "I agree."

"The way to get them is through you. See?"

"I agree," I repeated. "I have no problems with that." It was once again irritating to be lectured like a neophyte. I had experience in the bureaucracy; I knew that it had its share of the lazy, the drunks, the incompetents, and probably our share of those who opposed our form of government. This was life, and foreign intelligence services were, I knew firsthand, at work every day trying to recruit defectors in our government. The job of the FBI was to locate both the foreign agent and his recruit, and then turn them over to our judicial process. I certainly knew how this was done.

"But it isn't the press that bothers me," he rushed on, "it's the people within the bureaucracy that bother me. Those are the ones who have no excuse for leaks, right?"

Leaks again. I couldn't help envisioning a huge sieve, spilling our most sacred secrets all over Washington. How could this be the foremost topic on the mind of the president of the United States as he considered what many felt to be the second most important post in the government?

"Well," said Nixon after a moment's silence, "I think that under the circumstances—and I've just asked these questions to be the devil's advocate this morning—I think that you've got to make the decision. If you've got the health, if you've got the desire, and also if you feel that you can have the kind of relationship that I had with Hoover . . . which, of course, we shouldn't have had up to this point."

"No," I agreed.

"And you can't have it yet. Except, well, from the moment you're nominated, I think you've got to start cracking the whip. Having in mind, of course, that you don't want to crack any whips that are going to force some bastard to go out and testify against your nomination."

There. He's said it. I wasn't thinking about his whip-cracking advice; what I wanted to hear was the word "nomination," and now he'd said it. Twice. For the first time in this long meeting I began to feel that Nixon had finally made up his mind to send my name up before the Senate. Nixon continued.

"So you gotta be careful. But the moment you're confirmed, then I think we've got to have the kind of relationship we had with Hoover. You've got to watch everything around the world, in your own shop, and watch the papers to see what's in there. And when you think something's not right, for example, for Christ's sake, you can tail people, you know, from time to time."

"Sure, sure," I said. But it didn't slow him down.

"Suppose we've got some jackass in the State Department, some assistant to the secretary we know is a little off. So you tail him. You tail him because you're looking for the Israeli sabotage agent, right? Because you're doing it for his own protection. That's the way Hoover did it."

"Sure," I said again. "Those things can be done easily and can be done perfectly on the record." Nixon didn't have to tell me how Hoover conducted national security investigations; it should have been the other way around. I then began to give him an example, but as before, it was not of any interest to him at all. He quickly changed the subject.

"Well," he said, turning finally to Ehrlichman, trying to marshal his thoughts. He started several sentences, and then stopped, in a cryptic shorthand fashion that Ehrlichman seemed to understand. It made little sense to me, but then he settled down.

"I'd say, as far as the Watergate," he said, still looking at Ehrlichman, "I'd rather throw it all out there and not be defensive. The other side of the coin is, if we don't, they're going to call Pat in anyway." He turned back to me. "The Ervin Committee will call you in."

"Sure," I answered.

"So that's the feeling we have," said the president. "Now the question is—and I guess you and John will work that out—as to how and when the announcement will be made."

"Yeah," said Ehrlichman.

The president turned back to me. "How are your relations with Eastland? Is he for you?"

"Yes," I answered. "I'm positive of that."

"That's very important. Who else should be informed? Hruska, at least? Hruska?"

Ehrlichman interrupted. "Well, we haven't told the attorney general yet," he said. Nixon looked up at Ehrlichman, and then they both burst out laughing. That was pretty funny.

"Well, hell, the attorney general," said Nixon, still smiling. "The attorney general will support that. Let's talk to him, John. Do you want me to tell him, or Pat? Do you want me to tell the attorney general?"

"I think that would be good," said Ehrlichman.

"I'll tell him today," said the president. "He's coming to the cabinet meeting, so could you and Pat meet now and work it out? Time is of the essence, and I'd like to get this done like by today."

"All right," answered Ehrlichman.

"We've got to move fast," said Nixon, "because this motion's gonna leak. This damn Gray's a leaker." And he laughed again.

I was smiling, too. "Yes I am, Mr. President."

Then the president rose from his chair.

"Congratulations," he said, as I rose and shook his hand.

It was over; I was nominated. As we walked together to the door of his appointments secretary's office I tried to think of something to say, and as we reached Dwight Chapin's door I turned back to the president so that I could reiterate my strong belief that the leaks were not coming from the FBI. But Nixon had already turned and was walking back to his desk, where Ehrlichman sat waiting. I walked the rest of the way out of the White House in silence, unaware of my surroundings.

Yes, I thought, I was finally to be nominated as the next director of the FBI. But the manner in which this great honor had been bestowed upon me left me uncertain, bothered by the Nixon I had met this morning. I could not deny that I wanted dearly to head this magnificent group of men and women. I was eager to face the hostile senators and to lay the entire Watergate investigative file before them. I was ready to face a bitter confirmation battle to be able to serve my country again in a place of high trust. Nevertheless, I was off base on a morning that should have sent my spirit soaring to new highs.

Something was wrong. Nixon was not Nixon. Here was the president of the United States, just reelected by the second-greatest landslide in history, yet for thirty minutes he had lectured me on leaks, lie detector tests, cracking the whip, and developing a ruthless style of leadership. Every time I tried to say something of substance, every time, he cut me off. It was as if he didn't want to hear what I had to say; in fact, he seemed, in retrospect, to be afraid to hear it.

But still, I was to be nominated. And if I were to be approved by the Senate, I knew that I would be free to lead the FBI in my own way, through evenhanded example and discipline, and within the lawful framework of the Department of Justice.

When I reached the car, it was running, nicely heated against the chill February morning. Tom was in his place behind the wheel and Bea sat quietly in the backseat. I opened the door, and before Bea could say anything I put my finger to my lips and shook my head as I got in beside her. But the question wouldn't go out of her eyes, and her mouth silently formed the one-word query: *Well?*

I nodded my head, and I could see her relax. We said not another word all the way to Andrews Air Force Base. And I'm sure that Tom Moten never understood why this was the quietest ride we ever had together.

◾

This meeting, the first ever between a sitting president and his nominee to be the director of the FBI, was obviously one of great historical importance, yet in his memoir John Ehrlichman dismissed it in a single sentence.

> Almost as soon as we returned from San Clemente (where the weather was terrible) the President left for Florida to find the sun. In between, he nominated Pat Gray to be permanent Director of the FBI.
>
> —John Ehrlichman
> *Witness to Power*, 1982

Later, I obtained from the White House files a copy of Ehrlichman's handwritten notes of the meeting. They're six pages long and they match my version with precision. And why shouldn't they? The meeting was secretly taped and transcribed, copies of which are now available to every American.

There are two other important accounts of this meeting in print. One is contained in *RN: The Memoirs of Richard Nixon* and the other can be

found in *All the President's Men*. Nixon's can at best be described, politely, as an abridgement. Woodward and Bernstein's is blatantly false.
Let's look first at what Nixon wants us to believe.

> After Edgar Hoover's death in May 1972 I had
> named Pat Gray, then an Assistant Attorney
> General, as Acting Director of the FBI. Gray had
> earned a reputation in Washington as one of the
> most efficient, sound, and genial administrators in
> the city. As Acting Director during the summer
> and fall of 1972 Gray had overseen the Bureau's
> Watergate investigation. He was proud of the extent
> and intensity of that investigation, and he was eager
> to defend it in any forum.
>   I decided to nominate Gray to be the FBI's
> permanent Director, and I met with him on
> February 14 to discuss the post. I assured him that
> I was not worried about anything that might come
> out at his nomination hearings involving Watergate:
> "I'm not concerned about the substance, about the
> facts coming out," I said. My only concern was the
> condition he would be in after the partisan
> battering he could expect to receive in the hearings.
>   He responded that he was ready. "I'm not
> ashamed for it to hang out because I think the
> administration has done a hell of a fine job in going
> after this thing," he said. He told me that at the end
> of the first week he had called in the agents working
> on the investigation and "just gave them unshirted
> hell and told them to go and go with all the vim and
> vigor possible." He said that the week after the
> break-in even Larry O'Brien had said that he was
> very happy with the job the FBI was doing.
>   Gray was sure that he could convince even
> nonbelievers that the FBI had proceeded without
> showing favor in the Watergate investigation. He
> certainly believed it himself.

> *Diary*
> At least getting Gray before the committee he can
> tell a pretty good story. It is a true story of a
> thorough investigation and this of course knocks
> down the cover-up. As I emphasized to Ehrlichman
> and Haldeman and Colson, but I am not sure that
> they all buy it, it is the cover-up, not the deed, that is
> really bad here.
>
> —Richard Nixon
> *RN: The Memoirs of Richard Nixon*, 1978

Though he got the date wrong, Nixon remembered our meeting, that much is clear. But it's just as obvious that he chose not to tell us very much about it. Where is his recollection of his "directives," of his "crack the whip" advice? What about the leaks, the lie detectors? Where are they?

Still ringing harshly in my ears, more than thirty years later. That's where they are.

But though Nixon is guilty of a classic deception by omission, and Ehrlichman just avoided talking about it, Woodward and Bernstein did something far worse. They repeated a fabricated story, and then, when they were told that it was false, they chose to leave it in their book anyway.

I had a hint that this was coming well before the book was published. On January 30, 1974, Steve Sachs called me to discuss several things that had been happening. We talked about some of them, and then Steve said, "Also, Pat, Bob Woodward of the *Washington Post* called. He and Bernstein are writing a book. In it they will say that on the occasion of your visit to the White House, you said that you were taking the rap for Watergate and wanted the FBI job."

"Steve," I said, "that is false. *Insanely* false."

"I know," he said. "The implication is that you blackmailed the president in order to get the job."

I could hardly speak. I remembered what these two had tried to do to Angelo Lano, the case agent on Watergate; now they were about to do something even worse to me. "Steve," I said through clenched teeth, "tell those bastards that that is horribly, palpably false." And that's what Steve Sachs did, that same afternoon.

Here's what Woodward and Bernstein put in their book.

> What about Gray's nomination? asked Woodward. That didn't make any sense.
>
> Deep Throat said it made all the sense in the world, though it was a big risk. "In early February, Gray went to the White House and said, in effect, 'I'm taking the rap on Watergate.' He got very angry and said he had done his job and contained the investigation judiciously, that it wasn't fair that he was being singled out to take the heat. He implied that all hell could break loose if he wasn't able to stay in the job permanently and keep the lid on. Nixon could have thought this was a threat, though Gray is not that sort of guy. Whatever the reason, the President agreed in a hurry and sent Gray's name up to the Senate right away. Some of the top people in the White House were dead set against it, but they couldn't talk him out of it."
>
> So good Pat Gray had blackmailed the President.
>
> "I never said that." Deep Throat laughed. He lifted his eyes, the picture of innocence.*
>
> *Stephen Sachs, the attorney for Gray, told Woodward in early 1974 that the suggestion that Gray had pressured or blackmailed the President was "outrageously false." "He [Gray] went to the White House expecting not to get the job," Sachs said. "Nixon told him that he should be as ruthless as Hoover in stopping leaks and be aggressive in the use of polygraphs [lie detectors]." Sachs said that pressuring the White House was "not the way Gray handled himself with those guys. It was plain fear most of

the time. Now it makes perfect sense that some of those guys down there would think he might be pressuring because that's the way they operate, but not Gray."

—Carl Bernstein and Bob Woodward
All the President's Men, 1974

This passage in *All the President's Men* is a complete fabrication, as my account, Ehrlichman's notes, and the White House tape transcripts all show. The only question is by whom.

But on that February day in 1973, as Bea and I drove away from the White House, it wasn't even a question. Woodward and Bernstein had not yet written their book, and ahead of me lay my Senate confirmation hearings. Nixon was right. They were going to be bloody.

eighteen

"He's, he's out of his goddamned mind."

THOUGH WHITE HOUSE PRESS SECRETARY RON ZIEGLER DIDN'T formally announce my nomination to be permanent director until his press conference the next day, word of my Oval Office meeting with Nixon and Ehrlichman leaked fast enough for Jeremiah O'Leary to get the rumor into that same afternoon's edition of the *Washington Star*. And fast enough also for a UPI reporter to get a quote from Senator Robert Byrd of West Virginia saying that he would oppose the nomination, calling me "the bone of contention, the source of division" within the FBI. Byrd went on to say, "There is considerable friction within the Bureau."

Business as usual in the company town.

My confirmation hearings before the Senate Judiciary Committee were scheduled to begin on February 28, giving me and my personal staff less than two weeks to prepare. We went into high gear.

Back in May 1972, while Dick Kleindienst and I were awaiting the full Senate vote on our nominations to be attorney general and deputy attorney general, respectively, the columnist Jack Anderson published a memorandum from a lobbyist named Dita Beard in which she alleged that antitrust cases against the ITT Corporation had been settled by the Department of Justice in return for a substantial contribution by ITT to the upcoming Republican National Convention. A flurry of news resulted. Though both our nominations had received unanimous Judiciary Committee approval after our confirmation hearings in February, Dick felt that the Anderson column and others reflected adversely on his personal role in the antitrust settlement, so he asked the committee to reopen his hearings. Intent on clearing his name, Dick believed that he could march up before the committee and single-handedly resolve the matter once and for all.

He was wrong. The hearings continued for many days after Dick finished his testimony and soon became known as the "ITT hearings." The attitude within the department, at least among those of us who were presidential appointees, was that this whole episode was a tempest in a teapot created by the boastful writing of an arrogant lobbyist seeking to ingratiate herself with her bosses. We genuinely believed that we were the aggrieved public servants who were doing our jobs for country and president, while the Congress and the press attacked us for partisan purposes.

When the hearings finally concluded and Dick won his full confirmation in June 1972, we held a small party for him at the Justice Department. At the party I said that Dick had the strength of character and endurance to become a great attorney general. We believed in him, and all of us had suffered with him through the personal attacks he had withstood during his reopened confirmation hearings.

I wanted no part of that for my own hearings before that same committee. I refused to let the White House and the Department of Justice make up the members of my confirmation task force, whose job it would be to back me up and assist in the research on issues and answers bound to be raised by the senators on the committee. I had seen what just such a White House–directed task force had done to Dick back in May. The White House was furious and Dick tried to talk me out of it, but my mind was made up. This was going to be an all-FBI task force, and that's how I set it up.

Back in August I had established the Office of Planning and Evaluation as a new division to look into areas where the Bureau might improve itself, and I had promoted Dick Baker to be its first assistant director. Now I asked him and his division to work with Dave Kinley and several of my personal staff members on my upcoming nomination. I knew Watergate would be the issue, that the senators would have little interest in my qualifications or accomplishments within the Bureau, but I also knew that I would have the chance to place everything on the record. Dick, Dave, and the others strove mightily to put all the information together. It was a record of which I'm proud, and it's all there for anyone who wants to read it in the 714-page official volume of the Senate hearings.

On the morning of Friday, February 23, five days before the hearings were to commence, I called a meeting of all the senior FBI agents who had been involved in the Watergate investigation. I wanted to put their heads together in one room so I could prepare myself for what I knew would be a grueling and contentious set of questions. Charlie Bates flew in from San Francisco and Bob Kunkel came back from St. Louis. Joining them in my large conference room were Mark Felt, Bob Gebhardt, Jack McDermott, Dick Long, Angie Lano, and Charlie Nuzum, along with Dave Kinley, Mack Armstrong, and me. Like the early meetings I had held the previous June with Bates, Kunkel, and Felt, this one was "no holds barred." We started at 7:30 and went for several hours.

One of the first things I learned at this meeting was that Charlie Bates had kept a detailed running narrative of the early phase of the break-in investigation, including all the brainstorming conversations we had. It was enormously helpful. Bob Kunkel told us that he had assigned Angie Lano to be the case agent because Angie had worked burglaries. All agreed that everything looks like general confusion at the outset of big cases, particularly fast-moving ones like this. Bob Kunkel said that even though Chuck Colson's name had come up the first day, we did not go into the political aspects because we were trying to get evidence on a fast-moving criminal case. "We would have been murdered if we had gone into the political," he said. "We'd never do that without Department of Justice permission." All the others agreed.

We then went over the early delay caused by the confusion over the

CIA's interest in the Mexican money chain. Charlie Bates and Bob Kunkel were animated, still obviously annoyed by the CIA interference.

"We recommended to you that the president be informed," said Bob.

"And you agreed with us," Charlie added, nodding.

"I did agree with you," I answered. "At first I did that through Dean, but later I did it directly." I then told them about my call to Nixon through Clark MacGregor. It was the first time I had divulged this conversation to anyone besides Dick Walters.

Through the whole meeting Mark Felt said very little. At the end all present agreed that there never had been a case like Watergate. It was unique. Before they all left, Dave Kinley drew up a short memo for the record. It read:

> The handling of the Watergate investigation from the Headquarters level through the field operation level was done in accordance with procedures, both administrative and investigative, that are customarily employed in any major investigative effort by the FBI.
>
> Among the cases handled in the recent past in which similar procedures were followed are: the assassination of Martin Luther King; Capitol bombing, March 1, 1971; and major kidnapping cases such as the Barbara Jane Mackle case.
>
> The above is prepared with the concurrence of the following:
>
> W. Mark Felt, Acting Associate Director
> Robert E. Gebhardt, Assistant Director, General
>   Investigative Division
> SAC John J. McDermott, Washington Field Office
> SAC Robert Kunkel, St. Louis Office
> SAC Charles W. Bates, San Francisco Office
> Section Chief Richard E. Long, Accounting and
>   Fraud Section, General Investigative Division

SA Angelo Lano, Case Agent, Washington Field
Office
SA Charles A. Nuzum, Accounting and Fraud
Section

They all signed it.

I had resolved in advance that if the president saw fit to nominate me, I was going to make our work product, the entirety of our Watergate investigation files, available to any United States senator—not just those on the Judiciary Committee—to read in full. Two special agents would accompany the files, which filled two supermarket-type shopping baskets with what are known as FBI "raw files"—memoranda, teletypes, FD-302s, and other reports that are simply compiled, not yet checked or verified—and stand ready to answer any questions of a reading senator, or to bring those questions back to the Bureau for a fuller answer.

I informed Dick Kleindienst of this plan; I didn't ask him for permission. He didn't object. He knew that I would have to lay my cards on the table and respond fully and completely to the senators' questions. His own encounter with the Judiciary Committee had been too recent for him to forget. He knew what lay ahead of me. So did I: viciously partisan Democratic senators ready to destroy any Republican nominee, regardless of the facts.

I announced the offer on Wednesday, February 28, the first day of my hearings. Chairman Jim Eastland of Mississippi asked me what I would say if committee members wanted to see the FBI Watergate file, and I said I would let any of them have full access to it. I went on to say that I was well aware that this offer would shatter long-standing precedent, that I was making it anyway, but with the understanding that it would be in this one unprecedented case only—Watergate—and the offer stood only for United States senators, no one else. After that, I told the committee, I would zealously guard the

FBI's raw files and keep them closed. Though I had told Eastland in advance I would be making this offer, he still seemed a bit taken aback by it.

"There would be present an official of the Bureau at all times?" he asked.

"Correct, sir," I answered. "That is what I am saying."

"That no staff member would be permitted?"

"No, sir. I would not go beyond the offer that I have made because of the nature of these records."

"I certainly think—now these are the raw files?"

"They are, sir," I answered. "They are memorandums, the whole works. We have nothing to hold back."

If Jim Eastland had been surprised by my offer, the Nixon White House was aghast.

March 1, 1973   *Oval Office, 9:18–9:45 a.m.*

DEAN: I don't know if you've noted what Gray's position was up there yesterday or not?

PRESIDENT: Yeah.

DEAN: Giving the little store away, Dick, uh—

PRESIDENT: (Unintelligible)

DEAN: I don't know. I was very surprised by that.

PRESIDENT: Well what, you mean like saying—

DEAN: Saying that the FBI records, as far as he was concerned, were available to any Senator in the United States Senate.

PRESIDENT: For Christ's sake, ah, he must be out of his mind.

DEAN: Well, that was my reaction. He also said that, uh, uh, if they're not satisfied with any material that they're provided, he'll provide agents to come down and, and brief these people. So Dick, uh, Kleindienst last night—

PRESIDENT: Oh, we've got to get to Gray because . . .

PRESIDENT: But Jesus Christ if he gets down there and says that any Congressman—

DEAN: Well.

> PRESIDENT: Any Congressman he said?
> DEAN: Well, he said any member of the Senate.
> PRESIDENT: Of the Senate?
> DEAN: Of the Senate.
> PRESIDENT: Well . . . He's, he's out of his goddamned mind.

Only two of the one hundred senators took me up on my offer. Roman Hruska of Nebraska, whose daughter Jana was John Ehrlichman's secretary, and my good friend Lowell Weicker of Connecticut, both members of the committee, asked to read the file. Hruska was lucky; he got to read it while Angie Lano and another special agent were there to answer his questions. Weicker waited until after the seventh day of my eleven-day hearings, but by then it was too late. Before he got the chance, Nixon ordered Dick Kleindienst to have me "clam up" and rescind the offer.

nineteen

"The presumption is one of regularity."

THERE WERE SIXTEEN SENATORS ON THE JUDICIARY COMMITtee, nine Democrats and seven Republicans, including Democrat Sam Ervin of North Carolina who was already slated to head up the Select Committee on Presidential Campaign Activities. His televised hearings riveted the country later that year. He, along with most of the Democrats, came into my hearings declaring an outwardly neutral viewpoint. Most of the Republicans had stated in advance that they would support me. Only Robert Byrd had openly opposed my nomination before the hearings even started.

Prior to Senate confirmation hearings like mine, the custom and tradition in Washington is for the nominee to pay individual social calls on each senator. I did this without realizing at the time that each of the Democrats had a time bomb in his back pocket with my name on it, yet not one of them was other than cordial except Robert Byrd. Only he was honest enough to tell me to my face that he was going to oppose my nomination. The whole pre-confirmation ritual was like a goony-bird dance on Midway Island and I came to resent its hypocrisy intensely.

I never did learn why Byrd opposed me. Surely he had underlying motives, but they weren't outwardly apparent. Byrd had a long history of extreme conservatism—he was a self-admitted former member of the

Ku Klux Klan—and was an admirer of J. Edgar Hoover. Several times during the hearings he would say that he had nothing against me personally and could easily see his way clear to voting for me in some other position but not as director of the FBI. I now know that he was close to Tom Bishop, whose Crime Records Division empire I had closed, and it could very well be that Bishop was feeding Byrd a lot information that was incorrect. In a column published in January, Evans and Novak had predicted this without naming any names. I'll never know.

The other likely source for Byrd was the columnist Jack Anderson. Anderson, by his own admission to me as well as in his 1973 book *The Anderson Papers*, is on record saying that he did all he could to defeat my nomination. Anderson had a big hate on for me from the day I entered my service with the FBI. I don't believe it was personal. Anderson just disliked the FBI and would have attacked anyone who had been named to follow Hoover. Anderson had once loved the Bureau, when Hoover used to permit his underlings to feed him choice news goodies, which he could use to fill his columns and line his pockets, but for some reason Hoover turned off the spigot. Anderson was then forced to develop his own network within the FBI, which he did successfully.

Just where Byrd and the other opposing senators got their information I never learned. Some of it was leaked from inside the Bureau; that much is beyond question because it was available nowhere else. In many of those cases the leak was incomplete—just enough material placed in a senator's hands to cast me in a poor light but not enough to fully explain the circumstances and clear the taint. The other indication that the senators had been well stocked with answers before they even asked the questions was their lack of surprise or follow-through, even when I dropped what to the rest of the world was a bombshell.

On the first day, right after I delivered my opening statement, Jim Eastland handed the questioning over to Sam Ervin. The senator from North Carolina set the political tone immediately. In rapid sequence, he asked me about the supposedly partisan speeches I had made leading up to the election last November and the files the FBI had kept on members of Congress. I assured him that I had given no political speeches and that I had dismantled Hoover's Congress-tracking system that had been in place since the early 1950s. As backup I submitted documents for the record. He asked a few pro forma follow-up questions and then turned to the main event: Watergate.

One of the first things he asked me about was the October allegation in the *Washington Post* that at the Republican National Convention in Miami, Donald Segretti had been shown his FBI interview reports. I told him that we had indeed interviewed Segretti but that the FBI certainly hadn't shown him any reports.

"I take it," said Ervin, "that if any such event occurred . . . it was not given by you or with your knowledge or consent."

Ervin was satisfied and I could have left it at that. But I felt the FBI's reputation was on the line for the leaked Segretti interviews, which I knew had not come from the FBI because we had looked into it. Segretti had been interviewed in June, and the *Post*'s allegation was that he had been shown his interview reports in August. Those FD-302s had not only been given to the prosecutors in June, but I had also given them to John Dean in July for his separate inquiry for the president. So I didn't leave it there. I offered an explanation of where the leak might have come from.

"It was not done with my knowledge or consent," I answered. "But I can go into it further if you want me to explain how it possibly could."

"Yes," the senator said. "I would like to have that."

I then laid out the sequence of decisions I had made in the early stage of the investigation, starting with the summary that Mark Felt had wanted to send to Bob Haldeman two days after the break-in and which I had stopped. I told them of the reports that we send normally to Henry Petersen and his U.S. attorneys.

"Then," I continued, "I think it was the middle of July, about the nineteenth, I was asked by the White House, by John Dean, to provide them with a letterhead memorandum because he wanted to have what we had to date because the president specifically charged him with looking into any involvement on the part of White House staff members. I asked my legal counsel to prepare a memorandum regarding whether or not we had a duty to send any material to the White House. The answer came back: on our own initiative, no; in response to a directive from an individual acting for the president of the United States, that is another matter and we do. Later on Mr. Dean asked to review the interview reports of the Federal Bureau of Investigation, and I submitted those to him. So you see the possibility here, Senator, and I think what is being driven at in this, the allegation is really directed toward Mr. Dean having one of those interview reports and showing it to Mr. Segretti."

It was the first time Dean's name had been mentioned in connection with Watergate and the FBI. Until then he had been entirely in the shadows, dealing directly with me and with Mark Felt. Yet it seemed to slip past Sam Ervin almost unnoticed. The senator went on to other questions.

Phil Hart of Michigan picked it up a few minutes later when it was his turn. "Now, tell me again," he said, "help me to understand, why it would be possible that a Bureau file or files would be in the hands of somebody at the Republican Convention."

Once again I went over the series of actions I had taken, starting with my refusal to let Mark Felt send our investigation summary directly to Bob Haldeman at the White House, continuing through my asking for a legal opinion on whether the FBI could or should do that, and ending with my acceding to John Dean's request for our Watergate reports after the FBI's Office of Legal Counsel had issued a memorandum to me saying that on our own initiative we had no duty to furnish anything to the White House, but on official request from the White House we had to comply. I finished my long summary to Senator Hart by saying that when we in the FBI saw the newspaper report that Segretti had been shown his FD-302, the standard FBI interview report form, at the Republican Convention, I called John Dean and asked him about it and Dean had told me he knew nothing about it.

"And why did I call John Dean?" I asked, anticipating the next question. "Because he is the only person over there who had custody of the reports."

The larger import of what I had just announced in this public hearing—that John Dean had been given FBI reports on Watergate—seemed to escape Hart as well. He was more interested in the report getting out than in the fact that I had given it to the White House: "Did you ask him if he knew who might have had them with him? Did you ask him whether anybody had done it?"

"No, I didn't," I answered, "because the thought never entered my mind. You know, when you are working closely with the office of the presidency the presumption is one of regularity in the conduct of the nation's business."

Though it was now well into the afternoon, the main event of this long day still lay ahead. Robert Byrd, who had been absent from the proceedings, had finally made his appearance and was eager to get the nod from Jim Eastland to begin his own private inquisition. But it was getting late and the hearings had been going since 10:45 a.m.

"We will recess now—" began Eastland, but Byrd cut him off in mid-sentence.

"Mr. Chairman," he interrupted in his high West Virginia accent, "until when will you recess?"

"Ten-thirty tomorrow morning."

That wasn't acceptable to Byrd. "Could we not pursue this for a little while?" he whined. "I have waited all day patiently and I only have a few questions. I may not be able to be here tomorrow."

Eastland relented, and we all paid the price. Byrd's "few questions" kept us there until 6:30 p.m. He started with a short speech saying he had already made up his mind to oppose me because of my political connection to Nixon. "Now, I have no secret files," he intoned at the end of the speech. "All the information I have has been gleaned from press accounts which are available to the public."

And gleaned they were. Should anyone ever want to look into the nature and extent of the press leaks in the Watergate case—or into the veracity of Byrd's claim that press accounts were his sole source of information—all that researcher need do is take his many detailed questions as a guide. On this day and the others to follow, his questions to me named names, cited dates, and referred to specific FBI documents and grand jury testimony. He knew details of my travel methods, the names of special agents who had left or been transferred, whom we had questioned and whom we had not. He took special interest in Tom Bishop, Charlie Bates, and Bob Kunkel, asking why Bishop had left the Bureau and why Bates and Kunkel had been transferred. I explained each instance, but declined to give the specifics of Bob Kunkel's disciplinary transfer in the open hearing. He asked if there were any others associated with the Watergate investigation who had left and I answered that one man had resigned voluntarily. I didn't give his name.

"Was anyone else associated with Watergate transferred?" he kept pushing.

"I cannot recall any others."

"Was Mr. Charles Bolz?" Byrd clearly had inside information. He was reading from a list.

"No, he was not transferred."

Byrd sat up straighter. He thought he had me here. "I beg your pardon?"

"He was not transferred," I answered. "He was the man I was referring to, since you raised his name." To Byrd's obvious disappointment, I then provided the details of Charlie Bolz's personal decision to take a job at the Department of Housing and Urban Development. I had, in fact, tried hard to talk him out of it.

For the next hour and a half, Byrd hammered away with detailed, picky questions about the FBI's Watergate investigation. When did the FBI first learn that James McCord had worked for both the CIA and the FBI? Did we check into press reports that he was "plugged into" the FBI? Why not? And so on. In many cases, I simply could not answer at that level of detail, but in every one of those cases Dave or Barbara made a note of the question and we later supplied a detailed answer for the record. (And for the record, though McCord had once been an FBI agent, he had left the Bureau in 1951 and was not "plugged into" the FBI. His closest remaining contact was his old friend Donald Guthrie in

Birmingham, Alabama, as I learned when I had chosen to take the high road and not pursue the connection.)

Other questions from Byrd were so broad he seemed to be fishing for something. "Did you have contact with anyone employed by the Committee for the Reelection of the President?" Again he seemed disappointed when my answer was a straight "no." But his follow-ups always indicated that he was working from a scripted set of questions to which it seemed he thought he already knew the answers.

"When did you first learn of Mr. Liddy's involvement in the Watergate break-in?" he asked. Again, I had to tell him that I didn't have that kind of detailed information with me. "I will have to find the exact time that George Gordon Liddy's name was delivered to me, Senator."

"And from whom," he demanded.

"And from whom, yes."

"Were you aware that Mr. Liddy was a former FBI agent and that he was finance counsel for the Committee to Reelect the President at the time of the Watergate break-in?"

"No, I was not. I did not even know Mr. Liddy."

That surprised him. "You did not know him personally?" he asked.

"No, sir, I did not."

"Even through the Committee to Reelect the President?"

"No, sir. I did not."

This was clearly not the answer he was expecting. But it was the truth. I was under oath.

Byrd then launched into a long, tightly detailed series of questions about the ITT–Dita Beard matter that had been so difficult for Dick Kleindienst in his own hearings before this same committee. It was also a favorite topic of Jack Anderson and I have little doubt that Anderson was the source of Byrd's attack on me here. Once again I had to repeatedly defer my answers until Dave Kinley and the rest of my confirmation task force could go back to the files and dig out the answers.

Having failed to draw blood with that tactic, Byrd turned back to Watergate. In rapid sequence he demanded to know exactly what I knew about the details of what we had learned from our interviews of Alfred Baldwin, the burglary lookout; William Timmons and Dwight Chapin of the White House; Robert Odle and Glen Sedam of CREEP; and Donald Segretti again. It was impossible to answer him on the spot. Those were details that had been handled well below me in the FBI chain of command.

Not satisfied with his earlier attempts to connect me to CREEP, he turned back to the same topic.

"Did you ever discuss any matter relating to the investigation of the Watergate affair with anyone on the Committee to Re-Elect the President?"

"No, sir," I answered again.

"With Mr. John Mitchell?"

"No, sir."

"Or with anyone from the White House?"

Finally, Byrd had stumbled onto pay dirt. The question I had been expecting all along was now on the table. He had asked it as a follow-up throwaway and already he was looking at his notes for another line of questioning.

"Yes, sir," I said.

He looked up, surprised. "Who?"

I knew that what I was about to tell him was going to shake up all the candles in the church: "John Wesley Dean, counsel to the president, and I think on maybe a half dozen occasions with John Ehrlichman."

Had Byrd been paying as much attention to my answers as he apparently was to the expected ones in the notes his staff kept passing to him, he might have realized what I had just told him. But he didn't. He turned without follow-up to the last few of his prepared questions. He had missed it completely.

But the rest of the world hadn't. Here's how Barry Sussman, who was in charge of the *Washington Post*'s coverage of Watergate from its first day, put it in his very accurate book *The Great Coverup*, published a year later.

Several senators on the Judiciary Committee, including Byrd, had apparently made a decision to challenge Gray's nomination as a reminder to Nixon that despite his tremendous election victory, he could not have everything he wanted. But there is little reason to believe that any senator was prepared to ask questions that would have elicited information as sensational as that either volunteered by Gray or prompted by his utterances.

By March 1, the second day of the hearings, the conduct of John Dean had become as important in the proceedings as that of Gray, the man whose nomination was under consideration. . . .

In less than three weeks the Watergate coverup was to be exposed to the public and a coverup of the coverup begun in the Oval Office.

—Barry Sussman
The Great Coverup: Nixon and the Scandal of Watergate, 1974

Sussman's perspective, of course, was that of a newspaperman on the outside looking in. Things that were sensational to the public were old news to the U.S. attorneys, FBI agents, and members of the grand juries that were continuing the spadework of the Watergate investigation. As I told the senators at these hearings, we in the FBI looked carefully at every press report on the case, and what we saw consistently was that the "revelations" in newspaper and magazine stories were four to eight weeks behind their original discovery by the federal investigators. The difference was that we were required to keep the evidence and our leads private while we acted upon them in order to obtain valid convictions in federal court, and the press was free to do just the opposite. Their motivation was to "uncover" the crimes and dirty tricks on their individual front pages in order to sell newspapers. We had to get it right while protecting the privacy of innocent bystanders. The Watergate press operated without those restrictions, free to print rumors, hearsay, and the leaks of anonymous sources without restraint. And without penalty.

I left the Dirksen Senate Office Building that evening after the long day's inquisition only to learn that radical members of the American Indian Movement had seized the small town of Wounded Knee, South Dakota, at gunpoint, "reclaiming" it in the name of the Sioux and demanding a reexamination of broken federal treaties. It was the beginning of a seventy-one-day standoff, and for the rest of my confirmation hearings I would have to alternate between defending myself and the FBI against the partisan jabs of the Democratic senators on the Hill and trying to oversee the federal response to an armed insurrection 1,500 miles away.

It would prove to be an eventful three weeks.

twenty

"You are getting to me."

THE SECOND DAY OF MY CONFIRMATION HEARINGS STARTED with Senator John Tunney of California, but the main event was to be Ted Kennedy of Massachusetts.

"Mr. Gray," Kennedy began without preamble, "some of the areas which I will touch on have been touched on by other members of the committee but, with your indulgence and patience, we will review some of those areas."

Indulgence was required by law—I had to be there if I wanted to become director of the FBI—but patience was something I had to draw from within. Kennedy's "review," like the hearings themselves, would continue off and on for three weeks. Repetitive, argumentative, aggressive, and frequently impolite, Kennedy's interrogation matched Byrd's on every level.

But first, the developing crisis at Wounded Knee was on everyone's mind, including Kennedy's: "Could you just, before getting into some other questions, could you tell us the latest on Wounded Knee?"

"Yes, sir, the latest word is that I ordered another experienced SAC in there to assist the SAC I have now in there, and we also have information that Senator McGovern and Senator Abourezk and some of their staff members are going out in U.S. Air Force aircraft. Right at the time I left FBI headquarters, the last memorandum handed me was that the situation was 'stable as of this moment.' But I don't know what it is right now."

"The memorandum ought to show I have a staff member on that plane, too," Kennedy said.

"Yes, it does. I already mentioned the senators, but you are correct."

"This week's *Time* magazine contains information about alleged wiretaps on newsmen, according to the article, requested by the White House, authorized by the Justice Department, installed by the FBI. How would you respond to those charges?"

I had seen the article but I had never heard of these wiretaps. When I asked about them, no one in the FBI seemed to know anything about them, either. As a beginning to my detailed answer I tried to put the matter in perspective: "I would have to say, first, that with regard to the general matter of wiretaps—"

"No, just on these charges. How do you respond specifically. I will come on to general wiretap questions later on. How do you respond?"

So much for my full answer. "When I saw this particular article, I checked the records and the indexes of the Federal Bureau of Investigation, and I am told that the Department of Justice checked the records of the Internal Security Division of the Department of Justice. There is no record of any such business here of bugging news reporters and White House people."

"Well, is that the full answer?" Kennedy demanded.

"That is my answer. Yes, sir, that is my full answer."

And so it went. I tried mightily to give full answers like I tried to do with this one, but rarely would Kennedy be interested in them. Political points were there to be made, and that trumped all else.

But, as I was to learn later, the *Time* article was on to something that had actually happened before my tenure, one of the Nixon White House's deepest secrets about which I knew nothing. The magazine had gotten wind of the wiretaps placed on the telephone lines of certain newsmen and White House staffers to determine the identification of leakers of national security information from the files in Henry Kissinger's National Security Council office in the White House. These were the so-called Kissinger wiretaps that Bill Sullivan had run for the White House with Hoover's approval before Sullivan was fired. They were also, as I later surmised, the subject of the whispered conversation between Nixon and Ehrlichman in our Oval Office meeting on February 16.

This answer that I had just given Kennedy—that I knew nothing about the Kissinger wiretaps—would later be the basis for a full-fledged investigation by the Watergate Special Prosecution Force, whose zealous young prosecutors (egged on by Kennedy and his staff) would try to indict me for perjury. But I hadn't lied. As I sat there in the committee room, answering his questions under oath, all of my answers to Ted Kennedy were honest and truthful, even if he didn't believe me. Which he clearly did not, since he wouldn't let it go.

"And you never felt you had to follow up?" he pushed.

"I testified that I did not feel that."

"Or to do any other kind of investigation?"

"No, sir. Since I have been sitting in that chair, I have been signing all the paperwork that is involved in these national security taps and since May—"

"This is a crime?" he cut me off. Again, Kennedy wouldn't let me give him a full answer.

"Of course it is a crime." Wiretaps of American citizens without a valid court order were illegal.

"And you didn't feel you had to do anything more to review it?"

"No, sir."

"This is a serious allegation, it charged a crime, and you didn't feel that you had to do anything more than receive a call from—"

Ted Kennedy knew the law as well as I did. He and his fellow liberal Democrats had been first on the list of those demanding that J. Edgar Hoover be reined in from sending his agents into areas without judicial oversight and clear direction. But now, with the shoe on the other foot and a room full of reporters, he was trying to pretend that I was derelict by not sending my agents out to investigate an unsubstantiated news account. It was time for me to cut him off.

"The proper place to make this charge, you know, is with the U.S. attorney and not a magazine if there is any verity to it, Senator."

He knew he was trumped here, so he folded and tried another deal.

"Well, I don't know whether we would be as far as we are now in the Watergate if we didn't have the press write about it. Wouldn't you agree with that?"

"I am not saying anything against the press at all. And I further disagree with you about your statement. We would have been exactly where we are with or without the press because from day one, as I testified yesterday, I realized that the credibility of the Federal Bureau of Investigation was at stake—"

Kennedy tried to cut me off again, but Jim Eastland cut *him* off, saying, "Wait a minute, let him finish his answer." It didn't work. In the end Kennedy and I simply had to agree to disagree on this, the first of many topics that found us on opposite sides.

The confirmation hearings dragged on, intermittent and subject to the whims and schedules of the committee members. Eventually the hearings would spread over ten different sessions between February 28 and March 22. I was kept on the hot seat for the first five in a row, after which a series of other witnesses held forth for a couple of days, and then I was brought back for three more intensive sessions.

On Thursday, March 8, the first of my two multiday sessions came to an end. Kennedy, having gone through a litany of names of men in the Nixon administration with whom I had had some sort of personal or professional contact over the years, tried to use this as another mark against my confirmation.

"Obviously," he orated, speaking as much for the gallery as to me, "there has been general speculation again in some newspapers that this has really placed you almost in an impossible position in terms of doing the kind of work and job that you would be called on to do, despite the association or knowledge or work relationship that you had with many of these men, yet if you didn't do it because of the appearance of either those associations or relationships that would put an unfair burden upon you. Can you understand that sense of concern that others might have about having you investigate people whom you had this working relationship with, are knowledgeable of and friends with over a period of a number of years? So to speak, have served in the trenches with. Should people be concerned about that? Do you understand this concern?"

I had been ready for this question from the beginning. "Yes, indeed," I answered. "I understand the concern, Senator Kennedy. I think it is a valid concern. But I don't think this is the first time in the history of our government that this kind of a situation has occurred, where people have been placed either in cabinet officer positions or bureau chief positions. We have been able to operate this government because this government relies on people doing their job. If we begin to believe that people can't do their job, our institutions are in real trouble—and those of us who are in these jobs have got to contribute all we can so as not to default. I view a default on the part of leadership as far more serious than some of the really major crimes that are committed today because that default in leadership can hurt this society grievously. I appreciate your concern, and I do think it is a valid concern. But I think that it can be overcome, and we have been overcoming it, sir, in our government for many years."

That was the right answer, and it was as old as Washington, D.C. The question had been settled long ago. Still, Kennedy wouldn't let it go: "But it is the first time that has taken place in the FBI, isn't it?"

"Oh, no question, this is the first time." I had had enough. This was too hypocritical from a man whose own brother had been attorney general when his other brother was president. I let him have it. "But not in the Department of Justice. There have been many attorneys general in the Department of Justice who had political connections."

"I know of some."

"These men are going to go in there and do a crackerjack job."

"You are getting to me," Kennedy said. "Thank you, Mr. Gray."

It apparently got to Jim Eastland, too. He gaveled the morning session closed and I went back to work.

twenty-one

"Does the FBI have automatic weapons effective up to fifteen hundred yards?"

On Friday, March 2, my first day off from questioning by the Judiciary Committee, the Wounded Knee uprising intensified. At 2:30 that afternoon, Dick Kleindienst called.

"Pat," he asked, "does the FBI have automatic weapons effective up to fifteen hundred yards?"

"If we don't, we'll get them, Dick."

I hung up and called Mark Felt. "We'll get them," he said.

Here was potentially the worst-case scenario I had envisioned back in September when the members of the Cabinet Committee on Terrorism had dumped all the responsibility on us in the FBI. The militants now gathering in Wounded Knee were reported to have with them an M-60 heavy machine gun. The FBI wasn't armed to go to battle, but the governor of South Dakota had refused to federalize the National Guard. It was going to be the FBI or nobody. Deputy attorney general Ralph Erickson was in overall command and SAC Joseph Trimbach from the Minneapolis field office was our man in charge on the ground, since Wounded Knee fell into his territory. He had already obtained ten M-16s from the National Guard and was trying to get extra body armor for the fifty special agents already in the area. Roadblocks had been set up.

Militants were flowing into the area as we tried to assess and stabilize the situation. By that Friday night there were sixty-two special

Gray's notes of a call from Kleindienst and his resultant call to Felt, discussing weapons for the siege at Wounded Knee. March 2, 1973.

agents, forty-five U.S. marshals, and twenty-seven agents from the Bureau of Indian Affairs (BIA) on the scene, with fifty more special agents on the way. In response, the American Indian Movement (AIM) militants had set up their own defensive perimeter and we pulled ours back to add a cushion. No one—at least on the government side—wanted shooting to break out.

On Saturday morning Dick Kleindienst called. "I hear there's a caravan of fifteen hundred Indians on the way," he said. "I don't want a war out there."

I didn't, either. "Where did you hear that, Dick?" It was the first I'd heard of the caravan.

"It's a rumor we've picked up."

"Well, get me more info on it if you can. My men need to know what they're facing."

"I will," he answered. "What's this I hear about a Sixth Army military advisory team out there? Is that true? I don't want to call in the army."

"They're there at my request. I wanted a military assessment of the situation. We're not calling in the army."

Dick told me to keep the military presence low key, and then we rang off. I immediately called Bob Gebhardt at FBI headquarters and asked him what he knew of the 1,500 incoming Indians.

"I've heard a news report to that effect, but we don't have anything more than that," he answered.

"Tell Division Five to do whatever is necessary to confirm or deny the 1,500 Indians coming in a caravan," I ordered. "What's the current situation?"

"We've had some gunfire, but it's stable now," reported Bob. "Earlier the Indians were firing their M-60 machine gun at our armored personnel carriers at the roadblocks, but now there's no more shooting. Our communications setup is working, but the fifty additional agents are still not there. Snow's slowing them up."

Two hours later Bob called back. "We've got word back on the 1,500-Indian rumor. Eight field offices have reported in and the consensus is that there are 105 or 106 Indians on their way from Nebraska and Denver. Also, Joe Trimbach surveyed the area with a colonel from the Sixth Army. The colonel recommends against using his troops. They would need 4,500 to do this. The alternative is to use their APCs and choppers to carry our men."

"Tell Trimbach to decline the offer," I told Bob. "I just don't want to risk the life of one special agent in a situation like this. This is not a terrorism situation."

By then Dick Kleindienst was at the Burning Tree Club playing golf. I left a message with the pro shop for him.

I spent most of that afternoon on the phone, relaying my orders to the special agents in the field in South Dakota. Even as I spoke, they were being shot at, though so far only their automobiles had been hit. I reiterated my orders: not to risk the life of a single special agent. "Let the negotiations soak and simmer," I said.

By Sunday we had ninety-eight special agents, one hundred U.S. marshals, and twenty-seven BIA officers in place. It was twenty-five degrees at night, and the men manned their roadblocks in eight-hour shifts commanded by four SACs I had ordered in from different field offices. Off duty they had to drive to motels twenty-five to fifty miles away, sharing the rooms and sleeping in shifts.

This was the first time the FBI had ever been required to set up and maintain a paramilitary presence, and though morale was high, the special agents were poorly equipped. All had been trained to be investigators, not combat troops, and their standard weapon was a handgun. Assistant Director Ed Miller spent days trying to get military weapons and it was a bureaucratic mess.

"We have the biggest problem you ever heard of getting our hands on rifles," he told me. "It's going to require two million dollars to prepare ourselves for something like this. We don't have a training facility. If we're going to be ready in the future, we're going to need a combat village."

Every aspect of the situation argued for restraint, and that's what I ordered. But our job was to contain and minimize the problem, and that meant staying in place between the militants already inside Wounded Knee and those coming in from the outside. Word from a local gun shop owner was that the Indians were using scoped hunting rifles, which were effective at hundreds of yards. We needed to be armed with more than pistols in order to defend ourselves against these radicals who kept firing at us even though we made no move to advance against them. The SACs on site asked the local special agents to bring their own personal long guns if they had them. Meanwhile I issued specific orders: No frontal attack. No special agent's life is to be jeopardized. Fire only in self-defense and at a specific target who has fired on us first. The FBI's long-standing shooting policy was to remain in place: Shoot only in self-defense or to protect innocent lives, and then shoot to kill.

On Sunday afternoon Trimbach reported that the agents in the field were fully occupied in maintaining a defensive perimeter. No investigative work was being done at all. "The Indians want to set up a government there," he said. "Many militants are coming and going, and that gives us an opportunity to get some informants in there to let us know what they're planning."

Before I gave Trimbach the okay to do that, I asked Bob Gebhardt, Mark Felt, and the four on-site SACs to gather their views on the concept and execution. Before they all got back to me, Dick Kleindienst called on Sunday night to say that there was a possibility of a settlement. "Ralph Erickson is negotiating it," said Dick. "Between eight and six tomorrow, any Indian who wants to leave should be permitted to do so." I issued those orders and relaxed a bit. The Wounded Knee insurrection would continue without resolution until May, but at least for now I could turn back to my confirmation hearing testimony, which was scheduled to resume on Tuesday.

One of the few witnesses scheduled to testify against my nomination in the coming week was the columnist Jack Anderson, whose researcher Les Whitten had been arrested by FBI agents in January for possession of government documents that had been stolen from the Bureau of Indian Affairs. Whitten was caught by our men with a box of the documents in his hands as he was loading them into his personal car, but a federal grand jury had declined to indict him. Not content with this miscarriage of justice, Anderson decided to vent his anger on me personally and had been granted opposition witness status by the Judiciary Committee. Needless to say, the irony of having to deal with an armed Indian insurrection in South Dakota and at the same time defend myself against the utterly false accusations of one of their more bombastic sympathizers in Washington was not lost on me, or on any of us in the FBI.

The case arose as a result of the theft of thousands of documents from the Bureau of Indian Affairs when it had been ransacked by AIM militants in November, the same group that was now firing scoped hunting rifles and an M-60 machine gun at federal agents manning distant roadblocks in Wounded Knee. In January Jack Anderson had printed excerpts from various of these documents in his column, and we had been directed by the Department of Justice to conduct an investigation.

We endeavored to track down these documents in many parts of the country, sending leads to several field offices. We weren't having much luck until we caught a break. An undercover officer with the Washington Metropolitan Police Department learned that the documents had been sent from Rosebud, South Dakota, to Pembroke, North Carolina. He and an activist named Anita Collins were supposed to go get them and bring them back to a private house in the Washington area where they were to be sold to a representative of Jack Anderson for $100,000 to $200,000. When the undercover officer asked Collins what they would do if they got caught with the papers, she said, "We say we are returning these to the government." The Washington police passed this information to the FBI.

Collins and the informant picked up the documents and brought them back to Washington. They handed them over to an AIM member named Hank Adams, who kept them overnight in his home. That area was under FBI surveillance. We had information that the transfer was to be made that evening or the following day, and when an individual showed up as predicted we waited until the documents were brought out of the house and the people actually had them in their possession before we moved in to make a valid arrest, which had been authorized in advance by the assistant U.S. attorney overseeing the case. Les Whitten was the individual who had come to get the documents and had one of the three boxes in his hands when our agents arrested him.

It seemed as good a case as it was possible to make, but the grand jury disagreed. Though Jack Anderson in his career had printed many unlawfully leaked grand jury documents, when it came to what was said to get him and Les Whitten off the hook, the testimony remained tightly sealed. Instead of providing the usual leaked documents in his column, Anderson simply shouted "First Amendment!" Both he and Whitten testified against me at my confirmation hearings; in fact, Anderson did far more than testify—he personally lobbied individual senators against me.

My good friend Ed Morgan, a prominent Washington lawyer who strongly supported my nomination and who was also a friend of Jack Anderson's, called me to say that I was being severely harmed by Anderson.

He wanted to arrange a private meeting between Anderson and me so that Anderson could get to know me the way he did. In particular he wanted me to explain to Anderson that Whitten's arrest had been above-board and by the book.

"Ed," I said, "I see no value in meeting with him. No gain can come of it."

"I can tell you this, Pat. Jack Anderson is killing you on the Hill and I see no value in *not* meeting with him."

I hung up and gave this some thought and called Ed back. "All right," I said, "I'll do it, but I still think nothing is going to come of it."

So it was arranged. Tom Moten drove me out to Ed's beautiful home in Kensington, Maryland, a few days after Anderson's and Whitten's testimony against me. We met for almost two hours and spent virtually the whole evening on the topic of Whitten's arrest. Anderson admitted to me that he had indeed been speaking to senators on the Judiciary Committee and doing everything he could to convince them to oppose my nomination on the basis of the arrest of Les Whitten. At the end of the meeting, Anderson told me that he had changed his mind, that I had established to his satisfaction my bona fides.

"I'll go back on the Hill," he promised. "I'll speak to those same senators and try to right the wrong I have done to you."

Ed Morgan was pleased, and so was I. But not for long.

Jack Anderson never lived up to the personal promise he made that night. Instead, he let his inflammatory and false testimony against me stand. Though he now knew it was false, he never corrected it, and as far as I know he went back to not one of the senators he had lobbied to vote against my nomination.

What he did was wait three years and then file a civil suit against Richard Nixon, me, and anyone else he could name, claiming that we had all conspired against him. The suit was summarily dismissed when he could provide no evidence to corroborate his delusions, all of which were refuted by the facts I presented in my defense, the same facts I had shown him at Ed Morgan's house.

Here's how Anderson put it:

There is a footnote to the Les Whitten episode. Because one of my reporters had been arrested on the streets by the FBI, I stepped out from behind my typewriter for the first time since taking over the column and helped to line up the Senate opposition to Patrick Gray. I wrote a column on February 21, 1973, attacking Gray. "We hope the Senate," I wrote, "will refuse to confirm him." Throughout his confirmation hearings, I worked behind the scenes, planning strategy and making calls to senators. Gray's confirmation hearing was heavy with helpful liabilities, of course, but to the extent that this prominent false arrest added to the considerations that forced Gray's withdrawal, it was a vindication for Whitten and a victory for press freedom.

—Jack Anderson
The Anderson Papers, 1973

I'll leave it to others to decide whether this was a "victory for press freedom." As a measure of the honesty and personal integrity of Jack Anderson, I have decided. He lied about me to the senators in private, to his readers in public, and under oath in my hearings. And then he lied to me to my face while Ed Morgan listened. My contempt for him is total.

Meanwhile, the senators themselves were busy sharpening their knives for my return engagement before the Judiciary Committee. This time it would get even nastier.

twenty-two

"Let him twist slowly, slowly in the wind."

FROM THE FIRST DAY OF MY CONFIRMATION HEARINGS I HAD reported back to the White House after each session. The president had nominated me, and it seemed to me that he and his top aides had every right to be kept abreast of how the proceedings were going. In my calls to John Ehrlichman he would listen carefully, ask a few questions, and then hang up. Dean was essentially the same. And though I never spoke directly to him about the progress of the hearings, Bob Haldeman was kept up to date by Ehrlichman and Dean so he could in turn keep Nixon informed. What none of them let on to me was what they were saying behind my back.

March 6, 1973   *Oval Office, 9:40–10:05 a.m.*

NIXON: What's your judgment as to how Gray is handling himself?

HALDEMAN: I don't know. Dean says he's not doing well, that he's letting too much out . . . Dean has been hitting him hard and Kleindienst has, too. Kleindienst disagrees with him, as I understand it from Dean.

NIXON: Oh. Kleindienst, what's he think?

HALDEMAN: He doesn't think he should. He thinks he's being too outgoing on this stuff.

NIXON: Well, [Gray] says . . . a lot of people at the Bureau are disturbed and they're going to get to the bottom of the Watergate thing.

HALDEMAN: Yeah, I understand that.

NIXON: . . . You know, we might have been better to follow the first hunch and put Jerry Wilson in.

They certainly did not like my testimony, yet they really knew nothing of my work at the FBI, including my efforts to open its windows and make it more responsive to Congress and to the public at large. Like the senators on the Judiciary Committee, they were interested in only one event: Watergate. Unlike the senators, the last thing they wanted was to discuss it in public. That same day, Dean talked to Ehrlichman on the phone. Their problem now was that the senators might want to hold up my confirmation until they could get Dean and possibly Ehrlichman himself to testify at the hearings, now that I had blown Dean's name onto the front pages and told the senators I had also discussed Watergate with Ehrlichman.

"It makes me gag," Dean told Ehrlichman. The hearings might drag on while the senators tried to get Dean before them under oath, he suggested, and my confirmation might be held up indefinitely until the courts ruled on whether White House people should testify. Ehrlichman knew he didn't want that. The answer was to leave my confirmation in limbo.

"Well, I think we ought to let him hang there," said Ehrlichman. "Let him twist slowly, slowly in the wind."

The next day, Nixon was fuming at my willingness to answer every question and to back up my answers with FBI documents and memos. He called Dean into the Oval Office and told his counsel that he had an idea: force Gray to commit perjury and then remove him for doing it. The plan was to get a senator to ask me about the FBI bugging of Nixon's campaign plane in 1968, the rumor Nixon had harped on during my meeting with him and Ehrlichman in the Oval Office three weeks earlier. Nixon assumed I would deny knowing anything about it, and then Nixon could say, "Aha, you just lied under oath. I told you about it. You did know about it." Then he and the conspirators could yank my nomination.

March 7, 1973   *Oval Office, 8:53–10:12 a.m.*

NIXON: Let me tell you how this is done, the way I would do it . . . I'm going to make him lie, because I think Gray's not handling himself well . . . "Mr. Chairman, I am concerned about the White House being used for political purposes . . . Mr. Gray, do you have any knowledge that the White House has been doing it this year?" . . . And then repeat it, see? Then I would go on, but mainly I would go into this stuff that is new. Everybody knows about what happened in the Kennedy thing and rooting the reporters out of bed and all that sort of thing. But people do not know some of this other crap, about how Johnson used the FBI . . . And then Gray lies. He lies, and then we will be willing to call and tell him because he lied under oath and then withdraw his name. Do you get my point?

DEAN: Exactly . . .

NIXON: . . . I ordered him when he was in this room. I directed him. I said you are to give a lie detector test to every individual who may have had anything to do with electronic bugging of the President's plane in 1968. No, goddamn it, he hasn't done that . . . He didn't do it, did he? Has he used lie detector tests?

DEAN: No, sir. . . .

NIXON: But . . . how about it now? My view is that we should—now, what the hell, where's Kleindienst in all this? What in the name of God is he doing?

DEAN: Kleindienst has been totally unable to control what he calls a bull-headed Irishman in this whole thing. We have tried. They had—before the hearings started, they had sit-down sessions to plan this whole strategy . . . It's beyond Dick's control.

NIXON: Now listen. I want all communication with Gray cut off. That's the other thing. Give him the cold stuff for a while.

DEAN: All right.

NIXON: It doesn't do any good to talk to him . . .

It certainly did not do any good to talk to me if the purpose was to get me to do anything other than lay it all out on the table. The plan never hatched, but it would have failed anyway. Like every other question I was ever asked under oath, I would have answered this one with the truth. Had I known anything about this conversation—the president of the United States conspiring with his counsel to induce the acting director of the FBI to commit a felony—I'd have resigned immediately and gone public with it, just as I had told Mark Felt and Charlie Bates I would if the CIA continued to obstruct our investigation without explaining its reasons in writing.

At about the same time that Nixon and Dean were plotting against me, Henry Petersen called. In the course of our conversation, Henry casually mentioned that in a December meeting he had held concerning a motion by Howard Hunt's lawyer to suppress some evidence for the Watergate trial, John Dean had taken Henry aside and told him that he, Dean, had given me some separate documents from Hunt's safe. Henry told me that after Dean assured Henry that the documents were unrelated to Watergate, he told Dean to take the matter up with me.

"Did he ever do that?" Henry now asked.

Dean had not asked me about it in December, so I could truthfully say no to Henry's question. But I certainly did not tell Henry that Dean had given me any files. Even if he had asked me point-blank, I would have denied it. My instructions, which had come directly from Dean and Ehrlichman, had been that these national security documents "should never see the light of day." In my many years of handling top national secrets I had learned and adopted this golden rule: The best way to protect a secret is never to let anyone know that you possess it.

But it was now clear that though Dean and Ehrlichman had ordered me to keep the existence of these documents secret forever, Dean was now openly talking about them. Angry, I called him.

"Did you tell Henry Petersen that you gave me two of the files that Hunt had been working on?" I demanded.

"Yes, I did," he said. "Do you still have them?"

"No, John, I don't," I answered. "You said they were never to see the light of day and they won't. I burned them."

"Did you read them?" he asked.

"No," I told him, still seething. "Did you tell Henry the whole story? Did you tell him that you gave them to me in John Ehrlichman's presence and told me that they had absolutely nothing to do with Watergate, were sensitive and classified with national security overtones, should not become part of the FBI files, were political dynamite and clearly should not see the light of day?"

"No," he said sheepishly.

"Now, listen to me," I said. "If those files had nothing to do with Watergate, then you ought to be saying that you turned over Howard Hunt's files to the FBI. Period. If the idea was for you to be able to say that you turned over all of Hunt's files to the FBI in order to keep these two secret, then fine, I understand that. If they're national security files, then you ought not to be talking about them at all. But if you're going to talk about those files to somebody like Henry Petersen, then you jolly well better lay it all out for him and tell him under exactly what circumstances you gave them to me and what the purpose was in doing that. Otherwise, stop this nonsense right now of saying, 'I turned over two files to the acting director and the rest to the agents.'"

There is no question that I was angry with Dean, yet I had no suspicions as to his motive because saying that he had given all of Hunt's files to the FBI was what he had said he would do if called upon to testify about them. The problem was that he was now separating the files in his statements but not clarifying that those he turned over to me had absolutely nothing to do with Watergate.

The next day I called John Ehrlichman to keep him abreast of my confirmation hearings. The senators were asking probing questions about my delivery of FBI Watergate reports to Dean, and I fully expected them to get around to asking me about Dean's delivery of the contents of Hunt's safe to the FBI.

"I am being pushed awfully hard in certain areas," I said to Ehrlichman, "and I'm not giving an inch—and you know those areas. I think you've got to tell John Wesley to stand awfully tall in the saddle and be very careful about what he says and to be absolutely certain that he knows in his own mind that he delivered everything he had to the FBI and doesn't make any distinction. This is absolutely imperative."

"Okay," said Ehrlichman. "Keep up the good work, my boy."

I had no intention of volunteering to the Judiciary Committee my receipt and destruction of those files, and I didn't. As I later told the whole nation before the live television cameras of the Ervin Committee hearings, "I would not and did not make any false statements under oath but I acknowledge that I purposely did not volunteer this information to the committee." There is no doubt that the message I intended to give to Ehrlichman was that he should tell Dean not to disclose the delivery to me of those two files.

I justified my reticence not only because I still believed in the rectitude of the administration whose nominee I was and in the integrity of the men who gave me the files and instructions, but also because my brief look at the files when I burned them convinced me that they were State Department copies having nothing to do with Watergate. I had no way of knowing then that the files were fabricated, just as I had no way of knowing that as soon as I hung up after this call to Ehrlichman he would immediately pick up the phone and suggest to Dean that they leave me to "twist slowly, slowly in the wind." Both of those calls, like many of his supposedly private conversations, were secretly taped by Ehrlichman.

During my confirmation hearings and even during my entire service with the Nixon administration I had no just cause or good reason to suspect these men occupying the highest positions, counsel and assistant to the president of the United States, of wrongdoing. Subsequent events, of course, cast them in a different light and this taping of telephone conversations is just one small example of their degradation. I am ashamed of my defense of them in my confirmation hearings.

twenty-three

"We are going to have to break with Gray, who is killing us."

A WEEK LATER, WHILE I WAS STILL OBLIVIOUSLY CARRYING THE president's hod and battling my tormentors on the Senate Judiciary Committee, the president had another meeting in the Oval Office with Dean. By now they were plotting not only how to get rid of Gray but also how to use testimony from Bill Sullivan to destroy Hoover's image at the same time. Sullivan had written to Dean offering to testify.

In that March 13 meeting Dean told the president that Sullivan's testimony was going to change the atmosphere of both the Gray hearings and the upcoming Ervin Watergate hearings by showing that government institutions had been used in the past for the most flagrant political purposes. Nixon, being the pragmatic political animal, wanted to know Sullivan's asking price.

March 13, 1973   *Oval Office, 12:42–2:00 p.m.*

PRESIDENT: Why is it that Sullivan would be willing to do this?

DEAN: I think the quid pro quo with Sullivan is that he wants someday back in the Bureau very badly.

PRESIDENT: That's easy.

DEAN: That's right.

PRESIDENT: Do you think after he did this to the Bureau that they'd want him back?

DEAN: Uh, probably not . . . What, what Bill Sullivan's desire in life is, is to set up a national, or domestic national security intelligence system, a plan, a program. He says we're deficient. Uh, we've never been efficient, since Hoover lost his guts several years ago . . . That's all Sullivan really wants. Even if we just put him off studying it for a couple of years, we could put him out in the CIA or someplace else where he felt—

PRESIDENT: Put him there. We'll do it.

DEAN: I think that's what the answer is. I've never really—

PRESIDENT: No problem with Sullivan. We'll put him—I mean, he's a valuable man. Uh, now, would the FBI then turn on him, piss on him?

DEAN: There would be some effort at that. That's right, they would say he's disgruntled. He was canned by Hoover. He is angry, he's coming back. But that would kind of, I would think a lot of that would be lost in the, uh, in the shuffle of what he is laying out. I don't know if he's given me his best yet. I don't know if he's got more ammunition than [unintelligible] he has already told me. Those were just a couple off-the-cuff remarks.

PRESIDENT: Why do you think he is now telling you this? Why is he doing this now?

DEAN: Well, the way it came out is, when I, when the *Time* magazine article broke on the fact that it charged that the White House had directed that newsmen and White House staff people be, uh, subject to some sort of surveillance for national security reasons . . . I called Sullivan and I said, "Bill, you'd better come over and talk to me about that and tell me what you know." I was calling him to really determine if he was a leak. That's one of the reasons. I was curious to know where this might have come from because he was the operative man at the Bureau at the time. He's the one who did it. . . . [H]e came over and he was shocked and distraught . . . And then, and after going through his explanation of all what had happened, he started volunteering this other thing.

Sullivan had been the third-ranking official in the FBI before his bitter dispute with Hoover in the fall of 1971. Sullivan may have been right in that dispute, and I think he probably was. He wanted Hoover to step down and he dared to tell the old lion that he was destroying the Bureau. As smart as Sullivan was, and as experienced as he was in bureaucratic knife fights, he overlooked that if you strike at the king, you better kill the king. Sullivan thought his friends in the Nixon administration would back him against Hoover, but in the end Sullivan was expendable. Hoover locked him out of his office and forced him to retire. Bill Sullivan was heartbroken.

As their conversation continued, Nixon asked Dean how bad it would hurt the country to have the FBI so terribly damaged. Nixon overlooked that he had already damaged the FBI back in June 1972, when he generated and implemented the concept of having the CIA carry a false tale to the FBI on the Mexican money chain. Dean said that he thought it would be damaging to the FBI, but maybe it was time to shake the FBI and rebuild it, adding that he was not sure the FBI was everything it was cracked up to be. Dean did not have the slightest knowledge of the position of the FBI as an institution in our society. The president then replied, "If we can get [District of Columbia police chief] Jerry Wilson in there— What is your feeling at the moment about Gray? Can he hang in there? Should he?"

Dean did not respond. Later in the same conversation, Nixon answered his own question, saying that in his opinion Gray should not be head of the FBI. "After going through the hell of the hearings," Nixon said, "he will not be a good director as far as we are concerned." Translated from Nixonese, this meant that because I would not do or condone his dirty work, I was of no value to him. If Nixon ever thought that I would, he really did not know me. This was his error.

"I think that is true," responded Dean. "I think he will be a very suspect director. Not that I don't think Pat won't do what we want—I do look at him a bit differently than Dick in that regard. Like he is still keeping in close touch with me. He is calling me. He has given me his hot line. We talk at night—how do you want me to handle this, etc. So he still stays in touch and is involved, but he can't do it because he is going to be under such surveillance by his own people—every move he is making—that it would be a difficult thing for Pat. Not that Pat wouldn't want to play ball, but he may not be able to."

I never had and I never would "play ball," to use Dean's characterization. In fact, at the inception of the Watergate investigation, CREEP deputy director Bob Mardian was furious because of the intensity of our investigation and ordered Dean to tell me to slow it down. Dean did not comply with Mardian's wishes. He didn't dare to.

Yes, I did cooperate with Dean after both he and Ehrlichman told me that he was conducting an investigation for the president. Further, on at least three occasions, in response to my direct question, Dean lied, telling me that he was reporting directly to the president. All the world now knows that this was a bald-faced lie, that he was using my reports to try to disrupt the real investigation. Dean did not have my "hot line" for the simple reason that I did not have a hot line. I had a regular telephone in my apartment and a telephone connected directly to the FBI switchboard. I rarely called Dean during this period. He called me with one request for information after another regarding matters for the president, as he put it to me. In his conversation to the president, Dean said that if my nomination to be the director of the FBI was confirmed I would not be a good director. Why? Because he assumed that my people in the FBI would be watching me too much to permit the president to use the FBI as Nixon planned to use it (along with the Internal Revenue Service and other government agencies), that is, to aid his friends and harass those on the White House enemies list. Dean thought very little indeed of the FBI if he thought its agents would maintain surveillance of their own director. He certainly did not know my relationship with the magnificent men and women of the FBI. This is just another example of his own base character.

The plotting to get rid of Gray continued between the president and his distinguished counsel. At the same time, they and their henchmen were openly passing the word to me that I was doing a great job in my testimony. It was not until I read these transcripts of the presidential tapes that I learned the true state of affairs that existed during those days.

March 13, 1973   *Oval Office, 12:42–2:00 p.m.*

PRESIDENT: Well, you see, John—yeah. I know the situation. Ervin gets up there and, you know, gassing around, he was huffing and puffing about his being a great Constitutional lawyer and all. I guess it just makes us wonder about our first decision, doesn't it, [unintelligible] about sending Gray up. Probably a mistake, but then, we didn't anticipate—

DEAN: Well—

PRESIDENT: Or you think not. Who knows?

DEAN: Who knows? That's right. Uh, if you didn't send him up, why didn't you send him up. Because he was—

PRESIDENT: Right. I know. That's what they—

DEAN: That's true.

PRESIDENT: That's what they— You send somebody else up to take them on, not a big clown. You know what I mean?

DEAN: Yeah.

Nixon and Dean are obviously so worried about my truthful testimony before the Senate Judiciary Committee and my refusal to play their game that they are worried about me testifying later before the Ervin Committee. But that was to come later. Meanwhile the partisan pounding of my confirmation hearings continued.

I got so little assistance or counterbattery fire in support of my position from the Republican members of the committee, it was hard to believe that I was the nominee of a Republican president. Roman Hruska, Marlow Cook, and Edward Gurney tried, but they were no match for the Democrats, who were well organized and prepared and had obviously sorted out and assigned specific areas of inquiry to each senator. For eight long hearing days, I faced the Democratic barrage led by Ted Kennedy. He was ably assisted by Phil Hart, Birch Bayh, Quentin Burdick, John Tunney, and Robert Byrd, who was then running for—and soon to win—the post of Senate majority leader. We went at it with hammer and tongs with no quarter asked or given. No single one of them could have stood up under the inquisition they poured on me. They were in control. They had the votes. And I had to sit there and take it from men whose conduct quickly quenched the respect I had so long held for the office of United States senator.

On March 21, in a meeting with Nixon and Haldeman, Dean once again complained about my making my own decisions on how to handle my own hearings.

March 21, 1973   *Oval Office, 10:12–11:55 a.m.*

DEAN: He has been totally unwilling all along to take any guidance, any instruction. We don't know what he is going to do. He is not going to talk about it. He won't review it and I don't think he does it to harm you in any way, sir.

PRESIDENT: No, he is quite stubborn and also he isn't very smart. You know—

DEAN: He is bullheaded.

PRESIDENT: He is smart in his own way but he's got that typical "Well, by God, this is right and I'm going to do it."

DEAN: That's why he thinks he's going to be confirmed. He is being his own man. He is being forthright and honest.

This little exchange grew out of the president's press conference where he stated that no further raw data were to be turned over to the Judiciary Committee and that the attorney general had issued instructions to me to "clam up" and fall back on traditional Justice Department policy. I was silenced. I could no longer respond using material contained in the FBI's Watergate investigative files. I had received these instructions from Dick Kleindienst on March 19 and I still had to testify for three more days before a group of Democratic senators who were furious.

A week earlier Dean had told Nixon that I would play ball as a future director of the FBI, play the White House game against the "enemies list." But by March 21 he had learned his lesson the hard way. Gray is his own man and will not lie for the White House or for Dean.

At this same March 21 meeting, John Dean told the president of the United States, in the following unequivocal language, that the coverup was killing him: "I think that there is no doubt about the seriousness of the problem we've got. We have a cancer within, close to the presidency, that is growing. It's growing daily." Dean then went on to describe it in exquisite detail for his illustrious leader. The president feigned innocent surprise, yet he knew full well the skullduggery that had been afoot since June 20, 1972, when he elevated the third-rate burglary to the status of national scandal. He should have had the power in his hands to stop it then and there.

The president of the United States was powerless, however, to take the correct action because of his sponsorship of "the White House horrors," as John Mitchell called them. He had to contain the third-rate burglary and the horrors if he wished to continue to sit in the Oval Office. He embarked upon a course from which there was no turning back. He tried to tough it out, but he was not tough enough to keep his weaklings in the White House in line. He, too, learned the hard way that he had built his presidency on shifting sands, not on the solid granite that so many of us had expected and prayed for.

In that same eventful meeting of March 21, Dean complained to the president that my truthful testimony, under oath, to the Judiciary Committee had broken his cover. Since when has the counsel to the president of the United States had to operate covertly? More often than we the people would care to believe.

March 21, 1973   *Oval Office, 10:12–11:55 a.m.*

DEAN: I have noticed of recent—since the publicity has increased on this thing again, with the Gray hearings, that everybody is now starting to watch after their behind. Everyone is . . . getting their own counsel. More counsel are getting involved. How do I protect my ass.

PRESIDENT: They are scared.

DEAN: That is bad. We were able to hold it for a long time. Another thing is that my facility to deal with the multitude of people I have been dealing with has been hampered because of Gray's blowing me up into the front page.

PRESIDENT: Your cover is broken?

DEAN: That's right.

I did not realize then that I was giving the president's counsel such terrible heartburn. We in the FBI did not know a cover-up was on or that Nixon and Dean were at the center of it. I just knew that I was taking a terrible beating from the Democratic senators and I knew that I was testifying under oath. Not for any man, not even the president of the United States, would I commit perjury.

It was not until the following day, March 22, that I realized that Dean was hurting, but even then I did not have any inkling that a cover-up existed. On that day, I testified before the Senate Judiciary Committee for the last time. Byrd took the floor and went on the attack. At the end of one long series relating to the evidence we had obtained from Howard Hunt's White House safe, he asked this question:

> SENATOR BYRD: Going back to Mr. Dean, when he indicated that he would have to check to see if Mr. Hunt had an office in the Old Executive Office Building, he lied to the agents, didn't he?
> MR. GRAY: I would say, looking back on it now and exhaustively analyzing the minute details of this investigation, I would have to conclude that that probably is correct, yes, sir.

This answer produced pandemonium at the White House and glaring headlines in the press. Dean was distraught, as I was to learn later that very same day.

I could answer so emphatically because I had already prepared for this question, which we expected from Roman Hruska, not Byrd. Hruska was the only senator who had taken me up on my offer to review the entire Watergate file in time to actually do so before I was ordered by Dick Kleindienst to rescind the offer. Special agents Angie Lano and John Clynick had taken the entire file—twenty-six sections, one subsection, the summary book, and the testimony analysis book— to Hruska's office at four in the afternoon on March 6. The senator spent until ten that night reading it in the presence of the two agents and came up with a couple of questions that he told Lano and Clynick he intended to ask me about at the hearings. One was why a portion of

Alfred Baldwin's FD-302 had been excised, and Clynick was able to tell him that those pages contained portions of conversations illegally recorded in Watergate phone taps and were thus not to be disclosed under an existing U.S. Court of Appeals ruling. Hruska accepted that answer, and then he asked Lano and Clynick essentially the same question that Byrd was to ask me two weeks later. Here's how a portion of the official FBI memo describes Hruska's second question.

TO : Mr. Baker   DATE: March 7, 1973
FROM : R.E. Gebhardt
SUBJECT : CONFIRMATION

. . .

2. The Senator questioned concerning the apparent conflict in statements by John Dean, Legal Counsel to the President, and Fred Fielding, Assistant to the Legal Counsel, regarding the existence of Hunt's office at the Executive Office Building (EOB) and Hunt's personal effects.

Dean was present during the interview of Charles W. Colson, Special Counsel to the President, on 6/22/72, when Colson said Hunt had an office in the EOB. During this interview Dean interjected that he was not sure Hunt had an office and that Dean would look into this matter and let the FBI know.

However, on 6/27/72, Fielding told us that on 6/20/72, he and Dean reviewed the contents of the two cardboard cartons containing Hunt's personal effects, which cartons were taken from Hunt's office at EOB.

This apparent contradiction led the Senator to believe that Dean had lied to us on 6/22/72, and the Senator questioned what the FBI did about this. He was advised that this information was furnished to the Assistant U. S. Attorney, Earl J. Silbert.

ACTION: For information.

How Byrd ended up with this arrow in his own quiver, I never asked. Hruska was a Republican, a Nixon partisan whose own daughter was John Ehrlichman's secretary. The chance of him having passed it along to an arch-Democrat like Byrd seems remote. As I noted earlier, I later came to believe people in the FBI and elsewhere were keeping Byrd well stocked with damaging questions, which this certainly was to Dean. This memo was circulated in the Bureau, but in reality the question could have come to Byrd from anywhere, including the U.S. attorney's office.

Robert Byrd held the floor the entire morning, did all of the questioning, and then summed up his inquisition by placing on the record his reasons for opposing my nomination. It was a typical public relations ploy for consumption by the constituents back home, and it was quite a laundry list. I can hardly say that I was thrilled to hear this former Ku Klux Klansman take me apart piece by piece without any real or fair chance to respond to each of his specific reasons. I differed then with each of his reasons and I do today. But there was little that I could have said that would have changed his opposition to my nomination. I had testified day after day and he was not moved. His mind had been cast in concrete.

After I completed my morning testimony, I returned to FBI headquarters to have lunch with my personal staff. Dean had telephoned before I got there. I knew it had to be about my response to Byrd's question, and I was not at all in a hurry to respond. I had more important matters at hand, namely to go over my morning testimony with my staff and prepare for the afternoon session. I could call Dean at the end of the day. He would be hollering, screaming about my testimony to Byrd, which was sure to be the headline in the evening papers.

Apparently the White House counsel was very nervous. He telephoned again less than fifteen minutes after I got to the office. This time I did speak to him, interrupting my lunch to do so. Dean was hysterical. I could actually hear him panting as he spoke to me, and I could picture him frothing at the mouth. He wanted me in the afternoon session to retract my answer to the last of Byrd's series of questions from the morning. He said my agents had it all wrong. He did not lie to them. He just answered a question other than the one they asked.

"John," I said, "the record is clear. I have just reviewed the record of what you said to the agents and there was no other way I could answer Byrd's questions without perjuring myself."

He pleaded with me to change my testimony, but I refused. He said the headline was sure to ruin him and I had to retract my testimony. I again refused. Upon my return to the luncheon table I briefed my staff on this telephone conversation with Dean and they were incensed to learn that Dean would resort to this tactic. Later, as Watergate unfolded and I learned in the newspapers of Dean's full role in the cover-up, I realized that perjury was not taken too seriously by him.

That realization should have come to me that very day. Dean and Dick Moore, a special assistant to the president, called Dave Kinley and Chuck Lichenstein, my own special assistant. Their plea was the same: Get Gray to change his testimony. He really doesn't understand. Dean did not lie. Both Dave and Chuck told them there was no chance to persuade me, nor would they try to do so because the facts were too clear. In the context of Byrd's questioning there was no other possible truthful answer.

Dean made one last attempt. Just before two o'clock, Dick Moore called me at Dean's request to renew the plea that I retract my testimony because it was not accurate. I had a great deal of respect for Dick, whom I had first met when he came to the Department of Justice as a special assistant to John Mitchell. I liked him personally. I did not resent his call on Dean's behalf. Dick pointed out how much the evening headlines would hurt the president as well as Dean. Again I said that I would not change or retract my testimony. I told Dick there was no other possible answer and I would not debate with the committee members the fine points of Dean's argument. Dean had told the agents he would have to check out whether or not Howard Hunt had an office in the White House. At the time they questioned him, he not only knew Hunt had an office in the Old Executive Office Building of the White House, but he had also caused Hunt's effects to be removed from that office to his own office where he and his assistant, Fred Fielding, sorted out the material. Our records clearly indicated that Dean had lied. When Byrd's questions set up the scenario and he put the ultimate question to me, I told him the truth.

My refusal to retract this testimony, I believe, was the motivating power that sent Dean scurrying to his lawyers and brought him to the brink. He was ready to make the best deal possible with the prosecutors to save his own hide—or at least as much of it as he could. Contrast this performance with his remarks to Nixon in their March 13 meeting where Dean maligns Hugh Sloan—the young CREEP treasurer with detailed knowledge of the cash disbursements to Liddy, Segretti, and others under investigation—using these words: "He's scared, he's weak. He has a compulsion to cleanse his soul by confession. We are giving him a lot of stroking."

The transcripts of the presidential tapes shed further light on this grim episode. That afternoon, while I was on the Hill finishing my last day of confirmation testimony, Nixon, Haldeman, Ehrlichman, and Dean sat down with John Mitchell, who had been called in to meet with them in the president's hideaway office in the Old Executive Office Building.

Mitchell was greeted warmly by these dear friends who would soon be plotting how to throw him to the wolves—the federal prosecutors— in order to take the heat off themselves. Mitchell, the "big enchilada," as Ehrlichman famously nicknamed him behind his back, was sitting down with men who held all the cards.

Ehrlichman started off by saying, "Eastland is going to postpone any further hearings on Gray for two weeks and allow things to cool off a little bit. He thinks Gray is dead on the floor." Translation: Even if the committee reported my nomination to the full Senate, I would still lose the confirmation vote.

March 22, 1973   *Executive Office Building, 1:57–3:43 p.m.*
PRESIDENT: He's probably right. Poor guy.
HALDEMAN: Gray's the symbol of wisdom today. He accused your
    counsel of being a liar.

DEAN: He may be dead 'cause I may shoot him. [Laughter]

PRESIDENT: How's that?

HALDEMAN: He said, yes, he thinks John Dean did lie to the FBI when he said he wasn't sure whether Howard Hunt had an office in the White House.

Later in the same meeting, the discussion turned to how to give the upcoming Ervin Committee as little information as possible.

PRESIDENT: Well, let's talk about Gray. . . . He's [laughs] a little bit on the stupid side, to be frank with you . . . maybe Kleindienst ought to counsel him and talk to him.

DEAN: He has and he listened to him. John Ehrlichman talked to Kleindienst last night and said that's where Gray was getting his guidance.

EHRLICHMAN: The whole trouble is that Dick gives him guidance which is very general. Something like this comes up and Gray overreacts—it's almost a spasm reaction. . . . It was the opposite of what Kleindienst told him.

PRESIDENT: I know it. He shouldn't have even needed guidance on that. The director of the FBI should have even known, second nature, that you never turn over raw files to a full committee.

EHRLICHMAN: I talked to Dick Saturday night and he just was beside himself because of that. "Hell, we covered this," he says, and he was really obsessed on it.

Indeed, we had been battling within the administration as to what documents from the FBI Watergate Investigation Report to turn over to the lawyers for the Ervin Committee, which was scheduled to hold its hearings in May. The instructions to me had been only to turn over summaries of our FD-302s, and if they later asked for more information we were allowed to turn over any specific FD-302 they desired. To me and my people in the FBI this was a senseless procedure, and I said so to Dick Kleindienst. The preparation of the summaries would have required a huge number of wasted man-hours, since the Ervin Committee counsels were certain to ask for the FD-302s. Moreover, the order created the impression that the FBI and the administration had something to hide. We in the FBI did not suspect the administration really had much to hide—this was long before the blanket came off the cover-up—and we were proud of our Watergate investigation and not the least bit afraid to let its details see the light of day.

Now, at their March 22 meeting, Nixon, Mitchell, Haldeman, Ehrlichman, and Dean saw the possibility that their blanket might not work if Dean were to be called before a congressional committee or a grand jury. So he was directed to write a report of his nonexistent investigation for the president. Dean agreed, and the conspirators discussed with him how to write it.

"I am talking about something we can spread as facts," said Dean. "You see, you could even write a novel with the facts."

The next day, after their "Dean Report" plot was hatched, Nixon called me. The call was indeed a surprise. I was having lunch in the director's conference room with Dave Kinley, Chuck Lichenstein, Mark Felt, and assistant directors Nick Callahan, Bill Soyars, Bucky Walters, and Bill Cleveland. Marge Neenan came in quietly. As was her custom, she handed me a plain 3 x 5 card on which were typed the words, "The White House is calling. The President wishes to talk to you." I took the card, asked those at lunch to excuse me, went into my private office at the end of the conference room, and picked up the phone.

"Mr. Gray," said the White House operator, "the president is calling." Normally, these are magic words to any American who hears them. I was no different. I had spoken on the phone with him only twice before.

Nixon came on the line. It was a buck-up call. He told me that he knew the terrible beating I was taking up there, that it was very unfair. There will be another day to get back at our enemies, he said, and there will always be a place for me in the Nixon administration. I thanked him, and I distinctly remember his parting words: "You will recall, Pat, that I told you to conduct a thorough and aggressive investigation."

I remember the words so clearly because I had the eerie feeling that I had heard them before, and there seemed to be a reason for Nixon to repeat them. Of course, I *had* heard them before. He had used them in our July 6 telephone call, when I warned him that Dick Walters and I thought that people on his staff were trying to mortally wound him.

I thought no more about the conversation and returned to the conference room to rejoin my colleagues at lunch. Now, using hindsight, I realize that the president—the president of the United States!—was engaging in the age-old bureaucratic game so prevalent in the nation's capital city: Cover Your Ass. He was trying to build up his alibi!

That day, March 23, the conspirators got another reason to start covering their posteriors, one to which Nixon had apparently been alerted when he called me. Judge John Sirica's sentences for the seven original burglary defendants—all of whom had pled guilty in January—were to be announced in open court. Knowing that "Maximum John" was planning to throw the book at him and faced with many years in federal prison, one of the burglars caved, just as we and the U.S. attorneys had planned and hoped for. In open court that Friday, Sirica read a letter that James McCord had sent to him and to the *Los Angeles Times* three days before. The letter claimed that he and the other defendants had been pressured to keep quiet, that perjury had occurred at their trial, and that as-yet-uncharged government officials were deeply involved. The investigation that had never stopped even after the seven guilty pleas now revved up to an even higher plane.

For the next week I turned back to the regular business of the FBI. Watergate leads from the ongoing grand jury were followed. Wounded Knee continued to "simmer and soak" with occasional shooting but no bloodshed. Dick Baker, Dave Kinley, and the rest of my confirmation task force kept up their work, but with time now for the other pressing demands of their grueling jobs. The workload of the FBI is truly endless. Every one of its thousands of ongoing investigations could use more manpower. Meanwhile our budget was under review by the House Appropriations Committee. The paperwork was staggering, the pressure to perform intense, the dedication of the special agents and other professionals in the Bureau unyielding.

Meanwhile, at the White House, fear was beginning to show. In a meeting on Tuesday, March 27, with Bob Haldeman, John Ehrlichman, and Ron Ziegler, Nixon tried to come up with a game plan to avoid the Senate inquiry into Watergate and a way for Ziegler to present the president's case to the press. After Ziegler left the room, Nixon launched into a hopeful monologue describing a scheme by which I would come in and plead with the president to withdraw my nomination. The three top men in the White House then discussed how to get rid of Dick Kleindienst and Secretary of State Bill Rogers, one of Nixon's oldest personal friends.

In the midst of all this devious plotting, Nixon said, "The only thing I would say on Kleindienst at the moment is tell him that we are going to have to break with Gray who is killing us. We need to know what Gray is going to do. Can we handle it that way?" Later the president said to Ehrlichman, "Of course you have to change Gray. You know that. Kleindienst, I think you have to ride with that awhile. I don't think you can just kick the attorney general out like that, you know."

Two days later, on Thursday, March 29, I went to the White House after work to meet with John Ehrlichman and Bill Timmons, who was in charge of congressional liaison for the administration. We met in Ehrlichman's office ostensibly to discuss how many favorable votes I had in the Senate Judiciary Committee. We also talked about who from the FBI should testify before the upcoming Ervin Committee hearings. As I was to learn later, this was part of the Nixon orchestration of the easing out of Pat Gray. At the time, though, I believed they were realistically interested in the two questions. I told them both that I was the best qualified person to testify for the FBI regarding the conduct of the Watergate investigation and that I was proud of it.

Of course, on that date I did not know what Ehrlichman knew of Dean's description of the "cancer" growing within the White House and close to the presidency. Now I believe Ehrlichman was really fishing to determine how much, if anything, the FBI did know of Dean's revelations. We knew nothing, sad as it is to relate that fact.

By the time of this meeting, Nixon and his co-conspirators had already made the decision to "deep-six" me, and they were beginning their manipulations to place me in the position of requesting that the president withdraw my nomination. My good friend Dick Kleindienst and the chairman of the Senate Judiciary Committee, the arch-segregationist Jim Eastland of Mississippi, also had their assigned roles to play in this little charade, the guillotining of a presidential nominee without him ever knowing the blade was passing through his neck. Not one of these national leaders had the guts or the common decency to look me in the eye and tell me that I was now a political liability. The doorknob in the sock was used when I was not looking by men who knew that I was an idealist, a patriot who loved his country.

During the next two weeks, I had quite a few conversations with Dick Kleindienst on the subject of my nomination. These conversations occurred, I believe, on direct orders of the president. Nixon did not have the moral courage to withdraw the name of his own nominee. Behind my back he was cutting me off, but he had to preserve the image of support for me. Why? I'll never know, except that it was vintage Nixon, going through a charade to preserve his press image that was at best negative.

In one of our conversations, Dick was in a very melancholy mood, which I now can understand. Then I did not. I didn't know of the White House horrors that had been going on for nine months since the burglary. Maybe Dick did, maybe he did not, but he knew more than I did from the inception. And one of the most important details was one he never chose to relate to me. On the very first weekend that the burglars had been caught, G. Gordon Liddy had come rushing up to Dick on the golf course at Burning Tree and tried to pass a message that Liddy claimed was from John Mitchell concerning the burglary. Dick shooed him away but never passed that incident along to me or anyone else in the FBI. It took us two weeks to positively identify Liddy as the mystery man seen with Howard Hunt prior to the burglary, a passage of time that, had we been able to shorten it, might have allowed us to crack the case much sooner, before Dean and the other White House conspirators had time to erect their defenses. In a wide conspiracy like this one, your best chance at cracking it is to get at the key individuals quickly, before they can coordinate their alibis, and here was a chance we never got.

In this conversation, Dick was really more than melancholy. He was openly grieving as he discussed the tragedy of Watergate. Dick said the situation was very grim, grim enough to cause strong men to contemplate suicide. The attorney general of the United States then went on to say that many fine people would be hurt deeply by Watergate. I could sense that he was under enormous tension as he spoke to me, that he was burdened by information he could not bring himself to relate.

Earlier that week, Bea had been to lunch at Tully Plantation with Marnie Kleindienst and Donna Walters, whose husband, Johnnie, was the commissioner of the Internal Revenue Service. Marnie mentioned what nice young people she thought John Dean and Jeb Stuart Magruder were, and the talk had then turned to what the three of them would be doing in the future. "If Dick's not in jail," Marnie had said. Both Bea and Donna knew enough not to follow that line of thought, but it crossed my mind now as I talked with my very unhappy friend.

Dick Kleindienst was extremely intelligent, hardworking, and very popular in the Department of Justice. He was a religious man and the last person I would expect to be discussing suicide. I liked Dick a lot and I respected him. So I tried to cheer him up: "Dick, I know you are a strong Christian and I certainly know that remark doesn't apply to you."

As the next week went by with no word on the resumption of my hearings, it began to become apparent to Dave Kinley, the others on my confirmation task force, and me that a positive Judiciary Committee vote on my nomination was becoming less likely. Every day, Assistant Director Dick Baker would canvass the senators and their staffs, seeking indications of which way a particular committee member was leaning. By the end of the week, our head count showed a tie vote, which would not be enough to report my nomination out of the committee to the full Senate. Dick and Dave saw little chance of changing any of the "nay" votes to a "yea," and eventually neither did I. Not wanting to drag out a doomed process that was eating manpower and getting in the way of finding a permanent director for the FBI that I had come to love, I knew what I had to do.

On April 5, I called the president and asked him to withdraw my nomination.

twenty-four

"Is there anything else you ought to tell me?"

On the evening of Thursday, April 5, Bea picked me up at 6:45 in the Department of Justice courtyard. We had already made plans to drive to Connecticut for the weekend and spend the night along the way with our dear friends Burt and Lois Klakring, who were then living in Annapolis. One of the most revered and highly decorated submarine skippers of World War II, Burt had earned three Navy Crosses, a Silver Star, and a Bronze Star for his courageous exploits in the Pacific. He had graduated from the Naval Academy fifteen years ahead of me and was later to have a Perry-class guided missile frigate named after him. Lois wanted us to pick up the beautiful Lady of the Lake statue that she had kept in her garden for many years and which she was now eager for Bea to take back to Connecticut for our own garden there.

As I took the wheel and we drove through the department gates and entered the light Washington traffic, I told Bea that I had called Nixon and sent a letter to the White House requesting that the president withdraw my nomination to be director of the FBI. Bea was, I believe, expecting this sooner or later. It did not shock her nor did any tears flow. Bea, along with most of the wives of the higher officials of the Justice Department, had attended the reopened ITT-Kleindienst hearings involving the Jack Anderson column and the Dita Beard memorandum.

Having observed at first hand the inquisitorial tactics of the senators, Bea had attended only the first day of my own confirmation hearings before that same committee.

I told her we would be going back to Connecticut permanently and to my law firm just as soon as a successor was selected. She was pleased and delighted. At the same time I knew that she was hurt because I was hurt.

After dinner that evening in Annapolis, the FBI operator tracked me down at the Klakrings to connect a call from Bob Haldeman. He just wanted to say how sorry he was for the way things had turned out. It was a cordial call. It was also among the last of that variety from anyone in the White House. Things were about to get adversarial between the president, his men, and me.

On Sunday, April 15, Bea and I drove back to Washington after another weekend in Connecticut. When we got to our apartment, the white light on my Bureau phone was flashing, indicating a message was waiting. The FBI operator said Mr. Ehrlichman had called but there was no message and no need to call him, he would call me.

An hour later I called the FBI operator again to be sure there was no additional message from Ehrlichman. There wasn't, so I went to bed. A half hour later, at 10:30, the FBI phone rang.

"Pat, this is John Ehrlichman."

"Yes, John. Good evening."

"Did I find you at home?"

"Yes, I'm at home."

"I wanted to tell you that John Dean has apparently decided to make a clean breast of things with the U.S. attorney. One of the questions that apparently they've been asking him is about the envelopes that he turned over to you."

"Yeah, well, he better deny that."

"Well, he's apparently pretty much on the record on that. I thought I'd better alert you to it."

"What the hell am I going to do about that?"

"I don't know. Is it still in being?"

"No."

"I see. I don't know."

"I was told that that was purely political and I destroyed it."

"I see, okay. Well, it probably was."

"Is there any way you can turn him off?"

"No. He's out of any orbit that we recognize around here. So I just wanted to alert you to it."

"What other things do you think he's going to talk about?"

"Well, he's putting the best face on his relations with Petersen that he can, because Petersen has sort of moved in on the prosecution."

"Was he doing things with Petersen, too?"

"Yes."

"I see."

"You might want to take a look at your hole card where he's concerned, because I don't know all the ins and outs of your relationship or, you know."

"The only thing I can do with this is deny it."

"Okay."

"You're not going to back him up, are you?"

"I can just say I don't know anything about it except what he told me. But he has spent all day today with the U.S. attorney. So that's about all I have to tell you for the moment. I'll keep you posted if I can."

"Okay, John. Thank you very much."

Twenty minutes later, Ehrlichman called again.

"Pat, John Ehrlichman again. I've been giving some thought to our conversation. I just don't think that there's any way to do anything but level on this if you're asked. There are just too many collateral facts. If it's the fact that that was just full of stuff irrelevant to any business of the Bureau, why, you know, that's reason enough."

"Well, that's what I was told. But I didn't look at it, John."

"Right. I just don't see how you could get yourself crossways in the testimony in this thing, for fear you'll get caught up in it. So I just encourage you to just state the facts."

"I'd state it a different way, that at no time did he indicate that this was from Hunt's material."

"Yeah. So you didn't know where it came from?"

"No."

"I see. Just that it was papers that he wanted to turn over to you?"

"Yes. That it was purely political things and had no bearing on the subject of Watergate."

"Uh-hmm, uh-hmm. I think if I were you I'd stick to that. I obviously can't tell you what to do, but I was a little troubled by our conversation and I didn't pick it up fast enough when you said that. So I just thought I better call you back."

"Yeah. I don't know all the other collaterals there are that are involved in this."

"Well, the thing is moving so fast, I'm frank to confess I don't, either. But I just hesitate to get crosswise on something of that kind. I'll talk to you later."

"Okay."

" 'Bye, Pat."

I was left aghast by these two phone calls, and I felt as if someone had hit me with a hammer. If Dean was talking to the prosecutors, that meant only one thing to me: Dean was in trouble. And if Dean, the counsel to the president, was in trouble it also meant a lot more people in the White House were in trouble. How high, I didn't know. It also meant that all those people at the White House and at CREEP had lied to my special agents who had interviewed and questioned them. We had been badly misled by the very people we had respected and trusted. We believed they were on our side and were as interested as we were in resolving the Watergate mysteries.

The shock to me was of horrendous proportions. Until that moment I had total faith and belief in the government of the United States and in the office of the presidency. I could not accept the fact that we in the FBI—and the American people—had been lied to so blithely by the president and the top officials of our government. The destruction of the two Hunt files, the lies of Dean and Ehrlichman about Dean conducting an investigation for the president and reporting directly to the president, and my resulting cooperation with Dean and the fulfillment of his requests in the name of the president were just too much for me to reconcile. The disillusionment and the hurt, as well as the feeling of being used and discarded by people who held high office in our government, and whom I had been trained over so many years to respect, were overwhelming.

I also knew that it was going to be rough on me personally as well as officially, now that I knew Dean either already had or soon would tell the prosecutors that I had destroyed the two Hunt files. I knew that I certainly would not be indicted for this, but it was a shameful performance on my part. Had I been like Hoover, I would have saved those two files and used them as leverage against Dean, Ehrlichman, and the president. Had I not been so loyal to the president and his office and believed so deeply in the honesty of high government officials, I believe I would have taken those papers directly to Henry Petersen when they were thrust upon me by Dean in Ehrlichman's office. But I was blinded by the same loyalty and trust that had carried me through a very successful career in the navy and into three of the highest offices in the Justice Department; I believed Dean and Ehrlichman as to the contents of the papers and was neither alerted nor suspicious.

Analyzed in hindsight, this unusual transmittal of files from the White House to the director of the FBI was a dead giveaway and I should have ordered my agents to interview Dean and all White House employees who were in the so-called inner circle, and interviewed them again and again until we cracked the case.

Of course, if I had done this I would have been removed from my office, but the president would have had an awful lot of explaining to do.

The next morning, Henry Petersen came to my office. He said that Dean told the prosecutors that he had turned over two of Hunt's files to me. I wasn't ready to give up yet. I denied it. Henry wasn't ready to accept my denial.

"Pat, John said that the files had nothing to do with Watergate. He said that Ehrlichman told him, 'John, you drive across the bridge every day. Throw them in the river.' Instead, John told us he gave them to you."

"That's bullshit, Henry," I said.

That night I slept little, if at all. I was extremely troubled by my denial to Henry, who had by now become a good friend. We admired and trusted each other, and I had broken that trust. I knew I had to undo the damage and tell him the truth. First thing the next morning, I called Henry and asked him to come to my office.

"Henry," I said when he arrived, "Dean did give me two files. I wasn't ready to admit that to you yesterday and I'm sorry."

"Do you have them here?" he asked.

"No. I burned them." I then went on to give Henry the full details.

"Do you know what was in them?" he asked.

"No, I didn't read them."

Henry paced back and forth in my office. "The assistant U.S. attorney will want you before the grand jury," he finally said.

"Fine, Henry," I said. "I'll go willingly and tell it to them straight."

For another week I thought about little else. I knew that I should call Senator Lowell Weicker. He was a warmhearted friend and had provided staunch and valiant support of me during my confirmation hearings. He had spoken out publicly endorsing my nomination and arguing eloquently on my behalf. I had a duty to tell him of these two files, yet the shame was so deep within me that it was hard to pick up the phone and call. Finally, I did, on Wednesday, April 25.

"I've got something to explain to you," I said. "And I believe it's going to take some time."

He came over at four that afternoon. We talked for well over an hour. I told him the manner in which I had received the files, that I had not read them, and then I told him that I had torn them in half and thrown them in the burn wastebaskets under my desk back on July 3 of the previous year. We discussed this subject at great length and he questioned me intensively on the entire matter. I persisted in my assertions to him that I had not read them and that I had thrown them in my burn wastebasket on July 3.

I hadn't immediately burned them, of course, and I hadn't done it here in my FBI office. I made these misstatements to him out of a sense of shame. Here was a man who had backed me to the hilt and I had let him down by not telling him about this earlier, when he had been named to the Ervin Committee. He had come to me then and asked what facts he should know as he prepared for his role on that committee, one that I was certain to be called before to testify, and I had withheld critical information from him. Now I was trying to present myself to him in the best possible light under extremely adverse circumstances, and I just could not bring myself to tell him that I had held on to the files for six months before burning them.

"One last question, Pat," he said as he got up to go after our long meeting. "Is there anything else you ought to tell me? If there is and you don't wish to, then just say so and I'll quietly walk away from supporting Pat Gray."

I told him that there was nothing else to tell him that I could think of at this time.

That afternoon only one or two press calls came into the FBI Press Office, and they were given a "no comment." It was the calm before the storm.

Weicker came back to see me in my office the next afternoon, Thursday, April 26. "Pat," he said, "I let the story out to a handpicked few journalists. Their stories ought to start appearing tonight, and tomorrow they'll be out for sure. You might be angry with me, but I believe this is in your best interest."

"I'm not angry with you, Lowell. It ought to be the other way around. You've got every right to have withdrawn all your support."

"Well, I haven't, Pat. Not by a long shot. I'm still in your corner."

I thanked him from the bottom of my heart, and he left.

That was the evening I described in the prologue to this book. Tom Moten and I were stopped on our way out by the GSA guard who told me that Henry Petersen had called and wanted me to call him back right away. It was to be my last night as acting director of the FBI.

After dinner that evening, and after devoting considerable thought to the situation, I concluded that I could no longer serve as acting director. I would have to resign, retain a lawyer, and defend myself. I wasn't alarmed at this point, but it was finally apparent to me that I had permitted myself to be sucked into a whirlpool and I was going to have to scramble to extricate myself.

The next day, Friday, April 27, I met with Dave Kinley and Chuck Lichenstein and told them I could no longer command the FBI. I then laid out the whole story for them. Both of them listened until I had finished. For a moment nobody said a word. Then Dave, direct and to the point as ever, had only one comment: "Mr. Gray, you are going to be indicted."

"Dave, I don't believe that to be the case at all," I calmly answered. "But I do believe that I have put myself in a position where I have to leave the FBI."

At the end of our hour-long meeting I called in Marge Neenan and dictated my letter of resignation. After that I called in Mark Felt, explained the situation to him, and told him I wanted to meet with him and all the assistant directors at 11:30, where I would explain it all to them and tell them that I was resigning.

At that meeting I told the assistant directors that Mark would brief them more fully, but I wanted to tell them myself that I would be submitting my resignation later that day and I wanted to say good-bye personally to each of them. I told them that I was keenly disappointed at having to leave the dedicated men and women of the finest investigative agency in the world. I could see that to a man they were very, very disappointed in me, and very angry. At the end of the meeting each assistant director came up to me, shook my hand, and said good-bye. It was a moving experience and toward the end tears came to my eyes. I had done a pretty good job of holding them back, but, as I shook hands with the last two or three, tears began to flow. It had to be obvious to each and every one of them that I was a deeply hurt and aggrieved human being, and that I was filled with shame because I had failed them. I was the captain and I had let my ship run onto the rocks. In my fifty-seven years it was the first time I had ever failed at anything, and it hurt more than I can describe.

I then gathered myself and had lunch with my staff, after which I called Larry Higby in Bob Haldeman's office and told him I was submitting my resignation and issuing a statement to the press. Larry wanted me to wait until Haldeman and the president got back from Mississippi later that day. I said no, I was submitting my resignation now and issuing the statement, which I then did. I left the office at 2:45 that afternoon.

My last day at the FBI was not hurried in any sense of the word. I had plenty of time to remove anything that I wanted to take with me. Just before departing, I handed my Bureau weapons, my credentials, and my shield to Mark Felt. I said good-bye to all of my staff and took my time leaving. I walked down the five flights of stairs with Tom Moten to the Justice Department courtyard, where Bea was waiting. Together we said good-bye to Tom, then we got in our car and started the long trip back home to Connecticut.

That trip would take a while. First Bea and I had to close up our apartment in Harbor Square. And I had to hire an attorney.

twenty-five

"Take it easy, Gray. We'll get our day."

ON MAY 10, TWO WEEKS AFTER I HAD RESIGNED FROM THE FBI, my new lawyer Steve Sachs and I appeared informally before Sam Dash, the chief counsel for the Ervin Committee; Fred Thompson, the minority counsel; and four of their staff investigators in the New Senate Office Building. It was the first confrontation with the men and women whom Steve Sachs would facetiously call our "tormentors."

In this preliminary evening interview that covered several topics, I told Dash and his staff about the early delay in the Watergate investigation caused by the contradictory series of claims and denials of CIA "interest." It was the first time anybody outside the White House, CIA, or FBI had heard of this. Surprisingly, not a word of it had leaked to the press.

It started innocently enough. Sam Dash was the first to question me, and he started right in on the much-publicized Hunt files, seeking details of how I got them. I told him that I had gone to Ehrlichman's office on June 28, 1972.

"What was the occasion?" he asked.

"That stemmed from a long chain of events," I answered. "But the thing that started the chain was a telephone call from Mr. Ehrlichman on the morning of the twenty-eighth. Prior to that time I had set up a meeting with Mr. Helms and General Walters for 2:30 that afternoon."

"What led up to the meeting with Helms?" he asked.

So I told him. Starting with the early-stage suspicion Mark Felt, Charlie Bates, and I had that this might be, among other possibilities, a CIA operation, I then laid out the whole story for the six investigators, all the way through to my call to Clark MacGregor and the return call from Nixon.

In the middle of the tale, which got interrupted and sidetracked many times by questions from the six, I said to Dash, "Something happened to cause General Walters to come and see me that quickly. I can't pin it down. I must have told John Dean of my call to Helms and Helms saying there is no CIA involvement."

Dash and his men moved on in their questioning to other Watergate details that seemed to interest them more than this episode, but the tale obviously leaked out of the supposedly confidential room to someone in the CIA. The timing was both accidental and exquisite. The House Special Subcommittee on Intelligence chaired by Representative Lucien Nedzi of Michigan was scheduled the next day to begin an "Inquiry into the Alleged Involvement of the Central Intelligence Agency in the Watergate and Ellsberg Matters." (The "Ellsberg matter" was the first clandestine operation of the White House "plumbers," seeking to discredit Daniel Ellsberg, the former National Security Council staffer who had leaked the Pentagon Papers to the *New York Times* in 1971.)

At this point the Nedzi Committee knew nothing about the CIA interference by Helms and Walters. All they wanted to look into was the equipment and aliases the Agency had provided to its former employee E. Howard Hunt, details that the CIA was happy to provide. They had a good paper trail for that minor problem. What the CIA didn't want to talk about was what I had told Dash, that the two top men in the Agency had been active in trying to slow down the FBI investigation into Watergate. And what they *really* did not want to reveal was the part that neither of them had told me or anyone else: that they had done so on White House orders.

The Nedzi inquiry ran its course tamely on May 11, meeting in executive session and finishing that same day without any revelations embarrassing to the Agency. But the CIA had by now been alerted to my revelations to Dash and his team. The Agency was about to be exposed as complicit in the Watergate cover-up and needed to do something fast. As luck would have it, the CIA-friendly Senate Armed Services Committee was scheduled to take closed-door testimony from the Agency on Monday, May 14. Here was a potential platform to spin the story their way before it got out of hand.

The CIA chose the Senate hearings to launch a defensive preemptive strike against me and the FBI, but the Agency had a small problem: Dick Walters was in China. Twenty hours later he was back, and a day after that he was before the Senate committee, armed with a series of "for the files" memos that he claimed to have written almost a year earlier, in June and July, when he and I had our series of meetings and phone calls over the Mexican money chain. I had never seen these memos. They detailed Dick's version of what he had never told me—that he came straight to my office from the White House where he and Helms had been given their marching orders to get Gray and the FBI to back off.

Stepping very carefully around the actual truth of what took place, Walters revealed his White House meetings and claimed to the committee that he had resisted John Dean's attempts to "compromise" the Agency. It was a bombshell. Though the testimony had been behind closed doors, Senators Strom Thurmond and Stuart Symington couldn't arrange a press conference fast enough: they called one for the next day and revealed much of Walters's secret testimony. When the story hit the papers on Wednesday, it was the first I had heard anything about Walters and Helms meeting with the White House before coming to me. I was incensed.

Gray's outraged notes on his copy of the *Washington Post*. May 16, 1973.

Just as incensed, apparently, was Lucien Nedzi. Just four days prior, in his own hearings on the same topic with all the same witnesses (except Walters, who hadn't yet been called back from China), none of this had been mentioned. At the end of that day Nedzi had said, "As there are no further questions, I want to thank all of you gentlemen for what I consider to be completely candid testimony and straightforward. Until further call of the Chair, the subcommittee stands adjourned."

It didn't stay adjourned very long. By 11:00 a.m. on Wednesday, a clearly annoyed Nedzi had the CIA brass back and on the defensive. James Schlesinger was now the director, having taken over after Nixon fired Dick Helms in January and packed him off to Iran as ambassador. Schlesinger, Walters, and William Colby, who had already been named to succeed Schlesinger as director, all bobbed, weaved, and skirted the truth. Walters actually lied.

> MR. NEDZI: General Walters, did you inform Mr. Gray of the sub-
> stance of all your conversations with Haldeman, Ehrlichman,
> and Dean?
> GENERAL WALTERS: I had only one conversation with Haldeman
> and Ehrlichman. I did inform him of the substance of that. Of
> the conversations with Dean, I told him of the general thrust.

Dick Walters never mentioned to me that he had even been to the White House, and he certainly never said that his false tale of CIA interest in the Mexican money chain was one that he was passing on from Haldeman and Ehrlichman. Not only had he failed to "inform me" of the substance and "general thrust," he hadn't informed me of the existence of the meetings.

"Take it easy, Gray," Steve Sachs said when I showed him the numerous falsehoods and discrepancies I had marked all over the issue of the *Washington Post* that had banner-headlined the story. I wanted to call a press conference. Steve knew that was a bad idea. "We'll deal with it when they call us," he soothed. "And don't worry, they will call us. We'll get our day."

Steve was right. This was going to be a long war and this was just the first skirmish. No need to waste firepower when the major battles still lay over the horizon. Victory lay not in newspaper headlines and press publicity but in full exoneration by the legal system that was trying to indict me along with the real criminals. This was a test, nothing more.

Steve and I appeared before the subcommittee ten days later, armed with documents, notes, and a lengthy written response to Dick Walters's "for the files" memos. Because this committee had met in executive session, I wasn't aware of Dick's testimony, or I'd have been more direct in my own. I liked Dick Walters, and I was still trying to reconcile what I knew he and I had said to each other with what I was now reading in these later-drafted self-exculpatory memos and in the news accounts of his testimony. All I could do was tell Nedzi and his fellow committee members that my recollection differed from that of General Walters.

The Nedzi hearings lasted for twelve weeks and ended with more questions than answers. "In his testimony, Mr. Gray raises two points which continue to trouble this subcommittee," the committee's final report said. I had provided Nedzi with copies of the notes I had written to myself the day I saw the *Washington Post* article that had so outraged me, and the committee's final report issued in October quoted the notes verbatim.

> With both Helms and Walters present, they acquiesce in this move to send Walters over to me a message they both know to be false. At least Helms does, because I talked to him on 6-22-72 and he said no CIA involvement.
>
> Why, upon his return to the CIA and learning that investigation of Mexican financial affairs (and what affair was it) would not compromise any CIA clandestine assets, did he not inform me? He had just told me that it would, and he did not tell me that senior White House people told him to tell me. Now he finds out that investigation will not compromise (on his return to the Agency that very afternoon) and he does not tell me???

"It remains a good question," continued the report, "why General Walters failed to assure Mr. Gray of the lack of CIA conflict in the Mexican matter immediately after it was so determined on June 23, 1972."

As to Walters's testimony that he failed to so assure me because he assumed John Dean would convey to me "that there was absolutely no CIA problem," the committee report came awfully close to calling it a lie. "To be charitable," the report said, "the best that can be said for that explanation is that it is rather strange. General Walters, by his own admission, was concerned that Dean was attempting to blame CIA for Watergate, and in that frame of reference, one could hardly expect Dean to be the vehicle for informing Mr. Gray that there was no CIA-Mexican connection."

The other point that "troubled" the Nedzi Committee was Walters's

testimony that he had informed me that he had been directed by senior White House people to tell me that CIA assets might be involved
in the Mexican money matter. "Mr. Gray was vehement in his statement that Walters did not mention 'senior people at the White House.'
The important aspect of that testimony is that Mr. Gray said he
thought Walters was speaking for the CIA."

This and a similar behind-closed-doors appearance before the
McClellan Subcommittee of the Senate Appropriations Committee
that same week, where I again told my version of the CIA interference,
were the first legal battles for Steve and me. We fought the CIA and
its congressional allies to a draw. Both had the power and resources
of the federal government behind them. All we had was each other,
my detailed records, and the truth, a template for our defense in every
Watergate legal battle we would fight together for the next five years.

At first I did not realize that I had my records. After I resigned, they
had been packed into boxes by my two secretaries, Marge Neenan and
Erma Metcalf, and had been picked up at FBI headquarters by two of
my sons. The records were detailed, voluminous, and accurate; they
gave Steve Sachs the ammunition he needed to fight off the zealots.

Neither my adversaries nor I knew at that early date what a magnificent advocate I had in Stephen H. Sachs—and later, after his election
in 1978 as attorney general of Maryland, his younger law partner Alan
I. Baron. Each man was, and is, a lawyer of outstanding professional
competence. Each was, and is, far more than an advocate of incompa-
rable persuasion. As each worked with me, a strong bond of mutual
trust and confidence arose and a warm friendship and affection grew
between us and among our families. More important, each of these
lawyers became convinced of my innocence as they dug and probed
for the evidence. That led to a deep, personal, and vibrant conviction
to see justice prevail in my defense. The humanity, compassion, and
intellect of these men infused into their human relationships with me
a rare quality of life, drawing renewed strength from a relationship
that originated purely by chance. Henry Petersen had recommended
Steve as an outstanding trial lawyer and warm human being and had

urged me to retain him. Henry and I were friends, but this one recommendation was an act above and beyond. It was a miracle.

From the outset Steve and I worked well together, even when he wasn't yet sure about his new client. And he wasn't at all hesitant to be hard on me when he had to be. "Gray," he would say, "today I am going to push your head around plenty while you relive and remember these dreadful events." Day by day the process went on. Notes, documents, letters, and records were examined and studied. Steve cross-examined me with the strength of a battering ram, leaned on me as heavily as a redwood tree, and comforted me in my worst hours. We delivered nearly 1,000 separate documents from my files to all kinds of federal prosecutors and congressional committee staffers. Steve was able to speak their language and deal with them in a logical and reasonable manner. I was not. I despised them.

Those first few weeks after my resignation were a terrible time. In one of my early meetings with Steve at his office in Baltimore, I told him of the raging suicidal torment I was battling, of the numerous times I had planned to leap from the roof of our Harbor Square apartment building. While I was telling him this, we were working together in a fourteenth-floor office in the Mercantile Bank & Trust Building in Baltimore. Steve had to leave me alone there in order to take care of another pressing matter. He was very concerned about my state of mind. As gently as he could, he told me to stay put.

"Gray," he said, "I'm leaving you here alone for a few minutes and I just want you to know that these heavy windows are sealed and unbreakable. There is no way you can leap from this building."

I told Steve that I had myself under control and would keep working until he returned. He will know when he reads this that he read my thoughts accurately on that day early in May 1973.

I handled this suicide nonsense myself. I had to do it alone, and I had to do it my way. Unfortunately, my acute depression could not be kept from my beloved wife, Bea, and she had to watch her stubborn husband battle this monster. Bea did all that any wife could do to help her husband fight my terrible malaise. My love for her, our sons, and our grandchildren kept me going.

I broke the horrible obsession without the aid of any formal counseling or psychiatric intervention. Hard common sense did it. I gradually came to realize that suicide would not restore my honor or my reputation. If I took my own life, there would be no one here on this planet to defend me. I had to defend myself. If not, I would be a convenient dead target for Nixon and his rats to dump on. I had to stay alive to fight this battle to protect my wife, my four sons, their wives, and my grandchildren. With the help of Steve Sachs and Alan Baron, that's exactly what I did.

The battle became very public in the summer of 1973, with the hearings of the Senate Select Committee on Presidential Campaign Activities, chaired by Senator Sam Ervin. On Friday, August 3, I appeared before the committee with Steve at my side and a long, carefully prepared statement in front of me. For almost two hours, while the nation watched on live television, I discussed the CIA obstruction and my burning of the Hunt papers. By the time I finished reading, it was too late for any questions.

On Monday, August 6, again on live television, I testified all day. Each of the seven senators on the committee grilled me, as did Rufus Edmisten, the deputy chief counsel, and Fred Thompson, the Republican minority counsel.

"In the service of my country," I told Edmisten, "I withstood hours and hours of depth charging, shelling, bombing, but I never expected to run into a Watergate in the service of a president of the United States. And I ran into a buzz saw, obviously."

The senators' questions were probing and detailed, as were my answers. It was the first time the country had heard many of the specifics of the FBI's investigation. Republican Edward Gurney of Florida finished his interrogation this way:

> SENATOR GURNEY: As I recall your testimony before the Judiciary Committee in your confirmation hearings, you testified that this was one of the most extensive investigations in the history of the FBI. Is that not correct?

Gray at the Ervin Committee hearings. Behind him, at left, is his attorney Stephen H. Sachs. August 3, 1973.

MR. GRAY: That is correct, sir.

SENATOR GURNEY: All right. Now, one final question. If that were so, and I certainly believe you, and I certainly know that the files of the FBI will show the extent of the investigation, why do you not think this led beyond Liddy and Hunt?

MR. GRAY: I do not know. I have asked myself that many times and I wondered, "Were the agents awed by the people that they were interviewing?" But when I asked the question—Did the agents ask tough questions?—I was assured that they had indeed asked tough questions. And one must conclude at this point in time that what was being told to the agents was not correct, was not accurate.

SENATOR GURNEY: Well, to put it another way, perhaps the reason why it did not lead beyond those two is because there was a massive cover-up involved and people were not talking and they were not telling the truth.

MR. GRAY: That certainly can be concluded at this point in time, Senator Gurney.

Sam Ervin was more philosophical in his conclusion:

> SENATOR ERVIN: Well, in view of your testimony here, just for your consolation, the 15th chapter of Psalms talks about the people, the kinds of people that are going to dwell in the holy hill of the Lord and it says among those that he who sweareth to his own hurt changes not, and I would say that you might lay claim to that lesson because of the testimony you have given before the committee here.
>
> MR. GRAY: Thank you, Mr. Chairman. May I just make an observation, sir? On the very first Sunday that I went to Mass after being appointed acting director of the Federal Bureau of Investigation, the lesson of the Mass, and the little leaflet that was passed out at Mass, was the story of Job, and for some strange reason I put that in my briefcase and I have kept it there ever since. [Laughter]
>
> SENATOR ERVIN: Senator [Howard] Baker . . .
>
> SENATOR BAKER: Mr. Chairman, I have found that I can contend with one sermon at a time, but to have both the chairman and the witness is almost more than I can bear. But I am sure my soul is salved and improved by the example.

At the end of my two days before the committee and the television cameras, minority counsel Fred Thompson turned to a serious question: the future of the FBI. He wanted to know my opinion on whether there was "a structural defect" in the current status of the FBI as a bureau within the Justice Department, thus requiring it to report directly to the president. I told him that I thought the FBI would be better off as an independent agency, reporting through oversight committees to Congress, not the White House.

"Under your recommendation, then," he said, "I assume the director would not be looking to the president as his direct employer, so to speak, as the situation exists now."

"That is correct," I told him. Senator Ervin then thanked me for cooperating fully with his committee. I was excused.

"The small white flag currently flying at 1425 K Street."

THE HEADQUARTERS OF THE WATERGATE SPECIAL PROSECUTION Force (WSPF) was located on the upper floors of 1425 K Street NW, in Washington, D.C. I was to go there more than a few times.

Fort Knox was no more heavily guarded than these offices. Never did I believe it was necessary. Instead, I believed the heavy guard, the television surveillance system, as well as the elaborate identification and check-in and check-out procedure were all part of the psychology of this office. It was designed to intimidate, to try to shake the confidence of those who were summoned to this prosecutorial palace. All it did for me was to increase my confidence, my morale, and my fighting spirit.

It did not take long before I was a target of the Watergate grand jury and the Watergate Special Prosecution Force for the destruction of the two Howard Hunt files. On national television on August 3, 1973, I had admitted the destruction before the Ervin Committee, and the whole world had heard my explanation. The facts, as I had told Dave Kinley in my FBI office the day I resigned, seemed to me to be straightforward. More troublesome, I thought, was the other prong of the WSPF investigation—the allegation that I had lied to the Senate Judiciary Committee and to the Watergate grand jury when I testified to each that I was not aware of the Nixon-Kissinger-Mitchell-Hoover

wiretaps of 1969. This had been Ted Kennedy's favorite topic in questioning me under oath during my confirmation hearings and I could
sense at the time that he and his staff were certain that I was lying. I
was not. Perjury is a felony, a serious criminal offense carrying a
penalty of five years in prison, a $10,000 fine, or both. Conviction of a
felony would also result in my disbarment as a practicing attorney and
the loss of my livelihood. The stakes were high in this modern-day version of the Roman Colosseum.

One of the most difficult problems in law, like anywhere else, is
proving a negative. How do you demonstrate that you really did not do
something? Or, even more difficult, that you really did not know
something? That's why the American system of justice assumes innocence before a court of law, precisely because it is so hard to prove. But
the law provides little such protection from indictment by a grand
jury, especially one run by a predisposed prosecutor. There, the prosecutor holds all the cards and the potential defendant almost none. In
the end the grand jury's decision to indict or not usually comes down
more to credibility and persuasiveness than it does to the facts, which
are often as elusive as memory itself.

Of the two battles I waged with the Watergate Special Prosecution
Force, the fight to avoid a perjury indictment over whether anyone in
the FBI had informed me of the Kissinger wiretaps was the most difficult and time-consuming. Steve and I called it the "Wiretap" investigation as a shorthand title to distinguish it from the far easier to handle
"Two Files" investigation of the Hunt files destruction. What made
"Wiretap" so difficult was that I knew absolutely nothing about the
Kissinger wiretaps except what I had read in press accounts, and press
accounts of anything associated with the FBI were so often wrong that
I gave them little, if any, credence. Thus, when *Time* magazine broke
the story just as my confirmation hearings were about to get under way
and two days before the Wounded Knee occupation began, I didn't
even look into it. I let Jack Hushen, the spokesman for the Justice Department, deal with it, which he did by issuing a press release in which
Dick Kleindienst, who also had never heard of the wiretaps, vehe-

mently denied the allegations. That was good enough for me. As I told the prosecutors and the grand jury, I had plenty of other things to think about.

Because I had had nothing to do with the Kissinger taps, and because I had been kept in the dark by people like Mark Felt who did know all about them, I had no documents to support my side of the argument. I had no notes of meetings about them. I had nothing on them at all. All I had was my word and Steve's skilled and tenacious dealings with the prosecutors.

Before I became acting director of the FBI, special agents illegally engaged in surreptitious entries, wiretaps, and mail openings. But in the 1960s, as J. Edgar Hoover grew fearful of his image as his career wound down, he sought to take the FBI out of the lawbreaking business. Hoover thought he had stopped this practice through written orders in 1966 and 1967. I thought he had, too. My colleagues in the FBI led me to believe that we had lost the capability to do the surreptitious entry, the "black bag job." Lies were fed to me orally and in writing while these very practices were going on behind my back, and had been going on since 1968. They continued to go on during my year in office despite my issuance of a written order prohibiting special agents of the FBI from gathering information or evidence by illegal means. In my order I merely quoted language that was already contained in the *FBI Handbook.* These activities also continued to go on long after I left the FBI, even though my successors William Ruckelshaus and Clarence Kelley also thought the practice had been stopped. Kelley was reduced to such a state of frustration that it drove him to confess that though he knew he could enforce an order as chief of police in Kansas City, he could not say the same as director of the FBI.

As Mark Felt said to me on the telephone during the Wounded Knee operation, and within the hearing of my special assistant Chuck Lichenstein, "They would not tell you the truth even if they were doing it." I had ordered Mark to run down an allegation that our special agents at Wounded Knee were tapping a telephone line used by the Indians. This had been reported to me angrily by Henry Petersen. Felt, the Hoover hard-liner, was again all too ready to condemn the special agent in the field, never the Washington claque in their high offices at headquarters.

The essence of the potential wiretap charge against me was the prosecutors' firmly held belief that I had lied under oath when questioned at my confirmation hearings by Senator Kennedy on my knowledge of these taps. Like Dick Kleindienst, I had no knowledge of these ultra-secret taps, which had been placed with the approval of Hoover in 1969 and removed long before I became acting director, but my tormentors thought that I had seen FBI records of them and would not admit it.

The day after Kennedy asked his questions at my hearings, I decided to look at the most basic records the FBI had. I called Assistant Director Ed Miller to ask where such records were kept. I did not know. I was looking for the actual wiretap records and the index if there was one. I knew the paperwork, the memoranda system of applying for permission to do a tap, receiving permission to do it, and terminating a tap, but I did not know the actual point of initiation and control of taps within the FBI and the type of basic records that were kept by the FBI other than the memoranda and the permissions received from the attorney general.

On that Friday morning Ed Miller and Section Chief Tom Smith brought over to my office a heavy filing cabinet wrapped in brown paper. They rolled it in on a mover's hand truck. They then demonstrated and explained the entire system of record keeping and mechanics to me while I made notes.

After they left, I looked through the entire set of records for the Washington and New York field offices and found no record of a single tap on a Washington newsman or White House official, and later that afternoon I called Ed Miller and had him come get the filing cabinet.

In answering Kennedy, I had relied on the fact that I knew the FBI paperwork procedure for getting permission from the attorney general for national security and Title III wiretaps and that no such request had crossed my desk while I served as acting director. Further, I was

Gray's notes of his briefing on the FBI's wiretap filing system. March 2, 1973.

absolutely convinced that Hoover would not have permitted such taps to be placed. Frankly, I believed that I was also on very safe ground in relying on the denials of the White House and the attorney general. Now I had looked at the records themselves and nothing was there. If there had been, I would have gone back to the hearings and corrected the record, the way I did many times on other questions where my knowledge had been less than complete when the senators had asked them in the hearing room. In this instance I let my testimony stand, and the prosecutors were trying to indict me for it. It was a high-stakes contest.

How high the stakes were I thought I knew, but I really didn't know until nearly three years later, when I received a long letter from Mark Felt. Mark had retired in 1973, a month after I resigned, when he finally learned that he would never become director. He was now writing his memoirs and had forgotten Barbara Herwig and Mack Armstrong's names, which he wanted to put in the book. After asking about them in the letter, he went on to say that the Watergate special prosecutor had threatened to indict him for perjury because he would not testify against me.

> The Special Prosecutor even had the Bureau investigate me for the leaking of documents to John Crewdson (of the NEW YORK TIMES). The reason for this is that one of the documents someone handed Crewdson was a copy of the February 26th memorandum that Tom Smith wrote regarding the 17 Kissinger taps and the Radford tap. I could not even remember this memorandum let alone personally handing it to you as the Special Prosecutor wanted me to testify. . . .
>   This is an interesting point. Very few people had access to that memo. Whoever gave it to Crewdson was shooting at you. I can't imagine Smith or Miller leaking it. I know I didn't. Could it have been someone on your staff? I know you will think this farfetched, but there are not many possible explanations.

As Mark stated earlier in that same letter, he didn't know my personal staff. We operated on a level of trust and mutual respect that he and his top-echelon FBI fellows could never fathom. As Mack and Barbara had said, "It's us against them, boss."

But Mark was right about Crewdson: someone had leaked the document to him. In the middle of January 1974 while the "Wiretap" investigation was in progress, Crewdson called Steve Sachs to say that he had heard I was to be named as a co-conspirator in the Watergate scandal. He wanted to interview me. Steve gave him our regular answer: "No."

"Suppose," Crewdson then said, "you were to receive in the mail in an unmarked envelope a copy of the FBI report on the White House wiretaps, would that change your mind?"

Steve's "no" was a little more harsh.

When Steve reported this conversation to me I was stunned. "That's blackmail," I said.

"No, that's bribery," said Steve. Such a man was Crewdson.

Felt had laid it on the line for the prosecutors; they did not believe him. He was, however, telling the truth. The first time that I saw this February 26, 1973, memorandum written by Thomas J. Smith of the FBI's Domestic Intelligence Division was when Francis Martin and Jay Horowitz, two of the lead WSPF prosecutors on this case, showed it to Steve and me during one of their interrogation sessions. And they didn't let us look at it very long. As I recall, it had "SECRET" stamped all over it. They treated it like the royal jewels of the Watergate Special Prosecution Force. We could not copy it or run away with it.

In the end, we didn't need it. We beat them with persistence, honesty, and what little documentation we had. It took time. In this boiling cauldron of intrigues and conflicting goals, the truth gets submerged and tumbled about; it's only when the heat lessens and the waters calm that the truth generally pops to the surface for all to see—if anyone is still looking.

At times I wondered if the WSPF prosecutors were interested in discovering the truth or if they preferred to prove things they presumed to be true. Here's an example. When Clark MacGregor testified before their grand jury, he claimed that my call to him on the morning of July 6, 1972, the one in which I asked him to pass a message to the president that Dick Walters and I were concerned about what some people in the White House might be doing in their boss's name, was made at two in the morning and that I sounded drunk. He further testified that he did not talk to Nixon about it. This was outright perjury, verified not only by my testimony and official call records, but by John Ehrlichman's contemporaneous notes of that same day, which show that Ehrlichman and Nixon discussed MacGregor taking my call, passing it along to the president, and that Nixon had as a result called me back forty-five minutes later.

On June 13, 1973, Ehrlichman testified as much to Representative Nedzi's Subcommittee on Intelligence.

MR. NEDZI: Did MacGregor talk to the President prior to the President making his call to Gray?

MR. EHRLICHMAN: Yes, sir.

MR. NEDZI: How do you know that?

MR. EHRLICHMAN: The President told me.

MR. NEDZI: Was the call to Gray motivated by the report of Mr. MacGregor to the President?

MR. EHRLICHMAN: I gather that it was.

MR. NEDZI: The President told you that?

MR. EHRLICHMAN: Yes, sir.

MR. NEDZI: What was the purpose of the call to Gray?

MR. EHRLICHMAN: He had, as I got it, asked Clark MacGregor to cause the President to call him so he could discuss with the President this question of an unlimited investigation.

MR. NEDZI: Whom did you get that from?

MR. EHRLICHMAN: The President.

Clark MacGregor committed an easily proved felony, yet he walked. He never had to face the same humiliation and torment that Dick Kleindienst and Bob Mardian, for example, dealt with. Dick, who had stepped brilliantly through the ethical minefield of Watergate without getting trapped by Nixon like his predecessor, John Mitchell—who went to federal prison for perjury and obstruction of justice—eventually pled guilty to the misdemeanor of refusing to answer congressional questions in the ITT case. The prosecutors hounded him until they finally found something, and it wasn't even Watergate related. He paid a $100 fine but was tarred forever. Bob Mardian had to go through the ordeal of being tried and convicted along with Mitchell, Haldeman, and Ehrlichman before finally prevailing on appeal and getting his conviction overturned.

Why did Clark MacGregor avoid the ax that he actually deserved while men who did not deserve it were vilified on the public pillories of formal investigation and its attendant reputation-killing press coverage? Because, I am convinced, the Watergate prosecutors had decided beforehand who was guilty, and they set out to get convictions. In my case, trying to get a conviction meant not publicizing that in this critical instance I had told the truth. Gray was big game, MacGregor was not. So what if MacGregor lied under oath in order to shield his boss, Nixon? Better to let that crime go if prosecuting it would show Gray to be an honest man and not the perjurer they so desperately wanted to indict.

In the summer of 1974, around the time Richard Nixon resigned the presidency, I got a call from Chuck Lichenstein. He had come to my FBI personal staff late in the game as a highly educated political scientist and historian, a realist not given to hasty judgments. He and I had first met in the Nixon campaign of 1960 and we had served to-gether in the Department of Health, Education and Welfare in 1969. I respected and admired him as a human being and a thinker. He was my friend, but he was not trusted by the Hoover hard-liners. It was his mind they feared, but their mistrust was put to me on the basis that he had not been cleared by a background investigation.

During the course of the "Wiretap" investigation, Chuck had been called in for interrogation by Jay Horowitz and Frank Martin. Now, in this telephone call, Chuck told me that he had been interviewed five months earlier "by your buddies on K Street." He said they had told him to be ready to come back in three days, but he had heard nothing more from them. Chuck reported that Horowitz and Martin had been in a much more philosophic, let's-just-talk-things-over mood. Chuck went on to say that he sort of respected Jay Horowitz, who had told him that he was utterly perplexed by Pat Gray, saying he didn't know if he had ever met a completely honest man. Chuck replied that Pat Gray took a bit of getting used to and hoped that Horowitz, too, got used to him. "Pat Gray is a man without hidden motives," he said to Horowitz.

As I said, Chuck Lichenstein was my friend. Not only had he known me a long time, but he knew who I was.

Finally, on September 19, 1975, I got a letter from Steve saying, "Enclosed is a copy of the small white flag currently flying at 1425 K Street."

This was the white flag:

Dear Mr. Sachs:

As you are aware, this office has sought to determine whether or not your client, Mr. Gray, violated any Federal criminal laws by virtue of his admitted destruction of certain documents from the White House safe of E. Howard Hunt. Upon the review of the applicable case law relating to the obstruction of justice statute (18 U.S.C. § 1503) and the statute dealing with destruction of records (18 U.S.C. § 2071), as well as other criminal statutes, the Special Prosecutor has decided not to bring any criminal charges based upon Mr. Gray's destruction of the Hunt files. This decision is based upon the Special Prosecutor's conclusions that there is substantial doubt concerning whether or not these statutes, as interpreted by case law, would apply to the facts developed concerning Mr. Gray's conduct.

Sincerely,
Francis J. Martin
Assistant Special Prosecutor

This was not a testimonial. It was, however, in the clear language of the federal prosecutors an admission that they didn't "have it." If they thought they had, and if they thought they could have beaten us at trial, they would have leapt to have the grand jury rubber-stamp their indictment.

I was jubilant, yes, but angry, too. Angry that it had taken so long for a decision to be reached. As early as February 1974, one of the WSPF attorneys had casually inquired of Steve Sachs whether I would plead guilty to a misdemeanor charge for the destruction of these two Hunt files. Steve answered emphatically, "No!"

Despite what the darlings of the media had to write and print about this episode, the trash in these two Hunt files did not constitute Watergate evidence. I knew it at the time and the prosecutors had now certified it. Even so, the false tale has continued in the media to this day. Three years later, *Time* magazine, inaccurate as usual, was delighted to report that I had returned to my law practice in Connecticut after withdrawing my name from nomination as Hoover's successor "because of growing opposition in the Senate. The chief reason: Gray had destroyed evidence in the Watergate scandal." These words were false, and the editors of *Time* had to know they were false when written.

The second white flag flew from 1425 K Street three weeks later. This time Frank Martin's letter to Steve ended this way: "The Special Prosecutor has reviewed the evidence developed during the course of this investigation and has determined that this evidence is not sufficient to prove beyond a reasonable doubt that Mr. Gray in fact committed perjury. Accordingly, the Special Prosecutor has instructed that you be informed that this investigation concerning Mr. Gray has been closed."

One final note on the "Wiretap" episode. The Kissinger wiretaps, and specifically the press leaks over them, were what finally drove Mark Felt from the FBI. Though he had been allowed to retire effective June 1973, Mark was actually fired by my successor, Bill Ruckelshaus. Though I never learned the details, Bill said he had fired Mark because he had caught him leaking information about those wiretaps to the *New York Times.*

twenty-seven

"And this is how your government thanks you."

I first learned that the Department of Justice was investigating FBI domestic surreptitious entries when Steve Sachs telephoned me on June 24, 1976. We hadn't talked in months and we spent a few minutes catching up. I was glad to hear from him, as always.

"The reason I called, Pat," he said, "is that Sandy Smith called me. He says it appears that domestic black bag jobs were carried out while you were acting director and he wants to talk to you about it."

"Tell him to forget it, Steve," I answered. "It didn't happen, and I wouldn't even talk to that bastard about the weather."

Smith didn't stop there. He tried me at my office, and then he called Bea at home. She said I wasn't there. That evening when I got home from the office I told her that it was about illegal domestic entries. We both breathed a sigh of relief and shrugged it off. Here, finally, was an inquisition that couldn't possibly touch us.

We continued in this blissful state for a few more days. I was certain that I could not in any way be involved. Unfortunately, that state of mind was changed radically a couple of weeks later when the newspaper and magazine articles began to appear. They said that illegal bag jobs had been carried out during my tenure by special agents with the permission of their superiors in Washington.

Out of the blue it now appeared that Steve and I might actually have to go back to battle stations, once again with John Crewdson somehow involved. In the *New York Times* on July 9, 1976, he and Nicholas Horrock wrote:

> Although there is no evidence that Mr. Gray possessed knowledge of the burglaries committed in his year-long tenure as acting director of the bureau, some of those close to the investigation believe that the chain of evidence, including written authorizations for "bag jobs" as they are known within the bureau, will ultimately lead to the top of Mr. Gray's intelligence division and very close to the acting director himself.

Ten days later I sent Steve the first of a long series of letters as I reviewed my files for relevant documents. Most of these we had both seen many times before in our dealings with the Watergate prosecutors and congressional investigators. We were back on the same old treadmill. It was a chore and a heartache to go over all of this old material again and bring back the hurtful memories and anguish of those dreary days. Bea and I had thought this painful routine was behind us and that the government had finally been satisfied with all its investigations of my conduct as an official of the Nixon administration. How wrong we were.

Steve and I learned that this investigation was being conducted in New York and Washington by the Criminal Section of the Civil Rights Division of the Justice Department. Bill Gardner was heading the investigation, and Frank Martin was a member of his team. One of the first things that Steve and I realized as my letters and enclosures began to flow to him was that we were going to be up to our ears in bona fide national security matters. We suspected early in the game that the intelligence agencies of the United States would play a large role in any final decisions flowing from this investigation. We were right.

Soon news articles were quoting Mark Felt, saying that I had announced a change in Hoover's policy barring domestic black bag jobs. Mark was quoted as saying that I had made this announcement at the first meeting I held with all the SACs of the FBI in May 1972, almost as soon as I had been appointed to the job, and that such bag jobs were now to be authorized with permission from FBI headquarters. This was preposterous. I had said no such thing, and Mark and every SAC at that meeting knew it.

The first targets of the prosecution were the special agents in New York, who actually carried out the black bag jobs in their attempts to locate the Weatherman fugitives who had eluded us for so long. But soon they raised their sights to just three men: Mark Felt and Ed Miller, who had admitted authorizing the bag jobs, and me, who not only hadn't even known they were happening, but had been told over and over again by these same two men that the FBI had lost the capability to do them. Now those same two men whom I had trusted so completely while I was in the FBI were both lying about me in order to save their own skins. It was a nightmare.

For almost two years Steve and I fought to stave off my indictment. Mark Felt and Ed Miller were guilty by their own public admissions early in the investigation and were certain to be indicted. Felt said publicly that I knew nothing about the Weatherman break-ins. That was true. He and Miller arranged their own system of communication in writing about these bag jobs and made certain that I did not see the documents. The only way they could save themselves from certain conviction was to try to show at trial that their actions, like those of the street agents they had ordered to do the actual work, had been approved by a higher authority. There were only three higher authorities: the president, the attorney general, and me. Nixon had been pardoned by Gerald Ford for any and all crimes while he was in office, and Dick Kleindienst was too far out of the loop for Felt and Miller to blame. That left me.

Ed Miller said I gave him verbal authority and, over the course of the investigation, came up with four different versions of when I was supposed to have done that. None were true. Miller knew that he had no such authority from me. Mark Felt's thin defense was that he relied on Miller's tale that I had given the authority. Mark, of course, never checked this with me. He didn't dare. He and Ed Miller had both heard my often repeated admonition that we in the FBI cannot break the law while at the same time being duty-bound to enforce it. They knew only too well that I had fired Wes Grapp for a much lesser offense. They knew what their fate would be had I discovered their black bag job operation. So they kept it a secret from me, just as they had from Hoover himself. If they dared to condone these tactics under the nose of the aging tyrant, they certainly would have no fear that a novice on their own turf would uncover their illegal activities. And he did not.

The investigation dragged on. And on. Barnet D. Skolnick, the assistant U. S. attorney for Maryland who had prosecuted Spiro Agnew, was brought in as special counsel when the Justice Department realized that it didn't have the in-house talent to handle a case of this magnitude.

All three of us were indicted by the grand jury. On April 20, 1978, I was arraigned along with Mark Felt and Ed Miller at the U.S. Courthouse in Washington. It was a press spectacle attended by 1,200 present and former special agents who stood quietly outside protesting the action. We were fingerprinted and mug-shot. As we stood side by side washing off the ink, Mark asked me how many years of government service I had.

"Twenty-eight," I answered curtly. I was in no mood to talk to him. My entire family was waiting for me outside, by a side entrance. All I wanted was to slip away without having to deal with the press.

"And this is how your government thanks you," he said.

I said nothing. *And this is how you thank me,* was what I wanted to say, *for all the times I protected you in the past, by lying about me now? By letting these maggots indict me for something you know I didn't do? You can go to hell.*

That November Steve Sachs won his campaign to become attorney general of Maryland. Alan Baron took over for him and did a magnificent job for me under very trying circumstances. One of Alan's first actions was to conduct his own investigation. He and his associate Bob

Levin fanned out across the country to interview the SACs who had been at the May conference in which I was supposed to have counter-manded Hoover's prohibition of bag jobs. None of the SACs remem-bered me saying that. One of them said, "If Gray had said that, it would have sent shock waves throughout the Bureau." But then Alan and Bob discovered a troubling trend. Many of the SACs they were interviewing had kept detailed notes of what I had said at the conference, but they had never been contacted by the prosecutors. "We would have told all this to the prosecutors months ago," they said. "Gray never said any-thing like that."

The prosecutors hadn't taken the trouble to confirm or deny the al-legations against me. Instead, they had let the allegations stand unchal-lenged before the grand jury that eventually indicted me. Nor did they call another grand jury when the prosecutors asked Alan Baron to write a memo describing his new findings so they could present it to their superiors in the Justice Department. The prosecutors now knew by a preponderance of evidence that I was innocent. They should have immediately exonerated me, but they did not. Instead, they let my in-dictment stand while they took Felt and Miller to trial separately. They were convicted on November 6, 1980.

A few weeks later, seven and a half years after I resigned from the FBI and left the service of my still-beloved country, our tormentors threw in the towel in the last fight they would pick with me, Steve Sachs, and Alan Baron. Not only did the government finally drop its case against me, but it also issued an open-court public exoneration. This was no small white flag, this was unconditional surrender. I would have thanked them for it three years earlier. Now it just made me angrier. They had known the truth for three years and had refused to drop the case until Felt and Miller were convicted. By keeping me under indictment they had prevented me from testifying against my accusers at their own trials. Of all the prosecutorial outrages I endured in that seven-year war, this was by far the most egregious.

Though my exoneration was a victory for the truth, it was no vic-tory for me. All I had ever done was to try to do my duty as I and the law saw it, to tell the truth when somebody asked a proper question about it, and to believe that men and women entrusted like I was with high office in this magnificent country of ours would do the same. To my lasting disillusionment, very few of them did. I had been idealistic and naive, and it cost me and my family dearly. That I, an honest man who sought only to serve his country and had been pilloried and ridiculed for it, was now free to contemplate that for the rest of his life was no cause for celebration.

Early in my association with Dave Kinley, he gave me a small clipping of the famous Thomas Jefferson quote "The whole art of government consists in the art of being honest." I carried it with me ever since. Were Jefferson to stride onto the scene today, he might say the current art of government consists in the art of picking the right prosecutor.

twenty-eight

"And got on with my life."

As the battle over black bag jobs wound down, my son Ed and I decided that I ought to write a book. I had spent the better part of four years deep in the cauldron as the Nixon presidency melted down. I had stepped into J. Edgar Hoover's office the day after he died. And, most compelling, there were many things of historical importance known only to me. For over a year we worked in earnest on the project, though I wasn't sure I really wanted to do it. As time passed I became more sure that I did not.

During the long ordeal of my involvement in the Watergate investigations, I was under court order not to talk. To have spoken of my role in those investigations would have compromised my legal defenses and the documentation that enabled me to emerge exonerated. By the time justice, law, equity, and ethics no longer required that my pen remain idle and my mouth remain sealed, it was late in the game. Watergate had happened eight years earlier and many books had been written about it. The public might not even be interested. Finally, I decided not to pursue the project.

I came to this decision with mixed feelings. For many reasons it was a story I had not wanted to write. For many other reasons, it was one I knew should be told.

The best reason to write was to set out the whole story for my wife, my sons and their wives, and my grandchildren and great-grandchildren. Parts of it they knew; many parts they did not. Enough rot had been poured on me by all forms of the media to blacken me and my family forever. To correct this, to remove the tar that covered me—some of it indeed self-inflicted—I knew I should write the story of my government service while I was alive and in full possession of my faculties and my documents.

On the other hand, my family had suffered much from the painful glow of unwanted publicity that had too often been cruelly inaccurate. It was hurtful indeed to look down the path that led to my appointment and resignation fifty-one weeks later as acting director of the FBI, and to recall the eight years of inquisition and harassment that followed. Four years of public service in the executive branch of the government during the presidency of Richard Nixon, after my twenty-four years of honorable and rewarding service in the United States Navy, was to change my life so dramatically, and with such disastrous consequences, that I still found it incredible that service in high positions of government could end in such a manner. Did we as a family really want to revisit all of that?

For a long time I did not want to write about the FBI. I did not desire to tarnish in any way the well-deserved reputation of fidelity, bravery, and integrity built up over so many years by the vast majority of the members of the FBI. These dedicated men and women served our nation honorably and faithfully. They still do. I respected, admired, and loved them then. I still do. They built the reputation of the FBI in spite of J. Edgar Hoover and his palace guard of hard-liners.

And yet I also realized that I might do greater damage to the reputation of the FBI were I to remain silent. For I knew that there existed, before and during my tenure, two FBIs: the well-disciplined, highly motivated corps of street agents contrasted with, and often at odds with, the inbred cadre who controlled FBI headquarters and operations from Washington. To allow the well-publicized and selfishly motivated actions of these Hoover-picked hard-liners to cast a pall on the public's view of the FBI as a whole would be a disservice, both to the FBI and to the country.

A book would also give me a platform to say the things I wanted to say to my fellow citizens. I wanted to speak to them as one who had seen the government's innermost workings during one of its darkest hours. And what I wanted to say was this:

For much of its history, with few exceptions, the government of the United States has been led by presidents—each a politician in his own way—who adhered more, rather than less, to the plain truth contained in the Jefferson quote Dave Kinley gave me: "The whole art of government consists in the art of being honest."

Recent presidents, more ruthlessly political than presidential, have ignored Jefferson's words. The American people are not without fault in this process. Apathy, indifference, self-interest, and often total ignorance of the political process have brought to the office of the presidency politicians who are not worthy of the trust placed in them by the small percentage of the American voters who choose to vote in a national election.

The same comments are applicable to Congress. Self-perpetuation in office rather than the public interest is the name of the game played by too large a majority of these national politicians. Again, they are aided and abetted by the apathetic and nonparticipating members of the American electorate. Bribery, thievery, voter fraud, and criminal convictions have not prevented their return to office or to a lobbyist position where they are able to attempt to influence their former colleagues. This is both a national disgrace and a national weakness that will eventually bring our government to its knees.

One among these recent presidents chose to ignore completely the words of Jefferson and was mortally wounded. Indeed, Richard Nixon may not have known of this Jeffersonian definition of the art of government. If he did, it was low on his list of options in the conduct of his office.

To listen to Nixon in action on the presidential tapes as he conducted the duties of his office in a major crisis was a profound shock. My disillusionment with him was total. At the same time, do we ask ourselves how different he was from any other politician? We, the people, seem to tolerate these modern-day vandals. Indeed, we go so far as to curry favor with them to advance our own particular self-interest and to hell with the public interest.

The public interest is a nebulous concept in the minds of far too many Americans. It was not so to those men, young and old, who drafted our Constitution. We are one nation, one people, and the public interest is served when our government acts to enrich the quality of life for all Americans, not just a select few. For too many years the era of the special interest groups has been gathering strength. Our politicians have recognized this phenomenon and adjusted their strategy and tactics to meet it. The prevailing attitude is apparent: To hell with the needs of the nation, I'll do what's necessary to keep me in office. I never had it so good!

Today, I am disenchanted with the vast majority of our politicians at any level of government. Unfortunately, I believe the preponderant majority of Americans share this disenchantment. A vote today is more often a vote against than a willing vote for.

During the period of my service in the Nixon administration, I worked long hours and performed whatever tasks were assigned to me to the best of my ability. Not for one moment did I ever have the slightest inkling that Nixon was conducting the office of the presidency in a manner that would bring to him, and to his family, sledgehammer blows of pain, suffering, and shame. He and his family endured these as he became the first man in the history of our nation compelled to resign its highest office. Nixon was brought to his knees because of his calculated violation of the trust reposed in him by the American people. He had defiled the office of the president of the United States from the moment he entered upon its duties. Regrettably, I have no sympathy for him. His perfidy defies description. Nor did I ever envision that Nixon was to be the spider who would weave the vast conspiratorial web of the Watergate cover-up that was to wreck the lives of so many other Americans who served in his administration.

Some actually turned out to be as evil as Nixon himself. To be near the "throne," to ingratiate themselves with its occupant, to bask in the reflected glory of his high office, and to advance themselves seemed to be their sole goal in life.

Others were motivated only by their trust and faith in the occupant of the office of the presidency, and by their desire to serve the people of the United States. All were consumed by the voracious appetite of a man determined to save himself no matter what the cost to others. His pardon by Gerald Ford was an act of charity by a sitting president who wished to leave far behind the problem of bringing his predecessor to justice. Nixon justly deserved to walk through the flaming coals of the prosecutorial fires that so many of us faced time and again. Instead, he was pardoned, pensioned, and rewarded for his perfidy. To his dying day the man was incapable of showing remorse.

In my own long walk through those flaming coals I did not cooperate with any prosecutor. Even the phrase "cooperate with a federal prosecutor" has a sinister ring to it. To the American people this signifies that the cooperator was looking for a deal. Not I. I asked for no quarter and gave no quarter. Throughout that long and arduous struggle I never sought any privileges or immunities, nor did I ever attempt to plea-bargain. Yes, I gave information and delivered documents to federal prosecutors. I did not do so to curry favor or invite leniency. It was my duty to do so. I conducted myself as an officer of the United States, which I was and am—an officer of the retired list of the United States Navy.

All of these were things that I wanted to say to the American people, and a book was the most thorough way to do that. But the writing and publicizing of that book would be costly emotionally, not just to me but to my family.

In the end, I decided not to pursue it. Enough was enough. My life was stable again and I wanted to live it out with Bea, enjoying our growing family as our sons married and had children. I continued to practice law, made a few speeches, kept in touch with all our navy friends and a select few from the Nixon and FBI years. In 1986, at the age of seventy, I cut back on my practice, and Bea and I decided it was time to leave Connecticut and start enjoying my retirement.

I carefully packed up and indexed all the files and documents, put them into storage, moved south, and got on with my life.

twenty-nine

"You're still smiling about it."

ON JUNE 13, 2005, MY FATHER SAT AT HIS DESK WRITING, AS HE often did, short notes to himself as he followed a train of thought. Like all of the other notes, these were in a firm cursive on a yellow lined pad, but now, for the first time in his nearly eighty-nine years, there was a visible waver in his otherwise rigid hand. He had pancreatic cancer, a late-stage diagnosis that he had received only the week before. He knew he was dying, but there was something he had to get done first.

Just two weeks before, on May 28, he had read the *Vanity Fair* magazine article that finally identified "Deep Throat," the mysterious secret Watergate source that had driven *All the President's Men* onto the best-seller lists, movie screens, and television sets for more than thirty years. Bob Woodward and Carl Bernstein had kept the secret all that time, but now it was out. Even they admitted that the source was W. Mark Felt, my father's second-in-command at the FBI during Watergate, the man who had many times denied the accusation, including to his own boss, face to face, and in writing. It had all been a lie, and now it was time to respond. My father began jotting his notes.

> Felt cannot have it both ways.
>
> In his *Vanity Fair* article he states that I was his protector.
>
> Then in his justification for going to W&B he says he could not trust me or the AG or the AAG Criminal Div.
>
> In my judgment his motive was twofold: revenge and get rid of Gray.

His train of thought was interrupted. By me. I was calling to say that I wanted to ask him a question. He answered it, asked how my family and I were doing, and then he went back to his notes for one last entry.

> Cynic: a person who believes that only selfishness motivates human actions and who disbelieves in or minimizes selfless acts or disinterested points of view.

It's the formal definition. He didn't have to look it up. He knew all about the cynics. He had been fighting them for his honor and good name since 1972 and now, called up one last time by the deepest personal attack of them all, the old Naval Academy boxer in him had to gather himself, take the measure of his opponents, reach back thirty-two years, and throw one more punch.

It was one he wouldn't get to finish. At least not with the full follow-through that had taken him to the eastern collegiate light-heavyweight championship back then. His cancer stepped in and stopped the fight.

But in those last five weeks of his life after the Felt revelation, Pat Gray was fully alive and completely engaged. Once again his old enemies were on television, rehashing their old untruths about him.

May 31, 2005   *ABC* Nightline

CHRIS BURY: Terry Lenzner, who was the chief investigator on the Senate Watergate committee, says Felt feared the Nixon White House was undermining his FBI investigation.

TERRY LENZNER, FORMER COUNSEL, SENATE WATERGATE COMMITTEE: And when acting director Patrick Gray came in, I think that his motive was that he thought that Gray was cooperating with the cover-up. And Gray, himself, took investigative files out of the bureau, involving the Watergate investigation, and threw them in the Potomac River.

June 1, 2005   *ABC* World News Tonight with Peter Jennings

DEAN REYNOLDS: He knew, for example, that his FBI boss, acting director L. Patrick Gray, was destroying evidence implicating White House officials.

TERRY LENZNER: He took files from the investigation at the FBI headquarters, drove to Memorial Bridge, and threw them in the river.

June 1, 2005   *ABC* Nightline

TED KOPPEL: Then there was the—the director of the FBI, Patrick Gray.

BENJAMIN BRADLEE, FORMER EXECUTIVE EDITOR, *WASHINGTON POST*: Yeah.

KOPPEL: You could have told him.

BRADLEE: You could have told him. He was the guy who was throwing secret documents into the Potomac River from a local bridge. I think you can forgive him for not going to Patrick Gray.

June 2, 2005   *CNN* Larry King Live

LARRY KING: What about those who are saying, Carl, that Mark Felt is a guy who wanted to be head of the FBI and all this was revenge?

CARL BERNSTEIN: I think that's a much too simplistic way to interpret it. He obviously felt an obligation to the truth. He felt an obligation, I think, to the Constitution. He realized that

> there was a corrupt presidency, that the Constitution was be-
> ing undermined, and he was disappointed about not being
> made head of the FBI, and he was disappointed that the FBI
> that he loved and revered was being misused as part of a
> criminal conspiracy by J. Edgar Hoover's successor, Patrick
> Gray III.

My father was outraged. He called me as soon as he had seen the transcripts.

"Ed," he said, "if Lenzner in his investigative capacity heard me make such a statement, he certainly would have reported it to the Watergate prosecutors, they would have confronted me with it in a grand jury investigation, and if I had really done that, they would have indicted me. There's no question about it. And that guy is just dead wrong."

Together we made plans for a full-scale media rebuttal. I sent out an e-mail to news directors and Washington bureau chiefs cautioning them against any more erroneous coverage and letting them know that L. Patrick Gray III was "alive, well and watching with interest." We got Ben Bradlee to retract on the air a week later, but Carl Bernstein and Terry Lenzner stayed in character: wrong and defiant. Bob Woodward, also in character, kept a lower profile; his comments on those early news shows were more guarded, and my father had no problem with them.

Alerted by my e-mail, Jake Tapper of ABC wrote an excellent piece for the ABC News Web site. In it, he interviewed Lenzner, who refused to retract, saying he had notes. Tapper's piece then went on:

> But Gray's attorney during Watergate, Stephen
> H. Sachs, vehemently disputed Lenzner's
> recollection. "It didn't happen; it's inconceivable,"
> said Sachs, "and I was with him at every single
> interview he had." Sachs said for decades he has
> heard his former client described as having
> dumped Watergate evidence in the Potomac, but
> it's simply not true. "If he had destroyed Watergate

evidence, he would have been indicted along with everyone else," Sachs said.

Lenzner told ABC News he would look for back-up materials.

"If he has notes that say that, they were doodles," Sachs said, "because it never happened."

ABC News was not able to find any references to Gray throwing documents into a river in the committee's final report or anywhere else as Lenzner, Bradlee and Bernstein claimed.

I e-mailed Terry Lenzner first, since he was not only the most flagrant spinner of the falsehood but he had done it twice on separate national programs. He answered right away, saying that he entirely agreed with my sentiment and had advised Tapper to go back to documents. "If my recollection is wrong," he wrote, "I will apologize and retract to your father and his family. But the trouble with the press is they need to get it right by going to original sources."

A week later I asked him if he was ready to apologize. He answered by e-mail: "Haven't found anything dispositive but have requested interview notes from Library of Congress—I'll keep you advised."

I tried a couple more times, but Lenzner stopped answering. His promised apology never came. Months later, while I was gathering documents for this book, I found in the National Archives a copy of the official Ervin Committee transcript of the interview of my father that Lenzner was talking about when he said he would request "interview notes from the Library of Congress." (The Ervin records are kept at the Archives, not the Library of Congress.) As Steve Sachs had told Jake Tapper, there was no mention of throwing anything in the river. It was dispositive. Lenzner's name was listed among those in the interview room, so I sent a copy of it to him, once again asking for his apology. The Gray family is still waiting for it.

Carl Bernstein wasn't much more accommodating when I asked for his retraction. "I have examined and reexamined and parsed repeatedly my quote from the Larry King broadcast," he e-mailed. "I remain certain it is accurate, including contextually."

"To me they clearly state that you include my father in a criminal conspiracy," I answered. "I look forward to your clarification." He didn't reply.

My father and I turned to a television interview of his own. For thirty-two years he had refused all contact with the media, but that was about to end. He knew it had to, and so did everyone else in the Gray family.

As we began working toward that, my father went in for a medical checkup on June 8. He had abdominal pain and to him it seemed worse than the recurring obstructions he had fought ever since his ruptured appendix in World War II. It was far worse. It was Stage Four pancreatic cancer. Like every other problem he ever faced, my father assessed and studied this one. He concluded that it was a fight he could not win. Declining treatment, he spent the remaining few weeks of his life at home.

We kept working. In the papers we had retrieved from their nineteen-year incarceration, my father steered me to the appropriate folders so he could reread them. Refreshed by the review but losing the battle to cancer, he had time for only one interview. We gave it to George Stephanopoulos for his Sunday morning ABC program *This Week*, and on Thursday, June 23, my father taped the interview before he was too weak to do it. It was a tour de force, honored with an Emmy nomination as one of the three best interviews aired in 2005. Here's one of the reasons.

June 26, 2005   *ABC* This Week

STEPHANOPOULOS: And when you hear those who worked in
  the White House at the time—Chuck Colson, Pat Buchanan—
  describe Mark Felt as a "snake" and a "traitor," even though
  you disagree with what the White House was doing then, you
  agree with that characterization, it sounds like.
GRAY: No.
STEPHANOPOULOS: No?
GRAY: No. I think he was treacherous only to me, a man who
  trusted him. That's all. That's a deep inner hurt.

STEPHANOPOULOS: And you're convinced—or tell me this. Had Mark Felt come to you directly, rather than to Bob Woodward, what would have happened in Watergate?

GRAY: I would have said to him: "Mark, you're the professional. What is going wrong here? Tell me and we'll make it right. What do you think is going wrong here?" And I hope he would have had the courage to tell me: "Oh, Mr. Gray, I think you're a political hack and I think you're bent on destroying this FBI investigation."

STEPHANOPOULOS: But he never said that to you?

GRAY: No.

STEPHANOPOULOS: He never complained about the conduct of the investigation?

GRAY: Never.

STEPHANOPOULOS: He writes that he did. He says he was pushing and pushing you and pushing you.

GRAY: That is totally false. He wasn't pushing me and pushing me and pushing me, because as soon as we didn't get that writing from the CIA, that investigation proceeded and I didn't have anything to do in the direct conduct of it thereafter.

STEPHANOPOULOS: Do you think President Nixon would have been impeached if Mark Felt had come to you rather than Bob Woodward?

GRAY: I think that the FBI investigation itself was heading down that track and they were proceeding at max speed, and I think yes, he would have been impeached as soon as that information started coming out, as it would have come out, and then as the grand jury made their various reports, I think it would have come out, and I think he would been impeached.

At the end of almost two hours of nonstop taping, Stephanopoulos asked my father for a summary.

STEPHANOPOULOS: Does it make you wish that you had never, back in 1960 when you left the navy, never gotten involved with Richard Nixon in the first place?

GRAY: I do indeed. I made the gravest mistake of my eighty-eight years in making that decision, because I was on the fast

> upward track in the United States Navy. The Chief of Naval
> Operations talked strenuously with me about not leaving the
> service.
> STEPHANOPOULOS: And you went on a different track.
> GRAY: I did.
> STEPHANOPOULOS: Still public service, but more political.
> GRAY: That's right.
> STEPHANOPOULOS: And that was the biggest mistake of your life.
> GRAY: It was. I put the rudder in the wrong direction.
> STEPHANOPOULOS: You're still smiling about it.
> GRAY: Well, you know, Mr. Stephanopoulos, life has its ups and it
> has its downs, and you take them as they cross the plate and
> you swing, and sometimes you hit and sometimes you miss,
> and I missed.

Two weeks later he was gone, slipping away in his sleep, my mother and my brothers Alan and Patrick at his side. My brother Steve was on his way but didn't get there in time. I was here in New Hampshire, working on this book, planning to come down that weekend.

On June 6, less than a month before he died and in the midst of our trying to rebut Lenzner, Bernstein, and the others who were lionizing Mark Felt at Pat Gray's expense, my father sent me a short note thanking me for something I had said in his behalf. "PS," he wrote at the end. "Sixty-five years ago I graduated from USNA and I am still at battle stations with my son."

All of my father's Watergate papers—every document, transcript, memo, and note that he and Steve Sachs and Alan Baron used to defend him from the ill winds that others tried to twist around him—will someday be available to the public. He had nothing to hide and he wanted it that way. That last little note to me won't be among them. That one stays here.

In September we gathered at the Naval Academy Columbarium in Annapolis where he was interred with military honors, the twenty-one-gun salute and taps echoing across the Severn River toward the playing fields and halls where he had found the values he carried with him for the rest of his life. It was a private ceremony, just family and very few others. Steve Sachs and Alan Baron were there. So were Marge (Neenan) Ralls, Dave Kinley, Mack Armstrong, and Barbara Herwig.

Richard Nixon was forced to resign the presidency in 1974 not because of the small-time Watergate burglary that had happened two years before, but because of the subsequent criminal cover-up in which he participated personally. No one disputes this. The "smoking gun" tape that finally sealed his fate was a recording of an Oval Office plot hatched on June 23, 1972, six days after the break-in. That plot was brazen: call in Dick Helms, the director of the CIA, and order him to ask his counterpart, Pat Gray of the FBI, not to investigate the Mexican money trail on the grounds that it would reveal legitimate CIA undercover assets. This was a lie but, for reasons never made clear, Helms and his newly appointed deputy, Vernon Walters, went along with it, lying to my father as they tried to accomplish the deception. Bound by an existing interagency agreement not to uncover each other's sources, my father had no choice but to comply.

But not for long. My father, who had been on the job for only seven weeks, kept asking the CIA men for more details, and when these didn't come he released his agents. Within days they tracked the money to CREEP, opening a trail that would bring down the president himself two years later.

There are many enduring questions about Watergate. One of them is why Richard Helms, who had been in the CIA since its inception in 1947 and had been its director since before Nixon took office, went along with the "smoking gun" plot while L. Patrick Gray III, who had been appointed by Nixon and had been in charge of the FBI for only fifty-one days, resisted it. That answer eluded my father. "As far as I'm concerned," he once told me, "the extent of lying by senior officials of the CIA has never been fully exposed."

Pat Gray came into the Nixon administration as one of its most loyal supporters. He ended up detesting Richard Nixon and the others who went willingly down the dark and dirty path to Watergate. He especially hated what they did to the country and the government he had fought for his entire life. But what he hated most was what happened to him as he learned the truth about them and the self-serving talespinners who bent the story afterward. It changed him. More important, it prevented him from completing the greatest task of his life, the reshaping and reforming of J. Edgar Hoover's FBI.

Had there been no Watergate, the FBI today would be a much different government bureau than it has become. It would be more open to legislative scrutiny, more responsive to public needs, and much less defensive and self-promotional. Those were the goals that Pat Gray set out for his tenure as FBI director, and he initiated them immediately. He called them his "thirteen avenues of inquiry" and they're on the record for any American who wants to look into them. He invited journalists to come in and ask questions. He brought with him bright young Justice Department lawyers and told them to analyze the FBI's compliance with laws and regulations across the board. He opened the ranks of special agents to women, hired the first ones ever, and dismantled Hoover's draconian disciplinary system. He shut down divisions, reassigned longtime headquarters executives, and replaced them with rising talent from the field. He began to steer the Bureau away from Hoover's fixation on communists and internal subversives and toward the country's more important and growing threat of international terrorism. And most important of all, he insisted that at all times and in every investigation, the FBI was required to stay within its legal boundaries. As he said before the men and women of every field office he visited, "The FBI cannot enforce the law on one hand and ignore it on the other. Ours is a government of laws, not men."

Watergate undid almost all of it, and it almost undid him. He had been FBI director for less than a year.

thirty

The Watergate Books:
Fact and Fiction

It's now nearing the end of the succession of first-person Watergate accounts. Most of the major figures have had their say, and the pattern can now be seen.

The books written by those convicted or who pled guilty to a crime will always be subject to reasonable skepticism no matter how detailed or entertaining. Their axes were all in need of some sort of grind. John Dean's *Blind Ambition* and Mark Felt's *The FBI Pyramid From the Inside* are the high and low end of this spectrum in both readability and sales. Pat Gray read and vetted them both. Neither comes out well. The former seems to have contained some inaccuracies, the latter was almost certainly a pack of lies.

The memoirs written by the prosecutors, judges, and investigators can be more confidently relied upon to be factual, but those witnesses were just that: witnesses after the fact. The same can be said for the historians. No matter how carefully they dug into the record or how many people they interviewed, it was still secondhand. My father read and annotated many of these books as well.

Then there were the journalists' accounts. The one that stands out, obviously, is *All the President's Men*. It's a terrific book. The story is gripping and the characters are memorable. It reads like a novel and translated seamlessly into a screenplay. But what gave it the legs to become an iconic best-seller and an Oscar-winning movie was the sleight of hand it got away with from the outset. In the book they wrote about themselves, Woodward and Bernstein aren't the after-the-fact voyeurs they were in reality; they're the main characters. In *All the President's Men* the Watergate conspiracy isn't unraveled by the authorities, it's uncovered by a pair of plucky reporters who wouldn't quit. The literary trick they employed to achieve that shift was as simple as it was brilliant: in the narrative they treat every new discovery as if they were the ones who first uncovered it. It simply wasn't true. They didn't uncover the crimes, they followed the investigation that had already uncovered the crimes. The advantage they exploited was their First Amendment press privilege to publish anything they wanted as soon as they heard about it. Thus their revelations in the *Washington Post* were always ahead of the legally constrained and tactically deliberate public announcements of the prosecutors. When the American people began to get a sense that there really was a conspiracy, they got their hints from the press, not from the government.

But of course that's true in any crime story. We always get bits and pieces of the prosecution's evidence long before the trial. In the much-later court testimony, we get the details of a story we already know, but it's nonetheless far more compelling than the pretrial publicity. The courtroom drama eclipses all those early news scoops. We end up knowing the judge, the prosecutors, the defendants, and the defense lawyers, but no one remembers the bylines of the reporters. So how did Woodward and Bernstein become so famous?

By short-circuiting the process. In the world according to *All the President's Men*, the government never was going to tell the tale. The prosecution was going to be stopped with the low-level burglars themselves, and the big shots were going to get away with it because everybody was in on the conspiracy, including the head of the FBI. Only through the pluck and grit of the two cub reporters was the evil scheme uncovered, the top dogs forced to resign, and the wheels of justice handed back to the honest lower echelons.

It was a great story, but it had one big problem: the prosecution hadn't stopped. The story line could hold water only if the book were published before the next round of revelations, indictments, and trials, including the biggest one of all: Nixon's impeachment trial. And that's just what Woodward and Bernstein did, writing it in 1973 and rushing the book out in February 1974, six months before the whole story came out and Nixon resigned. It was a brilliant move—not only did they get their story out before it was eclipsed by the impeachment trial, but its publication helped to drive the president from office before the trial could even start.

Even with that masterstroke, the book might still have fallen as flat as all the others that came out at the same time. According to David Obst, the literary agent who helped write the proposal in Woodward's apartment, the original concept was an insider's account of reportage in the style of Theodore H. White's *The Making of the President* books. There was no "Deep Throat" in the proposal. But before the first draft was finished, Robert Redford bought the screen rights for $350,000 and invited Woodward to dinner, where he introduced him to William Goldman, who was to write the screenplay. Goldman and Redford suggested a few changes. "Deep Throat" appeared and so did the dramatic story line.

What sets Woodward and Bernstein's story apart from, say, their boss Barry Sussman's much more accurate and insightful *The Great Coverup* (published the same year) is the fiction-like drama that appeared in later drafts as *All the President's Men* took shape. Late-night meetings in parking garages, warnings that everyone's life is in danger, clandestine encounters in out-of-the-way bars. Those are screenplay elements. They seem fabricated. So does "Deep Throat."

There is now convincing evidence that "Deep Throat" was indeed a fabrication. Bob Woodward has provided it himself.

In April 2003, Bob Woodward and Carl Bernstein sold their Watergate papers to the University of Texas for five million dollars. To be included were all their notes of personal interviews, with the proviso that notes of confidential sources would be withheld from public view until the earlier of (a) the death of that person or (b) "such time as Woodward and Bernstein determine it appropriate." In 2003, the identity of "Deep Throat" was still a closely guarded secret, so Woodward kept his notes of those conversations out of the original set of documents deposited at the Harry Ransom Center in Austin, Texas.

When Mark Felt was identified as "Deep Throat" by his own family in May 2005, the University of Texas announced that Woodward would deposit his Mark Felt interview notes later that fall. When I visited the Ransom Center a year later, in May 2006, to research the "Woodstein" archive (as it's called there), I was disappointed to learn that Woodward still had not deposited any of his Mark Felt papers. The archivists had no explanation for the delay. Instead, they steered me to what was already there, and I took away copies of some interview notes and documents.

In January 2007, Woodward finally deposited his "Deep Throat" papers, now identified by him as notes of his conversations with Mark Felt. There were only ten pages—eight typed and two handwritten—of interviews dated October 9, 1972; January 24, 1973; March 5, 1973; March 24, 1973; and an on-the-record interview in July 1973. The October 9 and March 5 meetings were marked "meeting with X" and the January 24 notes began "interview with my friend." The March 24 interview was completely unattributed. When I got my copies a few days later, I looked at them carefully.

The first thing that struck me was that some of the information passed to Woodward in these meetings could not have come from Mark Felt. On October 9, 1972, "X" told Woodward that immediately after the burglary, John Mitchell, the chairman of CREEP, conducted his own investigation.

Mitchell conducted his invest for 10 days and "was going crazy---we had guys assigned to him to help" w. Rep. invest. foudn all sorts of new things. irony tha Hunt assigned to invest. for ½ day---then pulled off and fired (June 18) "told to pack his desk and leave town forever." by Ehrilichman "no less a person than that."

I turned to my copy of *All the President's Men*. Here's how this interview appears in the book, as an exact quote from "Deep Throat" during one of their clandestine garage meetings.

> "Mitchell conducted his own—he called it an investigation—for about ten days after June 17. And he was going crazy. He found all sorts of new things which astounded even him. At some point, Howard Hunt, of all the ironies, was assigned to help Mitchell get some information. Like lightning, he was pulled off and fired and told to pack up his desk and leave town forever. By no less than John Ehrlichman."

It's close, but it's not the full quote. The authors left out one crucial statement that "X" told Woodward: "We had guys assigned to him to help." Why would they leave out such a critical bit of information? Most likely to shield Woodward's source, since it identified "Deep Throat" as being part of a group of insiders "assigned to help."

But the dropped quote also reveals who "X" could not be. If "X" were Mark Felt, then his "we" could only mean the FBI. But there certainly were no FBI agents assigned to an internal CREEP investigation of its own employees immediately after the break-in, the results of which were precisely what Mitchell and CREEP wanted to keep away from the FBI. If there had been FBI agents "assigned to help" who "found all sorts of new things," not only would the Watergate case have been broken during those first ten days, but the FBI's files would be filled with FD-302s of the resultant interviews. There are none.

The conclusion is inescapable: "X" could not have been Mark Felt. It was someone from outside the FBI, someone close enough to CREEP to be asked to "help."

Wanting to be sure of that conclusion, I turned to the next set of notes. On March 5, 1973, "X" said this to Woodward about the Kissinger wiretaps that had just been revealed by *Time* magazine:

> said that Mardian~~head~~ ~~an~~ headed an "out of channels" vigilante squad of wiretappers that did, as *Time* reported, tap phones of reporters, including Hedrick Smith and Neil Sheehan for several weeks after *Times* refused to stop Pentagon Papers publication. authorization by Mitchell and FBI only found out about it indirectly. said this was very closely ~~...~~ held knowledge and Gray could deny it under oath because his knowledge was "out of channels."

Whoever "X" was, he was wrong here. On March 5, 1973, my father knew nothing about these wiretaps, as he attested to under oath at his confirmation hearings that very week. And, as my father and the rest of the country learned later, there was nothing "out of channels" about the Kissinger taps, nor did the FBI find out about them indirectly. The wiretaps had been set up and run by the FBI with Hoover's full knowledge and John Mitchell's written authorization, back when he was still the attorney general. And according to FBI documents and Mark Felt's own autobiography, Felt not only knew all about the Kissinger wiretaps, he was assigned to lead the inquiry into their whereabouts when Hoover learned that Bill Sullivan had removed the transcripts from the Bureau and given them to Bob Mardian at the Justice Department.

This March 5 meeting with "Deep Throat" also appears in *All the President's Men*, but not on March 5. The authors decided to move it back to February 26, two days before my father's confirmation hearings were to begin, thereby making it appear in the book that "Deep Throat" was passing his own information to Woodward, rather than merely discussing what that week's *Time* had just reported, as Woodward's notes now demonstrate. And "X" wasn't wrong just on the Kissinger wiretaps. In the book this is also the meeting where "Deep Throat" indicated that my father had blackmailed Nixon in order to get nominated as permanent director, footnoted when Steve Sachs pointed out to Woodward how preposterous this was. Whoever he was, "X" had fed multiple falsehoods to Bob Woodward.

I then turned to the next item in the "Deep Throat" files, an interview dated March 24 without any attribution listed—not "X," not "my friend." I immediately saw a discrepancy with what "X" had said on March 5 about the Kissinger wiretaps.

```
doesn't know about the term "out of channels," but says
that the tappers included some present and former
FBI agents. (my source insists absolutely that
all were former agents.)
```

Clearly these two March interviews were not with the same person. "X" had used the phrase "out of channels" twice on March 5, and Woodward had then asked the other person about it three weeks later. When he got a negative answer to that question and a different version of who the wiretappers were, Woodward then noted to himself, "*my source* [emphasis added] insists absolutely that all were former agents," which is just what "X" had claimed on March 5. As Woodward's own notes demonstrate, these were unquestionably two different people, yet both interviews were included by Woodward in his "Deep Throat" notes and attributed to Mark Felt. Was it just a mistake?

As I looked more carefully at the March 24 interview, I realized I had already seen it. In fact, I already had a copy of it. It matched a document I had obtained back in May 2006 from Woodward's files of interviews with people he said were not "Deep Throat." This interview had caught my eye because the unnamed interviewee told Woodward that my father had learned of the Kissinger wiretaps from Mark Felt. This person was wrong about my father's knowledge of the taps, but some of the other details in the interview were at least partly accurate.

meeting Mar. 24 [1973]

one of reporters tapped was the NYT reporter who
broke the stories on the SALT talks.
about six reporters total; on June 19, 1972 when supreme
court decision against nat. security wiretaps, had
about two in and Felt said they better get them out.

all the tapping was Mardian's idea and Mitchell signed
orders at insistence of Hoover.

project began as early as 1971. Gray learned from felt
that the taps were there---but all Gray's information
was second hand so he can deny it, saying there are
no records.

The top portion of the newly deposited interview, from the "Deep Throat"
papers.

meeting Mar. 24

one of reporters tapped was the NYT reporter who
broke the stories on the SALT talks.
about six reporters total; on June 19, 1972 when supreme
court decision against nat. security wiretaps, had
about two in and Felt said they better get them out.

all the tapping was Mardian's idea and Mitchell signed
orders at insistence of Hoover.

project began as early as 1971. Gray learned from felt
that the taps were there---but all Gray's information
was second hand so he can deny it, saying there are
no records.

The top portion of the previously deposited interview.

I e-mailed Stephen Mielke, the manuscripts archivist in charge of
the Woodstein archive, and pointed out the overlap. Mielke went to
the folder in which I had found the previously deposited notes and
e-mailed me back with some new information. In the same folder, just
behind the carbon that I had, was a second typed carbon that started:

"from very high Justice Dept. official who is Dean
critic 'one of john's more visible attributes is that he is
an ass-kisser . . .' "

Mielke then pointed out that alongside it was a note in Woodward's handwriting that started:

> "Santarelli—Assoc. deputy Atty Gen—'One of John's more visible. ass-kissing . . .'"

Mielke told me that when he first catalogued Woodward's notes, he thought that these two typed carbons and the handwritten note were from the same interview, but he could not be certain of it. He also pointed out that the March 24 interview was the only set of "Deep Throat" notes deposited by Woodward that did not correlate to any of the "Deep Throat" meetings described in *All the President's Men*. (Earlier we had both noted that though there are seventeen contacts between Woodward and "Deep Throat" described in the book, Woodward has so far deposited notes for only four of them.)

I knew that Donald Santarelli, the official mentioned in Stephen Mielke's e-mail, had been in the Justice Department with my father, and that he was still practicing law in Washington, but I had never spoken with him. I called him on January 23, 2007, and told him that I was finishing this book for my father and wanted to talk to him. He proceeded to relate several stories that more or less corroborated what my father had already written. He said he liked my father and thought he got badly used by the Watergate conspirators because he naively trusted them. "How shall I put this?" he said. "Your father wasn't Italian enough."

When I asked him about Felt being "Deep Throat," he was just as adamant. " 'Deep Throat' is still a composite," he said. "It wasn't just Mark Felt."

I then sent Santarelli an e-mail and attached the notes from Woodward's interview of March 24, 1973.

> After our excellent conversation, can I test your
> patience with a specific question?
> Attached from the Woodstein archive at the U. of
> Texas is a page of notes by Woodward of his
> conversation with you on 3/24/73. The topic is the
> Kissinger taps, and you say that LPG learned about
> them from Felt. My father always denied that, and
> he did so under oath. As you may recall, my father
> was the subject of a criminal inquiry as to whether
> or not he committed perjury when he made those
> sworn statements. He was exonerated.
> I know it's 3 decades, but is there any chance you
> can recollect for me why you thought that Felt had
> passed the information to my father? You weren't the
> only one who thought at the time that it was true, and
> I'm trying to find out why so many people believed
> that, other than that it seemed intuitively likely.

On February 5, ten days after I sent him the Woodward notes, Santarelli called me back. "Sorry I'm so slow to respond," he said, "but this was a long time ago and I'm having trouble remembering the conversation. I remember having it with Woodward, but the details are slow to come back."

"But this was a conversation that you had with Woodward?" I asked.

"Oh, yes," he said. "This definitely was me. Bob would call me regularly and would ask me stuff like this." Santarelli went on to say that he dealt more with Bill Sullivan than he did with Mark Felt, and that he had learned about the Kissinger taps indirectly. "I just picked it up," he said. "I was never briefed on them."

Now that Santarelli had confirmed to me that the March 24 interview was with him, I e-mailed him again, pointing out that in the recent release of the "Deep Throat" notes, Woodward had included this March 24 interview. I asked Santarelli if he wanted to notify the Texas archivists of the error, or would he prefer that I did? He didn't reply, even when I called to follow up.

I then got in touch with Bob Woodward. After an exchange of cordial e-mails, he called me on March 8, 2007. We talked for an hour and a half, and he told me at the outset that all of it was on the record.

Though I did not disclose to him that I had been in touch with Santarelli, I did ask him point-blank about the March 24 interview. He had a copy in front of him and he read it again. "Yes," he said, "I see the internal inconsistencies with the March 5 conversation, but both are definitely Mark Felt."

"Could it have been Don Santarelli?" I asked.

"Absolutely not," Woodward replied. "He was gone by then, wasn't he?"

I told Woodward that at the time of the interview, Santarelli had recently left the Justice Department to run the Law Enforcement Assistance Administration. "That's what I thought," he replied. He then reiterated that all the notes he had just deposited at the University of Texas were definitely of conversations he had had with Mark Felt, including both the March 5 and March 24 meetings.

That can't be true. Not only are the two interviews plainly with two different people, but the March 24 meeting was with Donald Santarelli, by Santarelli's own admission. The March 5 interview certainly was not with Mark Felt, because it was with "X," the source whose information about the CREEP internal investigation proved he could not have been in the FBI, and whose information about the Kissinger wiretaps was so at odds with what Mark Felt actually knew. The conclusion was so inescapable I decided to give Woodward one more chance to explain it. On April 18, I e-mailed him.

> I've got a couple more questions on the DT notes as they apply to my book. If you'd rather discuss them over the phone, feel free, of course.
>
> 1. In your notes of the 10/9 meeting, X says: Mitchell conducted his invest for 10 days and "was going crazy—we had guys assigned to him to help" w. Rep. invest. found all sorts of new things.

> My question is this: By saying "we" Felt can only
> mean the FBI. Did he really say this? (I asked you
> this question in my 3/3 email but I don't think we
> discussed it when you called.)

Woodward answered the next day. "He did say that," he wrote, "and at the time I wondered about it also." He went on to explain that he thought Felt could have meant "former FBI agents because there was one who I think was named King who acted as bodyguard for Martha Mitchell. Did the AG have bodyguards then who were FBI agents?" Woodward then said he wished he knew more. So did I. For one thing, John Mitchell wasn't even the attorney general then and he certainly had no FBI bodyguards as head of CREEP. More important, nothing in Woodward's explanation had altered the apparent truth, that "X" could not have been Mark Felt, as Woodward has continued to maintain.

So who was "X"? At this point it no longer mattered to me. What did matter was that "Deep Throat" was not the single individual Woodward always claimed him to be, an assertion my father always dismissed out of hand without even looking into it. "Deep Throat" was instead the composite fiction that knowledgeable people like my father always insisted he had to be. "X," whoever he was, was just part of the fable.

Why is it so important that "Deep Throat" was a fictional character and not an actual person? For two reasons, one specific to Pat Gray, the other important for the rest of us.

First the personal. *All the President's Men* isn't just the title of a best-selling book and a major motion picture. It is a list of evildoers and Pat Gray is still on that list. Check the current paperback, first page, "Cast of Characters." Check the Web site at the University of Texas, which houses Woodward and Bernstein's papers and where L. Patrick Gray III is still listed prominently by Woodward and Bernstein as a "conspirator." Pat Gray isn't just a name on that list; his photograph was included with Nixon's and ten others' on the book's original dust jacket. Of those ten men, every one except Pat Gray either pled guilty or was convicted of a crime. As a list, *All the President's Men* needs to have one name removed.

But more important, like several recently disputed memoirs, the book itself needs to be reclassified. *All the President's Men* is today accepted as a factual recitation—and often *the* factual recitation—of how Nixon and his "men" were driven from office. Until Woodward and Bernstein sold their notes to the University of Texas there was no way to test the book's claim of historical accuracy. Those verifiable documents have provided the previously unavailable key. "Deep Throat" was a fiction. So, therefore, is *All the President's Men*.

In the year Pat Gray sat in the FBI director's chair there was a clandestine war being fought among those who wanted to take that position from him. Chief among those plotters was Mark Felt. Without Watergate it would have been a tight little backstage drama. It got Shakespearean only because the stage got lit up and the whole country starting watching. In that war Mark Felt used every reporter he could get his hands on; Bob Woodward was just one of them. In their reporting for the *Washington Post*, Carl Bernstein and Bob Woodward used every source they could get their hands on; Mark Felt was just one of them. But in the creation of their after-the-fact myth, *All the President's Men*, Woodward and Bernstein bent the truth to fit the dramatic needs of a movie. They invented a hero named "Deep Throat." And since every hero needs a villain, Pat Gray was recast as one. In *All the President's Men* he is a liar, a blackmailer, and a conspirator. In reality he was none of those.

Pat Gray was caught in the middle of this war for fame and riches, a noncombatant casualty who was never supposed to learn there was even a battle going on. But Pat Gray was nobody's noncombatant. Felt's ill-advised confession and Woodward's reluctant confirmation brought Pat Gray back to the place he loved more than any other: a battleground. This one was unfamiliar, but in the conflict between truth and myth the best weapons are facts and Pat Gray was well armed. He meant this book to be the vehicle for his assault on the many fictions he had to live with after Watergate. The high ground to be retaken was his own good name.

I once asked my father if he had ever read *All the President's Men*. Since he had read and annotated nearly every other book on Watergate, I assumed the answer would be yes. It was no.

"It wasn't important enough," he said. "I wanted to hear what was happening from those on the inside like I was, not what some reporter had to say about it."

I'm glad he didn't read it. But if he had, this battle might have been joined a lot sooner, and he would have been the one to write the last chapter of his book, not me.

A Note on Sources

WHEN RICHARD HELMS RESIGNED AS DIRECTOR OF CENTRAL intelligence in January 1973, he and his secretary spent his last ten days in office destroying his files. When my father left the FBI three months later, his secretary, Marge Neenan, spent the following week in his office segregating his personal papers from the Bureau's official files. She gave the official files to Mark Felt. The personal files she then packed into forty-five boxes that were carted to the basement of the Justice Department until two of my brothers retrieved them a few weeks later.

Armed with the contents of those forty-five boxes, my father began creating the narratives that appear here. Most of them he wrote out longhand, preserving each draft as he went. Sometimes he dictated a draft and then edited the typed transcriptions by hand. The first accounts, begun within days of his resignation, were for his lawyers as they helped him prepare his testimony before the congressional hearings and grand juries spawned by Watergate. Those writings were narrowly focused on the specifics of the events in question. For a short time in 1974 and again a few years later, as the last prosecutorial white flag was about to fly, he wrote more expansively, filling in personal details and observations. His background source for everything he wrote was his extensive archive of personal papers.

Two events led to the expansion of that archive. Because he knew that at his confirmation hearings he would be asked detailed questions, not only about Watergate but also about such events as the disbanding of Tom Bishop's Crime Records Division and the arrest of Jack Anderson's associate Les Whitten, my father first posed those questions hypothetically to his personal confirmation task force. The answers came to him in writing, backed by copies of FBI documents. Then, when he needed corroboration or amplification of an actual response he had given to a particular senator at the hearings, his team provided copies of backup material from the FBI files. Those answers and copies he took with him when he left the Bureau. The result is almost certainly the most complete set of Watergate investigative records outside the government, one that contains many personal notes and other original documents held only by my father.

The other event that added substantially to my father's archive was his indictment in the Weatherman black bag job case. In the two and a half years before the government publicly exonerated him by dropping the indictment in open court, my father was entitled to the discovery process. He and his lawyers used it to obtain copies of hundreds of otherwise locked-up documents and those, too, now reside in his personal files. They inform much of what is here.

The White House tape transcripts included here are from several sources. For his account of the Nixon-Gray-Ehrlichman Oval Office meeting of February 16, 1973, my father worked from a nearly unredacted copy of the official transcript that he received through the discovery process. For the Oval Office conversation between Nixon and my mother and father on May 4, 1972, I made my own transcript from a recording provided by the National Archives. For each of the other taped conversations, I used an official transcript provided by the National Archives, if one existed. Otherwise I used the version provided by Stanley Kutler in his 1997 book *Abuse of Power: The New Nixon Tapes*.

Bob Woodward's "Deep Throat" notes are courtesy of the Harry Ransom Humanities Research Center at the University of Texas at Austin, which houses the Woodward and Bernstein Watergate papers.

Acknowledgments

L. Patrick Gray III was not a man who left his debts un-
paid, his friends unthanked, or his gratitude unsaid. Had he lived
to write these acknowledgments himself, they might have rivaled the
book itself in length. To all those whose names remain on the unwritten pages that my father took with him when he died, let me say it for
him: Thank you. And to those of you who do find yourselves acknowledged here, let me say that, except for his family, which meant everything to him, there is no sequence. You're all at the front.

After his indictment in 1978 several of my father's friends banded
together to form the Pat Gray Legal Defense Fund. These friends, led
by Oscar "O.B." Nelson, knew that my parents had already sold their
home and spent all of their savings on attorneys' fees in the legal battles
of 1973–77; the Weatherman indictment was sure to ruin them finan-
cially. From an initial committee of thirty in southeastern Connecticut,
the PGLDF grew to one hundred committee members and eight hundred contributors throughout the country. Their financial and moral
support was immeasurable and enabled all of us in the family to hold
our heads high.

Many of the best years of my father's life were spent with his law
partners, Charlie Suisman, Max Shapiro, Butch Wool, Jim Brennan,
Dale Faulkner, and the others in his "beloved law firm," as he often

called it. He meant exactly that. He loved it and he loved them. They never wavered in their support, even when the government he had left them to serve turned against him. Instead, they welcomed him back with a continuing full share while he fought to protect his name. It was an act of pure generosity, fueled by their faith in him.

From the submarine service of the U.S. Navy, my parents developed their longest-lasting friendships. They formed a safe harbor during the storms of Watergate and a following sea of normalcy afterward. Among them were O.B. and MaryAnn Nelson, Burt and Lois Klakring, Joe and Madeleine Williams, Phil and Gigi Beshany, Murray and Betty Frazee, and so many others.

To those who had a hand in the preparation of this book, my father's gratitude commingles with my own. My wife, Rebecca; my brothers, Alan, Patrick, and Stephen; and my mother read early drafts and steered the project through the unmarked turns of its inception. Jennifer Unter could not have been a better agent when we finally gave her something to work with. Paul Golob's editorial skills made this a far better book than the one my father and I envisioned—and our sights were set very high.

Finally, to Steve Sachs, Alan Baron, and the others who stood with my father during and after Watergate itself and who find themselves included in this book, I know that he would have wanted expressly to say thank you here. I'll say it, too: Thank you. You kept him alive.

Illustration Credits

Index

About the Authors

L. Patrick Gray III (1916–2005) was acting director of the FBI at the height of the Watergate scandal, from May 1972 to April 1973. He had previously served in the Justice Department as an assistant attorney general and was a twenty-year veteran of the U.S. Navy.

Ed Gray, his son, is a freelance writer and the cofounder, with his wife, Rebecca, of *Gray's Sporting Journal.* He is the author of seven books and lives in Lyme, New Hampshire.